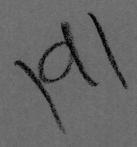

191

Handbook for Construction
Accounting and Auditing

HANDBOOK FOR CONSTRUCTION ACCOUNTING AND AUDITING

Henry G. Pansza

PRENTICE-HALL, INC.   **Englewood Cliffs, N.J.**

Prentice-Hall International, Inc., *London*
Prentice-Hall of Australia, Pty. Ltd., *Sydney*
Prentice-Hall Canada, Inc., *Toronto*
Prentice-Hall of India Private Ltd., *New Delhi*
Prentice-Hall of Japan, Inc., *Tokyo*
Prentice-Hall of Southeast Asia Pte. Ltd., *Singapore*
Whitehall Books, Ltd., *Wellington, New Zealand*
Editoras Prentice-Hall do Brasil, Ltda., *Rio de Janiero*

© 1983 by

Prentice-Hall, Inc.
Englewood Cliffs, N.J.

Library of Congress Cataloging in Publications Data

Pansza, Henry G.
  Handbook for construction accounting and auditing.

  Includes index.
  1. Construction industry—Accounting. I. Title.
HF5686.B7P33 1983   657'.869   83–9568
ISBN 0-13-372573-1

Printed in the United States of America

About the Author

Henry G. Pansza, CPA, is uniquely qualified to write about accounting and auditing practice in the construction industry. Not only has he spent twelve years as a construction contractor, which enables him to view the special problems of construction accounting from the inside out, but he also has extensive experience in professional accounting, auditing, tax consulting and management advisory services to the construction industry.

At present, Mr. Pansza is an active CPA operating his own firm in Oklahoma City, Oklahoma. In addition, he has taught accounting, income tax, financial management, and related courses at Oklahoma City University and Central State University in Edmond, Oklahoma. He is a member of the American Institute of Certified Public Accountants, the Oklahoma Society of Certified Public Accountants, and the National Association of Accountants. He is also a past president of the Association of Plumbing-Heating-Cooling Contractors of Oklahoma City, Inc.

Mr. Pansza's articles have appeared in professional accounting publications, including *Management Accounting*. He holds a Bachelor of Science degree in accounting from Oklahoma City University and a Master of Arts degree in economics from the University of Oklahoma.

WHAT THIS BOOK WILL DO FOR YOU

The *Handbook for Construction Accounting and Auditing* is a "hands-on" guide to both accounting and auditing practices in the construction industry. In a single, comprehensive volume, it offers a wealth of authoritative, fully illustrated techniques for designing, installing, operating, and auditing a successful accounting system for the construction contractor. Whether you are an internal accountant employed by a construction firm or an external accountant acting as auditor and consultant, you'll find in this *Handbook* the practical help you need to handle your workload more efficiently and effectively.

Here is just a sample of what this valuable *Handbook* offers you:

- It shows you how to choose the best accounting system for the construction contractor. You'll see which system does the best job from both a management and tax point of view—and whether a combination of systems may be the best approach.

- It outlines a unique task-cost approach to the knotty problem of percentage of completion contracts. Here at last is a simple, step-by-step method for handling income determination for construction in progress.

- It demonstrates how to design, install and operate a successful accounting system for the construction contractor—complete with detailed forms, records, processing techniques and methods of presenting financial information.

- It guides you step-by-step through the year-end audit, from the planning stages all the way to the completed audit report. You'll see what the contractor's accountant can do to save time for the auditor and money for the contractor . . . you'll find a complete set of audit programs, working papers, flow charts, and internal control questionnaires . . . you'll see how to prepare a polished, professional audit report—with a complete model report for ready reference.

- It steers you surely through the minefield of audit pitfalls peculiar to the percentage of completion contractor. You'll discover innovative procedures for handling this high-risk audit area that fill in the gaps left by prescribed auditing techniques.

- It offers tax tips of special importance to the construction contractor. You'll find valuable tax planning strategies that can save the contractor big money—and tax traps you can help him avoid.

- It explains how you can help the contractor map out a blueprint for financial success. You'll find a comprehensive game plan for helping the contractor establish a strong working capital position, improve his cash flow system, and make sound capital investment decisions.

The *Handbook for Construction Accounting and Auditing* is aimed exclusively at the special requirements of the construction industry—a business that is truly unlike any other. Because it gives you a complete picture of how the contractor operates and what his accounting needs are, this *Handbook* helps you tackle with confidence any assignment that takes you into the unique world of the construction contractor.

Henry G. Pansza

Table of Contents

Handbook for Construction
Accounting and Auditing

1

KEY PROBLEMS IN THE CONSTRUCTION ACCOUNTING PROCESS

Every industry presents special problems to the accountant. What he hears is the familiar cry: "We are different." Usually he shrugs this off, but occasionally he will encounter a business that is truly different such as the construction company. When this happens he has to stop and think. What makes this business different? How does this affect the accounting system? What special problems does all this present to the auditor?

This chapter contains a description, in general terms, of the world of the construction contractor—how he operates, what his accounting system looks like, and what effect it has on the auditor. In chapters that follow, problems are narrowed down to specifics so that both inside and outside accountants, as well as nonaccountants who deal with the contractor, and the contractor himself, will know how to handle each problem as it comes up.

HOW THE CONTRACTOR OPERATES

The construction contractor's stock in trade is his ability to take a set of plans and transform them into a finished structure. Working in a manner that often seems chaotic and confusing, the contractor really knows exactly what he is doing and where he is going. Beams sticking out into space, pipes coming out of the ground at odd places, duct work seemingly going nowhere, electric wiring a maze of "spaghetti"—all these things have a purpose and precision often lost to the untrained eye.

THE CONTRACTOR'S JIGSAW PUZZLE

When what appears to be unrelated pieces of a jigsaw puzzle finally come together, the entire construction team consisting of the architect, the engineer, the various crafts, the general contractor, the banker, the surety underwriter, and the owner can all share in the great satisfaction that only a completed construction project can bring. The job is finished. The dream has taken shape and is standing there for all to see and admire. But how did it happen? It's very much like putting together a jigsaw puzzle—little pieces fit together to form a task, tasks grow into phases, and phases fit together into the complete job.

What does all this mean to the accountant? It means that he has to keep track of each piece of the jigsaw puzzle. He must make sure that each piece wears a price tag, and that it is properly costed and categorized as it goes into its proper niche.

HOW CONSTRUCTION JOBS ARE PUT TOGETHER

Most products take shape in a manufacturing plant or in a fabricating shop, under close supervision and centralized control. The production effort associated with construction takes place in the field, at various construction sites scattered geographically in direct proportion to the size of the construction firm. What this means to the construction accounting process will be discussed in sections that follow.

ATTRIBUTES OF SMALL, MEDIUM, AND LARGE CONTRACTORS

The small contractor sticks close to home, while the medium-sized contractor reaches out across state lines to neighboring states. The large contractor works in several states, and is the international giant in several countries.

The bigger the contractor, the greater the scattering effect. Even the small-to-medium-sized contractor begins to scatter his work quite early in the course of his existence, feeling the need for some kind of centralized job control compatible with decentralized operations.

As the small contractor begins to grow, so does the need to delegate. First he must delegate to the job foreman, then to the project manager, or else to the project engineer, the area manager, or the branch manager and so on, in ever-widening spirals directly related to the growth of his operations. How does all this affect the contractor's way of managing his business? Let's begin with job control.

HOW THE CONTRACTOR VIEWS JOB CONTROL

Even at the first phase of delegation there is a peculiar management twist whereby the contractor, willing to give up a certain amount of personal contact with the job, is not willing to give up control of the job. The simple reason for this is that control over key decisions must be centralized in the construction industry. Only in this manner can the contractor assure proper coordination and performance of the intricate tasks that make up the project.

Decentralized operations and centralized decision-making describes the world of the contractor. Keeping this peculiarity in mind, one can understand why the contractor's management philosophy will be unique and why his accounting system will reflect such uniqueness.

THE CONTRACTOR'S BUILT-IN PROFIT CENTER

Scattered operations mean scattered record keeping. The novice accountant will be struck by this peculiarity. Actually, there is no great difference between a job site and a profit center. Within this microcosm, one finds all the ingredients needed to provide the contractor with that all-important comparison of planned versus actual costs. Planned data can be taken directly from the estimator's takeoff sheets. Actual data can be aligned with the takeoff with a minimum of effort. This, of course, is the essence of a good control system. This is also a golden opportunity to establish a fairly sophisticated information system, capable of providing both job control and feedback to the estimator. There is even a bottom line, in which the foreman's performance can be evaluated by comparing the actual gross profit produced by the job to the estimated gross profit shown on the takeoff sheet.

THE CONTRACTOR'S GRASS ROOTS CODING SYSTEM

A little digging around at the construction site will show that labor hours and costs, as well as other job costs, are subject to some kind of coding by the job foreman. The small home builder, general contractor, or subcontractor might be satisfied with a simple coding system consisting of a house number or a job number. The larger operator might go for something more elaborate, perhaps a coding system that follows the takeoff, phase by phase and even task by task, broken down by basic cost elements for ultimate input to a faraway home-office computer. Grass roots coding is peculiar to the construction business. How the creative accountant can take advantage of this grass roots peculiarity is covered in detail in chapters that follow. In the meantime, let's take a quick look at the general framework of the contractor's documentation, where all this coding takes place.

HOW THE CONTRACTOR'S DOCUMENTATION AFFECTS THE ACCOUNTANT

The contractor's *modus operandi* requires both extensive delegation and tight controls. To accomplish this, he relies on the established industry practice of requiring solid documentation of all phases of the construction job. Over time, the construction industry, in a manner somewhat similar to manufacturing plants, has developed the practice of making a single document do more than one job. In the accountant's language, this usually means using a document to satisfy both the cost process and the financial process. There is no set order. Time sheets will be used, first to prepare the payroll and later to post to job cost ledgers. Invoices go the job-cost route first, then take off for the accounts payable ledgers. Some systems do both jobs at the same time. This is true of some of the better computer systems using the data base concept. But even some modest write-it-once manual systems can provide side-by-side posting to both the cost and the financial process.

While the contractor's documentation presents opportunities for the accountant, as previously mentioned, there are also problems to be considered. In a way, the accountant tends to bring these problems on himself by being more finance conscious rather than cost conscious. Not only will such an accountant fail to see the need to reconcile one process with the other, thereby weakening internal control, but in the long run, he commits another serious error. He fails to give the contractor what he wants, when he wants it, and how he wants it. How to avoid this pitfall is covered in detail elsewhere in this book. But now let's look at the contractor's financial statements, and pick out peculiarities that might be hidden from the eye of the uninitiated.

HOW RETENTION AFFECTS ACCOUNTS RECEIVABLE

The contractor's accounts receivable might look the same as anybody else's, but they really are not. Under the AICPA definition, accounts receivable for the contractor include amounts retained by the customers, in accordance with contract provisions.[1] This is the familiar retainage or retention, usually ten percent, which is not paid to the contractor until the job is finished and the "punch list," consisting of complaints, has been worked off. One can well imagine the cash-flow problems generated by this peculiarity. One can also appreciate the need for the outside user of the financial statements to be aware of this problem and to insist on a separation of retention from net receivables. The auditor, too, has a problem in that he might not realize the importance of disclosing retention as a separate element of the accounts receivable whole, thereby failing to warn the user that retention is really in a different liquidity category.

AN OVERVIEW OF OVER- AND UNDERBILLING

Outside of the construction industry, accounts receivable are debited in a continuous stream as sales on account take place. But for nonconstruction industries, sales are not recorded until they are earned. Not so in the construction business. While the name is the same, we will soon see that there is something different in accounts receivable besides the retention problem explained in the preceding section. What happens is that, in the construction business, accounts receivable are debited for the full amount billed, whether earned or not. There is a different process for determining how much has been overbilled and how much has been underbilled, and what to do about it.

If billings have not been earned, we have an overbilling situation. If costs have been incurred and gross profit has been earned beyond that claimed through the billing process, we have an underbilling situation. For percentage of completion contractors, a very important series of plus and minus adjustments take place in the process of analysing each job in order to determine earned revenue. In effect, the analysis determines overbilling and underbilling for each job, deducting from revenue for overbilling and adding to revenue for underbilling. Exactly how this is done and what it means to the accountant, the auditors, and others is covered in detail in chapters that follow.

Basics of Underbilling

The AICPA recommends showing, below accounts receivable, an item entitled "costs and estimated earnings in excess of billings on uncompleted contracts."[2] In this book, you will find this item referred to as "unbilled costs and earnings." Debits to this account wind up as credits to earned revenues, thereby increasing this account.

Basics of Overbilling

Going over to current liabilities, you will find a related item called "billings in excess of costs and estimated earnings on uncompleted contracts."[3] We will call this item "unearned billings over costs." Credits to this account wind up as debits to the earned revenue account and will decrease this account.

THE CONTRACTOR'S INVENTORY ACCOUNT IS ALSO DIFFERENT

Normally the inventory account includes raw materials, work in process, and finished goods. In the construction business, inventory takes in only materials and supplies not allocable to construction in progress. Everything else is costed to the job and charged directly to cost of earned revenues, whether the material has been installed on the structure or not. Hence, material on the job site is recognized as a job cost for which the contractor may collect on a progress billing. But see Chapter 10 concerning uninstalled material that is not "unique" to the job.

HOW TO UNCOVER OVER- AND UNDERBILLING

Reference to previous sections will show that earned revenue represents a net figure that absorbs plus and minus adjustments for over- and underbilling. Therefore, the unwary outside user, as well as the untrained accountant, might not be aware of adjustments of great significance buried in this account. But a look at the balance sheet accounts will show where the plus or minus adjustments came from, such as unearned billings over costs, a current liability, or decreased earned revenues, or else from unbilled costs and earnings, a current asset, or increased earned revenues.

HOW THE ACCOUNTANT CAN HELP THE CONTRACTOR

Opportunities are many for helping the contractor. The accountant, trained in disciplined thinking and the organization of data, can be a big help. The nuts and bolts of the accountant's stock in trade are described in the chapters that follow, with special attention devoted to what each subject means to the contractor and his team. Many examples are given, but two are presented below to give the reader a feel for the constant interplay between the accountant and the operator.

In Estimating. Estimating is to a contractor what planning a sales pitch is to a salesman. There is a difference, of course. The salesman hits the psychology angle pretty heavily. As a superprofessional, he is dealing with a fantastic array of unknowns as he tries to figure out the mystery of what makes a person part with his money.

The contractor is a salesman too, but unless he is negotiating a job, his problem is more mathematical than psychological, even though he still engages in mind-reading when he has to figure out what his competitor is up to and how he can beat him to the punch with the lowest figure at bid time.

The contractor must reduce a complexity of plans, specifications, and alternates to dollar amounts. Unknowns must be changed to knowns, and where this is not possible, the danger of risk must be determined and a value assigned to it.

Can the accountant operate in this area? Of course he can. He must be ready, however, to go beyond the record keeping process and delve into the area of planning. He must be ready to leave the sure world of debits, credits, and balanced journals for the world of evaluating probabilities. Exactly how he can do this is covered in succeeding chapters.

In Refining Cost Factors. Long before a job has taken off, the accountant should begin using other jobs to refine labor cost factors. His work should start with an evaluation of the coding of time sheets, to see if the coding system can be made to follow the task pattern of the takeoff. This is merely one example of how the accountant can help to refine cost factors. Others are covered in great detail later. The principal point is that there are many other opportunities in which the accountant can help the contractor refine his estimating factors.

WHAT THE ACCOUNTANT CAN DO ABOUT JOB CONTROLS

Bringing a job "in the money," or, within cost estimates, is the secret of success in the construction business. The accountant's skill in the use of coded documentation is the key to helping the contractor control job costs. In the construction business, this is a must. The alert accountant knows that in the takeoff sheet, he has the basis for determining what a job should cost. All he must do is relate this information to the actual costs. This simple process is a powerful tool that the contractor can use to control job costs.

WHAT THE OUTSIDE CPA CAN DO FOR THE CONTRACTOR

This book presents, under one cover, the accounting methodology needed to give the contractor a solid, documented accounting basis to back up his financial statements. For the first time, a specifically prescribed accounting system is used as a basis for a direct tie-in to detailed auditing procedures that apply exclusively to construction industry audits.

The outside CPA is an invaluable member of the contractor's team. It is he who assures the banker, the bonding people, and other outsiders that the contractor's financial statements "present fairly" his financial position and the results of operations. The outside CPA can do a great service for the contractor, first by showing the contractor how to tighten his internal control, and second, by assuring outsiders that the contractor's figures mean what they say.

Special Guidance for the Outside CPA

This book will guide the auditor through the maze of documentation that constitutes the contractor's world, and will bring him through the entire auditing process, straight through to the final product—the audit report. The construction industry auditor will find detailed auditing instructions that adhere carefully to standards prescribed by the AICPA. While considering AICPA standards, the auditing procedures will go even further to prescribe in detail many innovative solutions to age-old construction industry audit problems.

The Internal Revenue Code contains problems that apply specifically to the contractor. Although not pretending to be all-inclusive, Chapter 12, the final chapter, will present tax tips, strategy, and pitfalls peculiar to the contractor. Since the auditor usually is also engaged to prepare the contractor's income tax returns, this chapter will serve as both a refresher and a stimulant to the auditor, and will help him wrap up the audit in the form of a good professional income tax return.

THIS BOOK IS FOR EVERYBODY IN CONSTRUCTION

Everybody connected with the construction industry will benefit from this book. The title suggests primary concern with construction accounting and auditing. But the book contains more than accounting and auditing. It constantly plays back the effects of what the accountants' efforts mean for management and the nonaccountants. In a real sense, this book reflects the experience of the author, who, in addition to being a practicing and teaching professional accountant, also spent over eleven years as a construction contractor. This means that besides being a handbook for accountants and auditors, this book also constantly looks at the utility factor—how the nonaccountants are going to use the information so carefully and professionally put together by the accountants.

ACCOUNTING BASIS IS NEEDED, BUT WHICH ONE?

As we proceed beyond the basic concepts, we realize that the accounting system forms the foundation for further management control, and also gives insights into the contractor's operations that are not usually afforded outside users of financial statements.

This brings us to the point of helping the contractor decide which accounting system he should chose. For although the contractor's accounting system is peculiar and must conform with certain norms that belong only to him, he still has certain options, particularly the choices affecting his tax returns. What these options are and what they mean to the contractor will be examined in the next chapter.

Notes: *Chapter 1*

1. *Construction Contractors*, p. 64, © 1981 by the American Institute of Certified Public Accountants, Inc., New York.
2. *Op. cit.*, p. 185.
3. *Ibid*.

2

CHOOSING THE BEST ACCOUNTING SYSTEM

When the contractor decides to go in business for himself, there are many decisions he must make. One of the most crucial is choosing the right accounting system. Here we have not only a bookkeeping decision, but one that has repercussions, the main one being the effect on how the contractor will pay his tax bill.

The problem of choosing the best accounting system is not apparent at the beginning. What happens is that the contractor's choice evolves from an innocuous start. What difference does it make, he asks himself, if I go on the cash basis, the completed-contract basis, or the percentage of completion basis? It could, and often does, make a difference. Let's see how it does.

THE CONTRACTOR'S EVOLUTIONARY PROCESS

The contractor started as a small operator. His wife did the bookkeeping part-time, while taking care of the kids. When the contractor hired his first employee, he was forced to start keeping payroll records. His wife went to the local Internal Revenue Service office and obtained a copy of Circular E, so that she could comply with various withholding and reporting requirements. She then called the state withholding people for instructions on how she could enroll the contractor, then called the state unemployment authorities to get the contractor into the state unemployment program.

PRIMITIVE BOOKKEEPING FOR THE CONTRACTOR

At first, the contractor could use his check stubs for almost anything he needed in the way of reporting requirements. Later he took on more work, and soon found himself with more than one employee and more than one job to look after. He went to the office-supply store and bought an armful of single-entry ledgers, one for each job. He had his wife write down labor and material costs, taking the information right off the check stubs. This was the beginning of his cost accounting system.

WHY THE CONTRACTOR LOVES THE CASH METHOD

If the contractor had already established his accounting system, having gone through the evolutionary steps described above, it would seem that he would have opted for the cash basis of accounting. Using such a system, the contractor has many powerful arguments for staying with it. For example:

• There is nothing wrong with a system that permits you to pay your taxes when you have collected the money you'll use to pay them.
• Paying your bills when you have the cash is the essence of good cash management. What's wrong with that?

WHAT CAN ACCOUNTANTS SAY AGAINST THE CASH METHOD?

Accountants have trouble refuting the cash method. In the early stages of a contractor's economic life, cash flow will dominate his thinking. Hard pressed to pay bills and meet payrolls, he will search for scapegoats. The blame will be placed not on poor profit performance but on "cash flow." Usually, the contractor will fail to conclude that cash flow problems stem from poor profit performance.

WHY THE CONTRACTOR WILL CLING TO THE CASH METHOD

As long as the contractor has cash flow problems, he will tend to cling to the cash method because he feels that he has a better control over the cash situation. This is a good point, but the accountant should point out several problems related to the cash method:

• The cash method does not measure performance.
• Banks, bonding people, and other outsiders don't like it.

THE PROS AND CONS OF THE CASH METHOD

Suppose that pro and con arguments are jotted down in this manner:

Pros by the Contractor	Cons by the Accountant
1. It's simple. You record the transaction right off your check stub.	1. It's often too simple: A simple picture is not always a true and complete picture.
2. Income is based on deposits. Costs and expenses are based on checks written.	2. For a true profit picture, income should be based on what is earned, not on what is collected. Costs and expenses should be counted when incurred, not when the contractor decides to pay for them.
3. Let's face it. You can manipulate this kind of system. Delay making a deposit and you throw income into the next accounting period. Delay paying your bills and you can defer your costs and expenses—and, therefore, your losses, to the next accounting period.	3. Manipulation is not only dishonest, but it also requires your personal attention. It can get out of hand. Your accounting system should measure income and expenses accurately and completely. Otherwise, you can't possibly know what's going on.

HOW THE CASH METHOD FAILS THE CONTRACTOR

Point 3 is the one that will bring the contractor around to discarding cash basis accounting. As his business grows, he will be demanding more complete and precise measurement of performance from his accounting system. He will be under pressure from his banker and other interested outsiders to show not only what he has collected, but what he has earned. A record of bills he has paid is fine, but what about bills that he has not paid? Internal and external pressure will grow, and the contractor sooner or later will have to abandon cash basis accounting.

TAX CONSEQUENCES OF CHOOSING THE ACCOUNTING METHOD

To a great extent, the contractor has the Internal Revenue Service looking over his shoulder as he chooses his accounting system. For example, the contractor should know that the IRS permits him to report income on long-term contracts, either on the completed contract method or the percentage of completion method.[1] A long-term contract is one that is not completed within the taxable year into which it is entered.[2] This definition changes for large contractors doing over $25 million a year. (See Chapter 12.) The IRS also permits any other accounting method, including the cash method, if the method chosen clearly reflects income. The catch is that both the taxpayer and the IRS must be able to prepare returns on long-term contracts from these records. Whether the ordinary cash-basis accounting system can do the job is questionable. At any rate, it is doubtful that it could, without extensive adjustments that would essentially convert it to an accrual system anyway.

WHY THE COMPLETED-CONTRACT METHOD MAKES GOOD TAX SENSE

The contractor will like the completed-contract method because it permits him to report gain or loss from long-term contracts at the time they are completed. This means that income and related direct costs on work in progress are both deferred, while overhead costs, called "period costs" in tax and accounting parlance, are immediately written off, regardless of whether they belong to work in progress or completed contracts. The rules are different for contractors doing over $25 million a year. Allocable indirect, overhead, or period costs—no matter what the big contractor calls them—will be phased out completely as currently deductible. This means that in a few years the percentage of such costs treated as currently deductible will be reduced to zero. Chapter 12 deals with this and other matters pertaining to the over $25 million-a-year contractor.

Suppose that the contractor was successful on a job with an estimated completion date of two and a half years from the contract's signing. Suppose that the job, by the end of the first accounting period, had progressed as follows:

	Collections	Cost	Profit
First year	$ 2,000,000	$ 1,500,000	$ 500,000
Second year	15,000,000	13,000,000	2,000,000
Third year	3,000,000	1,500,000	1,500,000
	$20,000,000	$16,000,000	$4,000,000

The IRS will permit the contractor to report no income or expense on this contract for the first two years. The entire $4 million profit is reported in the third year.

The contractor will be quick to list several advantages:

1. There is no guess work. I report profit after the job is completed, and I know exactly how much money I've made.

2. I don't have to worry about having to estimate my profit, and therefore, I avoid the risk of paying taxes on profits I might not make.

3. I like the idea of getting to use the money I collect, after I pay my bills, of course, without having to worry about paying taxes on it.

These are all good, practical reasons for the contractor's love affair with the completed-contract method. But not everything is peaches and cream.

THE BAD SIDE OF THE COMPLETED-CONTRACT METHOD

The accountant must be careful when, while playing the Devil's Advocate, he begins to recite disadvantages to the completed-contract method. He must recognize the fact that advantages are almost immediate, occurring as soon as the money starts coming in. Disadvantages are down the road. In the previous example given, they appear two and a half years from now, when the job is finished. There's lots of time to worry about them later. Nevertheless, it is the duty of the accountant to point out underlying risks that will surface sooner or later. For example:

1. There is a tendency to look upon the difference between deferred income and deferred job costs as real profit. It is easy to overlook the trouble ahead resulting from overbilling and cost overruns.

2. Deferred income and deferred job costs are balance sheet items. Transfer to the income statement, the normal place for evaluating performance, takes place only after the job is finished. By then it might be too late to do anything about poor performance.

3. It's fine to defer profit, and the corresponding taxes, until the job is finished. But what if several jobs are finished at about the same time, and all of a sudden the contractor has to come up with a large sum of money to pay taxes?

PITFALLS OF DEFERRED INCOME

Deferring income until a job is finished makes the contractor feel as if he might be in control of the tax situation. However, cold facts right out of Section 451 of the Internal Revenue Code might sober him up. For example, he will not be permitted to defer income beyond the completion date simply because he has not been paid, or because his warranty period is not up, or because he learns that someone up the line is having financial difficulties, and he therefore expects trouble getting his money.

HOW TO COPE WITH THE CASH FLOW PROBLEM OF THE COMPLETED-CONTRACT METHOD

If the contract is 99 percent complete, the concept of "substantial" completion will catch up with the contractor. At this point, he must report income and settle his tax bill. Cash flow problems, which looked so remote when he was deferring income, are suddenly knocking at his door.

The completed-contract method has its place, if used with the idea that deferral in meeting the tax bill means postponement and not cancellation. If provisions can be made for the inevitable cash drain at the end of the line, then tax deferral can be used as a discrete device for postponing cash settlement to a time when a more accurate determination of profit can be made.

THE COMPLETED-CONTRACT METHOD FAILS TO MEASURE PERFORMANCE

As in the case of the cash method, the completed-contract method suffers from an inability to provide a fair measurement of income, and therefore cannot be used internally and externally to measure the contractor's performance. The contractor who knows how to use financial data to find out what is going on will grow restless with it, and so will the banker and the bonding people. Inevitably, all these people will insist on an analysis of construction in progress. Bulk figures, shown as deferred income and deferred costs, will not prove satisfactory. Inevitably, the pressure will be on from all sides for an analysis of work in progress, presented in the classic format, so as to reveal under- and overbilling and their consequences.

WHY THE PERCENTAGE OF COMPLETION METHOD IS PREFERRED

This method recognizes income as a contract progresses, and therefore provides a more timely measurement of performance than either the cash or the completed-contract method.

There is a major problem involved here in that the measurement of income earned—and reported—depends upon the percentage of completion fraction. The numerator is costs incurred to date, and the denominator is costs incurred to date, plus estimated additional costs to complete the job. One can easily see how the percentage of completion fraction can be subject to much abuse. For example, the numerator can be overstated and the denominator understated. The result is an overstated percentage of completion, which in turn produces overstated income.

Working with Percentage of Completion Accounting: 4 Examples

At this point, let's assume that we will get the problem of percentage of completion accounting pretty well resolved, both from the internal as well as the external accountant's point of view, after the in-depth treatment given to it in Chapters 3 and 10. In the meantime, here are the key points to consider in evaluating and understanding the system:

1. Estimated gross profit, times percentage of completion, equals earned income.
2. Excess of billing over costs is offset against earned income.
3. Unearned amounts become a current liability, and are presented in the balance sheet as "unearned billings over costs."
4. If there is an excess in earned amounts after the comparison with earned billings over costs, the excess becomes a current asset and is presented on the balance sheet as "unbilled costs and earnings."

Example 1. Let's assume the contractor has a contract in progress in the amount of $500,000. At the end of the reporting period, costs to date are $250,000. Estimated costs to complete the job are $150,000. The analysis of work in progress can now be completed as follows:

Billings to date	$300,000
Excess billings over costs	50,000
Estimated gross profit:	
$500,000 − $250,000 − $150,000 =	100,000
Percentage of completion:	
$\dfrac{\$250,000}{\$250,000 + \$150,000} \times 100 =$	62.5%
Gross profit earned, $100,000 × 62.5% =	$ 62,500
Unbilled earnings	12,500

Unbilled earnings of $12,500 are debited to the current asset account, unbilled costs and earnings. The corresponding credit is to contract revenue.

It is easy to see that the estimated cost to complete the job is indeed a critical figure. If the contractor is the optimistic type, as most of them tend to be, and permits his optimism to influence estimated costs to complete the job here is what will happen:

1. He understates the denominator of the percentage of completion fraction.
2. He overstates percentage of completion.
3. He overstates estimated gross profit.

4. He applies an overstated percentage of completion to an overstated gross profit.[3]

Example 2.   Let's take another look at the illustration. Suppose that instead of $50,000, excess billings over costs had turned out to be $70,000. Then, instead of unbilled earnings of $12,500, the contractor would have unearned billings over costs of $7,500. This would become a current liability, and the corresponding debit would reduce contract revenue. One can imagine the mental gymnastics a contractor goes through as he tries to avoid the recognition of unearned billings over costs.

Example 3.   Assuming that costs to date are $325,000, and that the estimated gross profit is still $100,000, the percentage of completion is now:

$$\frac{\$325,000}{\$325,000 + \$75,000} \times 100 = 81.25\%$$

Gross profit earned is $81,250, and instead of excess billings over costs of $50,000, we now have costs over billings of $25,000. Unbilled costs and earnings are therefore $106,250, consisting of costs over billings of $25,000 and gross profit earned of $81,250. The entire amount of $106,250 becomes an increase to current assets and a corresponding increase to contract revenue.

Example 4.   Suppose that it turns out that only $35,000 of the $50,000 in excess billings over costs has been earned. The difference of $15,000 becomes a current liability under unearned billings over costs, with a corresponding reduction to contract revenue.

HOW THE COMPLETED-CONTRACT METHOD DISTORTS THE PROFIT PICTURE

Suppose Contractor A had chosen the completed-contract method to report income for long-term contracts. During the fiscal year, let us also assume that he had been successful bidder in a $5 million contract. At the end of the year, the contract was 55 percent complete. In the meantime, he had contract income of $2 million from a contract obtained and completed during the year. Gross profit was 10 percent, and general and administrative expenses amounted to $320,000 for the year. Here is what the income statement would look like:

Income from completed contracts	$2,000,000
Less cost of completed contracts	1,800,000
Gross profit	$ 200,000
Less general and administrative expenses	320,000
Net income (loss) before taxes	$ (120,000)

HOW PERCENTAGE OF COMPLETION DOES A BETTER JOB

If Contractor A had chosen the percentage of completion method, his income statement would have looked like this:

Contract income	$4,750,000
Less cost of contracts	4,275,000
Gross profit	$ 475,000
Less general and administrative expense	320,000
Net income before taxes	$ 155,000
Income taxes	75,000
Net income after taxes	$ 80,000

Contract revenue of $4.75 million consists of $2 million completed contract revenue, plus percentage of completion income of 55 percent of the $5 million long-term contract, or $2.75 million. This is quite a different story from the $120,000 loss reported under the completed contract method.

COMPLETED-CONTRACT METHOD vs. PERCENTAGE OF COMPLETION

Did Contractor A actually sustain a loss of $120,000, as reported under the completed-contract method? Of course not. What really happened was that the completed contract method did not measure profit being earned on work in progress, and therefore failed to show what was really going on.

What was really going on was that Contractor A was making a profit, not losing money, and that he faced a possible $75,000 income tax bill. Of course, he could possibly defer a good portion of this potential tax liability, as will be explained below by "keeping two sets of books."

From the contractor's point of view, another advantage of using percentage of completion is that it gives interim financial statements the ability to more effectively measure construction in progress. At the end of each month, going back to the example given above, the contractor would have evaluated progress being made on the $5 million contract by means of the analysis of work in progress. Finally, by using the task-cost analysis method, as explained in Chapter 3, he would have been able to use cost factors contained in his takeoff sheet to keep the job under control.

The month-by-month comparison of planned versus actual costs, carried out element by element, and made possible by the use of the percentage of completion method, will sharpen up the contractor's estimating factors. This kind of feedback, as has already been noted, is invaluable to the estimating department.

KEEPING TWO SETS OF BOOKS: ONE FOR TAXES, THE OTHER FOR MANAGEMENT

Most big contractors will use percentage of completion for management purposes, but will switch to the completed contract method for tax purposes. The reason for this is pretty obvious: the contractor does not want to pay taxes on estimated gross profits earned, a key figure in the analysis of the work in progress worksheet. No matter how careful he might be in estimating costs to complete a job in progress, he does not want to pay taxes on this estimate until the job is complete and all unknowns are resolved before settling his bill with the government.

One might call this common practice among construction people "using two sets of books." Theoretically this might be so, but in actual practice the books are kept on the percentage of completion so that the various evaluations required by bankers and bonding people can be taken right off the books. The conversion to completed contracts can be done on an income tax worksheet without disturbing day-to-day accounting operations. Contract revenue and contract cost of work in progress can both be deferred, along with other income-determining portions of the analysis of work in progress worksheet, including the tax liability, until a more precise determination of profitability can be made upon completion of the jobs.

HOW THE INTERNAL REVENUE FEELS ABOUT PERCENTAGE OF COMPLETION

While the contractor prefers the completed-contract method in figuring his tax liability, the IRS takes the opposite view, preferring percentage of completion because taxes are collected more quickly. However, both methods are permitted for long-term contracts, but a word of caution is in order. Choice of either the percentage of completion method or the completed-contract method is binding. Once a choice is made, the contractor is stuck with it, and changes to or from the chosen method require IRS approval.

The IRS Wants to Force the Use of Percentage of Completion

The Internal Revenue Service has tried before and will continue to try to force the contractor to pay his taxes on the basis of percentage of completion. At first the IRS argument was that if you use percentage of completion to manage, you should also use it to pay your taxes. The courts turned this down. Current arguments are less subtle, and go something like this: We need the money to close the budget gap, so let's speed up collections by prohibiting the use of the completed-contract method for tax purposes. The contractors strongly oppose such legislation. They will argue that in the construction industry, there is a huge gap between the earning of profits and their collection, especially in view of the practice of holding out a retention, sometimes amounting to as much as 10 percent, until the job is completed and "sold." Many times retention represents more than the net income of the job. The contractor can't see borrowing money to pay taxes on profits that, even if they turn out to be as estimated in the analysis of work in progress, are a long way off from being collected. The IRS has won a partial victory with respect to contractors doing over $25 million a year. How tax benefits will be stripped for these contractors is covered in Chapter 12.

HOW TO USE THE ACCOUNTING SYSTEM TO REFLECT MANAGEMENT POLICY

The accounting system is a management responsibility. It is up to management to decide what it should look like, what it should do, and how it should be used. Management must mold the accounting system by prescribing policy that makes demands on it, forcing it to perform in conformity with overall company objectives.

How the Contractor Should Use the Income Statement. Let's suppose that the AAA Construction Company enjoyed a good year and that the contractor was examining the income statement as shown in Figure 2–1. The contractor, although happy with his profit, will wonder whether it could have been better.

AAA CONSTRUCTION COMPANY
Income Statement
Year Ended December 31, 19___

Earned revenues	$2,500,000
Cost of contracts	2,000,000
Gross profit	$ 500,000
General and administrative expense	250,000
Net income before income taxes	$ 250,000
Income taxes	116,500
Net income after taxes	$ 133,500

Figure 2–1. *Income Statement, AAA Construction Company*

Actually, the accountant should guide the contractor's attention to a key figure, cost of contracts. What the contractor needs to know is if this figure is good or bad. The contractor might go one step further and ask himself, "Are job costs good or bad, and compared to what?" The accountant's answer should be, "Compared to what contract costs are *supposed* to be."

The contractor will be quick to point out that costs are supposed to be just about the same as the costs he came up with on his takeoff sheet; that is, the estimated costs used as the basis for the successful bids that won him the contracts.

How the Contractor Prescribes Accounting Policy. It might not look like it, but from what has gone on above, the contractor has made important policy pronouncements. He has defined what costs are supposed to be as compared to the takeoff sheet. He is on his way to establishing accounting policy, described as follows:

1. Labor, material, subcontractor, and miscellaneous costs will be broken down by jobs.

2. In each job, cost elements will parallel those used in the takeoff sheets.

3. Weekly control reports will be prepared, showing planned versus actual costs by job and by cost element within each job.

4. The job-cost system will be changed to incorporate this policy.

The Benefits of Contractor-Established Accounting Policies. Here is what can be expected from carrying out such policies:

1. The comparison of planned versus actual cost elements will sharpen up the cost factors.

2. Feedback to the estimating department will prove invaluable.

3. Sharing this information with the job foremen will give them challenging incentives to bring their jobs in "on the money."

4. The contractor, noting the good effects of his policy formulation, will take new pride in his accounting system and be inclined to continue the habit of providing valuable input.

5. The accountant will be elevated from the routine job of recordkeeper, to the satisfying and challenging position of directing the operation of the contractor's principal management information system.

Key Examples of Contractor-Established Accounting Policies. Examples are many. The contractor could establish policies for buying materials and equipment, for awarding subcontracts, for labor costing, for billing, for estimating costs to complete jobs, for profit planning, and for financial statement presentation. Such policies will have a profound effect in the shaping of the accounting system.

HOW THE ACCOUNTANT SHOULD REACT TO THE CONTRACTOR'S POLICY FORMULATION

Having stimulated the contractor into recognizing his role as policy maker for the accounting system, the accountant should be ready to respond. He should be in tune with the contractor's thinking, and should be ready to make the accounting system responsive to the needs of the contractor.

ACCOUNTING BASIS FOR THE PERCENTAGE OF COMPLETION CONTRACTOR

A very important need for the percentage of completion contractor is the establishing of a solid accounting basis. A key factor in income determination is the proper measurement of the percentage of completion of any work in progress. Exactly how to establish the required accounting basis, and how it leads to the solution of this complex problem, is the subject of the next chapter.

Notes: Chapter 2

1. IRS Regulations, Par. 1.451–3(a).
2. *Op. cit.*, Par. 1.451–3(b)(i).
3. Henry G. Pansza, "Task-Cost Analysis of Construction in Progress," *Management Accounting*, December, 1976, p. 42. Copyright © 1976 by National Association of Accountants, New York.

— 3

HOW TO SOLVE THE PERCENTAGE OF COMPLETION PROBLEM

Large construction contracts are invariably long-term. For these, the percentage-of-completion method will almost certainly be used. Each month, managers and accountants get together to analyze contracts in progress. The purpose is to determine for each such contract the estimated gross income and the percentage of that gross income earned.

A review of the principles and methodology prevailing in the construction industry indicates a need for a simple, step-by-step approach to the problem of income determination for construction in progress. The theme of this chapter is that such a need can be satisfied by the task-cost approach. This approach subjects work remaining to be done to a specific procedural analysis in arriving at estimated costs to complete the job.

This chapter will give the accountant and the auditor a down-to-earth explanation of the percentage of completion problem. An original approach to its solution will make use of those accounting techniques that are intended to dispell the haziness and confusion associated with this problem.

The accountant and the auditor will learn to solve the percentage of completion problem by the use of task-cost analysis. What it is and how it is to be used will be covered in detail in the sections that follow.

WHAT IS THE PERCENTAGE OF COMPLETION PROBLEM?

The problem is complicated by the fact that it can become many things to many people. For example, the contractor, conscious of stockholders, bankers, and bonding people looking over his shoulder, will wish to present the best possible profit picture. Stockholders will be suspicious of any substantial increase in earnings per share based on a significant build-up in unbilled costs and earnings, and so will the bankers and the bonding people. The latter in particular will tend to be critical, since bonding capacity is roughly the equivalent of ten times net working capital. Hence, a buildup in unbilled costs and earnings, which in turn means an increase in current assets, will be closely reviewed.

HOW BONDING COMPANIES LOOK AT CONSTRUCTION IN PROGRESS

Basically, formats prescribed by bonding companies for analysis of construction in progress are designed to answer the following questions:

- How much has been billed in excess of cost?
- How much of this has been earned?
- Is the earned amount fairly stated?
- How much is unearned, and therefore a current liability?
- Are unbilled costs and earnings, a current asset, fairly stated?

HOW THE COST-TO-COST BASIS CAN BE ABUSED

Getting back to the contractor, the cost-to-cost basis for determining percentage of completion becomes an irresistible opportunity to window dress. Cost-to-cost means that the numerator is the cost incurred to date, and the denominator is cost incurred to date, plus estimated additional costs to complete the job. Although there have been cases where contractors have been accused of inflating the numerator, the more common tendency is to deflate the denominator by understating the estimated additional costs to complete the job.

Now consider what happens to the percentage of completion fraction, and the dependent variables it affects, when the contractor ignores facts, gives way to optimism, and deflates the denominator by understating the estimated additional costs to complete the job.

- The denominator is understated.
- The percentage of completion is overstated.
- Estimated gross profit is overstated.
- An overstated percentage of completion is applied against an overstated gross profit.

EFFECTS OF UNDERSTATING ESTIMATED COSTS TO COMPLETE

The dramatic effects of understating estimated costs to complete is illustrated in Figure 3–1. The facts are as follows:

Contract number	978
Contract amount	$350,000
Billings to date	$240,000
Costs to date	$192,000
Estimated costs to complete:	
Realistic	$ 90,000
Optimistic	$ 55,000

Now let's go back to Figure 3–1, in order to evaluate the consequences of going from realism to optimism.

- Estimated gross profit jumps from $68,000 to $103,000.
- Gross profit percentage increases from 19 to 29 percent.
- Percentage complete is now 78 instead of 68 percent.
- Billings over costs:
    Earned:
        From $46,240 to the full $48,000, plus unbilled costs and earnings of $32,340.
    Unearned:
        From $1,760 to zero.
- Unbilled costs and earnings:
    From zero to $32,340.

Now, let's analyze the effect on working capital.

	Increase (Decrease)		
	Current Assets	*Current Liabilities*	*Working Capital*
Realistic		$1,760	$ (1,760)
Optimistic	$32,340		32,340

The adjustment resulting from the realistic estimated costs to complete is:

	Dr	Cr
Contract revenue	$1,760	
Unearned billings over costs		$1,760

CONTRACTOR'S CONSTRUCTION COMPANY
ANALYSIS OF WORK IN PROGRESS
19____

	(1)	(2)	(3)	(4)	(5)	(6)	(7)	(8)	(9)	(10)	(11)	(12)
Contract No.	Contract	Billings to Date	Costs to Date	Billings/ Costs	Costs/ Billings	Est. Costs to Complete	Est. Gross Profit	Percent		Billings/Costs		Unbilled
								G.P.	Compl.	Earned	Unearned	Costs & Earnings
978	$	$	$	$	$	$	$			$	$	$
Realistic 978	350,000	240,000	192,000	48,000	-0-	90,000	68,000	19	68	46,240	1,760	
Optimistic	350,000	240,000	192,000	48,000	-0-	55,000	103,000	29	78	48,000		32,340

Note:

(4) = (2) − (3)
(5) = (3) − (2)
(7) = (1) − (3) − (6)
(8) = (7)/(1)
(9) = (3)/3 + (6)
(10) = If (10) is less than (4) the difference is put in (11)
     If (10) is more than (4) the difference is put in (12) + (5)

Figure 3–1

The adjustment resulting from the optimistic estimated costs to complete is:

	Dr	Cr
Unbilled costs and earnings	$32,340	
Contract revenue		$32,340

Please note that unearned billings over costs is a current liability, while unbilled costs and earnings is a current asset. The impact on working capital is $34,100; that is, it changes from a minus $1,760 to a plus $32,340.

Is the example an exaggeration? Not necessarily. A contractor, desperate for bonding capacity, will be tempted to do just such a thing. After all, a $35,000 estimating "error" on a $350,000 contract is only 10 percent. In this crazy business, who can hold the contractor to a tolerance of less than 10 percent?

How Understating Leads to Trouble. The effects of deliberately understating costs to complete are insidious and pervasive. The contractor will be inclined to gamble that future performance will overcome the problems caused by his optimistic estimates. When the next cycle comes around and the expected improvement does not materialize, the frustration and anxiety will become unbearable.

When Optimism Comes to an End. There is danger that if the contractor applies his optimism to too many jobs in progress, he will have started a chain of events that will eventually trap him. There is no escaping the day of reckoning when a job is completed and the gross profit is a simple arithmetic fact. Is there a way to beat the sobering reality of completed jobs? The optimistic contractor will say, "Yes, keep the pipeline full. We need lots of work in progress. This might mean taking jobs cheap, but things will work out. My optimism will eventually be justified."

Let's look at Figure 3–1 again. Suppose the contractor stayed with his optimistic estimates, and gradually began to accommodate his thinking and judgment to optimism so that he accepted as real his estimated gross profit of $103,000.

Before he realizes what is happening, his accountant presents him with an analysis of completed jobs such as the one in Figure 3–2.

• Job 978 is now completed, and it turns out that gross profit is $68,000 and not $103,000.

• Total jobs completed of $3.5 million reveal an actual gross profit of $663,000, as opposed to the estimated gross profit of $990,000 consistently reported by the optimistic contractor.

Faced with the reality of the analysis of completed jobs, what options does the contractor have?

• He can take his lumps and adjust his profit by $327,000 through the following entry:

Dr Contract Revenue
   Cr Unbilled costs and earnings

CONTRACTOR'S CONSTRUCTION COMPANY Analysis of Completed Jobs ————————— 19__					
Contract Number	Contract	Cost	Gross Profit	Est. Gross Profit	Over (Under) Estimate
978	$ 350,000	$ 282,000	$ 68,000	$103,000	$ (35,000)
	$3,500,000	$2,837,000	$663,000	$990,000	$(327,000)

Figure 3–2

• He can try to offset the $327,000 decrease in profits, or part of it, by continuing to tamper with the analysis of work in progress.

Can Outsiders Cope with Understated Costs to Complete? How much he will be hurt by the problem depends a great deal on the skill of the outsider. If he defers decisions based on work in progress until he has had a chance to study the analysis of completed jobs, he can save himself a lot of trouble. If he knows how to use analyses of completed jobs to adjust for the contractor's optimism, he might even be able to prevail upon the contractor to become more realistic in his estimates of gross profit.

The outsider's problem is mostly an inability to grasp the plight of the contractor. The more desperate his financial condition, the more he will be inclined to take chances. And if he is successful in getting away with his deception, heaven help everyone concerned. If the cover-up succeeds, even for a short period of time, no one will ever be able to convince him to see things as they are and deal with problems as they occur.

WHAT IS TASK-COST ANALYSIS?

Most construction firms, even the smaller ones, will already have available through their accounting system the basic data needed for the successful application of task-cost analysis. Other than the normal documentation such as takeoff sheets, quotations, purchase orders, contracts, and subcontracts, a basic requirement is a simple job-cost system capable of producing cost data by job and cost element. Such a system would show the costs for each job, broken down by labor, material equipment, miscellaneous, and subcontractors. A handy and inexpensive addition to the cost ledger columns would be one for labor hours. If such a cost system is not in existence, it can be easily installed. Specifications for the contractor's basic accounting system, described in Chapter 5, will provide all the data required for the successful operation of task-cost analysis.

For the remainder of this section, the task-cost approach will be illustrated as it would apply to a fictitious mechanical contractor, simply because of the author's familiarity with this type of operation. However, it will be readily apparent that the principles and procedures described are easily adaptable to other trades in the construction industry, as well as to general contractors.

Analysis of Work in Progress. The first step is to prepare an analysis of work in progress. Most contractors are familiar with this analysis. The format shown in Figure 3–1 will satisfy the requirements of management, accountants, auditors, and surety, as well as providing the point of departure for task-cost analysis.

Estimated Costs to Complete. Column 6 of the analysis of work in progress, which shows the estimated costs to complete the job, is the key to successful analysis of work in progress. Miscalculation of this critical figure, intentional or not, is the main problem. Its solution lies in bringing to bear all possible analytical data available to the contractor through his accounting system, in a systematic procedure to reduce as many unknowns to knowns, in order to produce the best possible estimate of costs needed to complete the job.

HOW TO USE TASK-COST ANALYSIS

Each job listed in the analysis of work in progress is subjected to a careful analysis and evaluation of work remaining to be done versus amounts available to accomplish this work. The task-cost relationship is then used to arrive at estimated costs to complete the job. These are the amounts that are to be inserted under Column 6 of the analysis of work in progress.

Task-Cost Analysis Illustrated

Let us assume that we have taken one line of the analysis of the work in progress and have arranged the columnar headings vertically instead of in the normal horizontal arrangement. Let us further assume that the contractor's accountant has filled in the amounts for Columns 1 through 5 as follows:

XYZ MECHANICAL CONTRACTORS, INC.
Job 519—Travis Technical Facility
December 31, 19__

1. Contract Amount	$343,000
2. Billings to Date	247,000
3. Cost to Date	192,000
4. Billings over Costs	55,000
5. Costs over Billings	–0–

In addition to the above, the accountant also prepares the following analysis of Job 519:

	A	B	C	D
	Per Take-Off	*To Date*	*Balance Remaining*	*Costs to Complete*
Labor hours	(6,100)	(4,100)	(2,000)	
Labor costs	$ 85,500	$ 57,600	$27,900	
Material	54,500	38,400	16,100	
Equipment	82,800	52,300	30,500	
Miscellaneous	5,200	3,300	1,900	
Subcontractors	57,000	40,400	16,600	
	$285,000	$192,000	$93,000	

HOW TO NAIL DOWN ESTIMATED COSTS TO COMPLETE

The accountant works closely with the engineer, the estimator, and the manager to compute amounts to be entered in Column 6. The takeoff sheets, used to figure the job and bid it, are carefully reviewed to ascertain agreement with the amounts shown in Column A. Adjustments are made as necessary. The takeoff sheet is then analyzed, task by task, and those tasks already accomplished are checked off, together with corresponding actual manhours required to accomplish them. Finally, tasks remaining to be done are isolated, carefully analyzed, and, if necessary, verified with the job foreman, after which the best possible manhour estimate for each task is calculated. Methodology might include critical path methods, probabilistic models, engineered standards, or educated guesses, depending on the capability at hand.

Manhour estimates arrived at in this way are then totaled. Let us assume that the total manhours needed to complete Job 519 turn out to be 2,600, or

600 more than the balance remaining. This amount is entered in Column D. Later on, the accountant, using the latest data, plus adjustments to reflect anticipated pay-scale changes, will multiply the 2,600 manhours by the cost per hour thus arrived at, to come up with the labor costs figure needed for Column D. Let us assume that this turns out to be $36,300. This exercise completes the first two lines and the most critical part of Column D.

WRAP-UP AND ADJUSTING ENTRIES IN TASK-COST ANALYSIS

What is left to be done is a wrap-up that is relatively easy. For example, the next line of our worksheet, materials, can be figured pretty closely. Amounts in Column C are verified by examining purchase orders and isolating the material to be delivered. The estimator, engineer, or manager should be furnished this information, so that he can match what he has coming with what he has to do. Normally, material estimates on the takeoff sheets are reliable, the degree of reliability depending upon the level of completeness at the time of the job's takeoff. In our example, let us assume that an adjustment of over $800 was needed, bringing the Column D amount up to $16,900.

How to Handle Equipment Costs. Normally, the computation of equipment needed to complete the job is pretty cut and dried. When Job 519 was bid, equipment suppliers quoted fixed prices to the contractor. Therefore, the balance remaining in Column C should represent uninvoiced, and hence undelivered, amounts. This approach is the basis of the equipment delivery status report illustrated in Figure 5–5.

In our example, we will assume that the balance remaining in Column C represents uninvoiced, and hence undelivered, amounts. Therefore, we will move the $30,500 shown in Column C over to Column D. However, we must recognize that problems could develop during periods of inflation. For example, amounts shown in C might not necessarily satisfy the requirements of Column D. During periods of severe inflation, suppliers might try to hold prices good for only thirty days; therefore, delays in delivery could result in upward adjustments to Column D, with or without corresponding adjustments to Column A.

How to Handle Other Costs. Miscellaneous costs are estimated for specific line items on the takeoff sheets. Some line items are precise, task-oriented, and can be analyzed by procedures described above. Others are contingency items, and must be analyzed in terms of the latest information—whether the contingency has occurred or, if not, whether it will occur, and if so, whether provisions for its occurrence are adequate or need revision. We will assume a minor revision in the case of Job 519, going from $1,900 in Column C to $1,600 in Column D.

Subcontractors will quote fixed amounts, and except for unusual circumstances or errors, amounts shown in Column C will be used in Column D.

Column D can now be completed as follows:

	Needed to Complete
Labor hours	(2,600)
Labor costs	$ 36,300
Material	16,900
Equipment	30,500
Miscellaneous	1,600
Subs	16,600
Total	$101,900

HOW TO COMPLETE THE ANALYSIS OF WORK IN PROGRESS

The accountant now goes back to the analysis of work in progress and completes all the columns as follows:

Column	Columnar Heading	Amount
(1)	Contract amount	$343,000
(2)	Billings to date	247,000
(3)	Cost to date	192,000
(4)	Billings over cost	55,000
(5)	Cost over billings	–0–
(6)	Estimated cost to complete	101,900
(7)	Estimated gross profit	49,100
(8)	Percentage: gross profit	14.3
(9)	Percentage: completion	65.3
(10)	Billings over costs earned	32,062
(11)	Billings over costs unearned	22,938
(12)	Unbilled costs and earnings	–0–

Expanding the Procedure to Other Jobs. The procedures described above for Job 519 are carried out for all the jobs in progress, with the exception of small, short-term jobs that are normally handled on a completed-contract basis. See Figure 6–2, and the section on Small Jobs immediately preceding it.

Adjusting Entries for Work in Progress. Assume that the schedule of work in progress has been completed for all jobs, and that totals for all jobs include the following amounts:

Unbilled costs and earnings	$15,000
Unearned billings over costs	$26,000

Any amounts appearing in the asset or liability accounts, unbilled costs and earnings or unearned billings over costs, are first reversed with the net contra going to the earned revenue account. Then, the new amounts are placed on the books by the following adjusting entry:

	Dr	Cr
Unbilled costs and earnings	$15,000	
Earned revenue	11,000	
Unearned billings over costs		$26,000

REPORT PRESENTATION OF CONSTRUCTION IN PROGRESS

If procedures described in this chapter have been followed, the accountant can be sure that the amounts shown in his analysis of work in progress under estimated costs to complete, or Column 6 of Figure 3–6, will stand up to the closest scrutiny. Security underwriters will be the most pleased because they constantly clash with the contractor about facing facts in analyzing construction in progress. Bankers, creditors, and investors will also be pleased to have an opportunity to view in detail the inner workings of the construction firm. After all, it is not unusual for unbilled costs and earnings to make up a significant part of both current assets and contract revenue.

Balance Sheet Presentation of Construction in Progress. If the accountant, the contractor, and his staff have all done a good job in arriving at Column 6 of the analysis of work in progress, it seems only natural that they will want to follow through with a good presentation on the financial statements of the spin-off figures. These, of course, are unbilled costs and earnings, a current asset, and unearned billings over costs, a current liability. As a matter of good form, there must not be a netting-out on these two items, because each is significant. The net outcome reflected as part of contract revenue must be annotated so that the user of the financial statements will be able to tell how much has been added or deducted from income as a result of the analysis of work in progress.

What is the Proper Wording? The wording of the balance sheet items must be such that the user will not be left with any misunderstanding. The accountant's choice will depend on the preference of the users.

As an example, what we have been calling unbilled costs and earnings can be called:

Costs and estimated earnings in excess of billing on uncompleted contracts

or

Costs and estimated earnings in excess of billings.

Unearned billings over costs can also be given a more elaborate nomenclature such as:

Billings in excess of costs and estimated earnings on uncompleted contracts

or

Billings in excess of costs and estimated earnings.

Illustrations.   Figure 3–3 shows the more common method of presenting unbilled costs and earnings. Note the preferred method of showing accounts receivable and the reference to Schedule 1, shown here as Figure 3–4.

Figure 3–5 illustrates the method of presenting unearned billings over costs. Notice the reference to the analysis of work in progress, shown in Figure 3–6. Also, note that the statement of income and retained earnings shown in Figure 3–7 discloses what portion of contract revenue results from the net difference between unbilled costs and earnings and unearned billings over costs.

NOTES TO ACCOMPANY INTERIM FINANCIAL STATEMENTS

Not shown in the illustrations above are the various notes on significant accounting policies and analytical information normally accompanying the financial statements. If only a few items are involved in the clarification process,

---

CONTRACTOR'S CONSTRUCTION COMPANY *Exhibit A*
Balance Sheet
June 30, 19___
Assets

CURRENT ASSETS

Cash	$ 192,300
Accounts receivable (Schedule 1)	797,400
Unbilled costs and earnings (Schedule 2)	230,000
Inventory of materials and supplies not applicable to contracts	45,200
Prepaid expense	20,100
Total current assets	$1,285,000
PROPERTY AND EQUIPMENT (Schedule 3)	750,000
OTHER ASSETS (Schedule 4)	10,000
	$2,045,000

Figure 3–3

CONTRACTOR'S CONSTRUCTION COMPANY   *Schedule 1*
Receivables on Uncompleted Contracts
June 30, 19___

	Completed Contracts	Progress Billings, Completed Contracts	Retainage Not Currently Due	Total
Castile Industries, Inc.	$ 48,000	$	$	$ 48,000
Wright Rubber Co.	66,500		73,100	139,600
Newkirk School		35,500	32,600	68,100
Total	$581,600	$65,300	$150,500	$797,400

Figure 3–4

CONTRACTOR'S CONSTRUCTION COMPANY   *Exhibit B*
Balance Sheet
June 30, 19___
Liabilities and Stockholders Equity

CURRENT LIABILITIES

Accounts payable		$ 180,000
Notes payable		250,000
Income taxes payable		56,000
Accrued expenses		33,000
Unearned billings over costs (Schedule 2)		255,000
Total current liabilities		$ 774,000

OTHER LIABILITIES

Long-term debt	$490,000	
Contested liability	50,000	540,000

STOCKHOLDERS EQUITY

Common stock—authorized 100,000 shares par value $1; issued and outstanding, 75,000 shares	$ 75,000	
Capital contributed for common stock in excess of par	150,000	
Retained earnings (Exhibit C)	506,000	731,000
		$2,045,000

Figure 3–5

CONTRACTOR'S CONSTRUCTION COMPANY

Analysis of Work in Progress

June 30, 19___

Schedule 2

Job No.	Job Name	Contract (1)	Billed to Date (2)	Cost to Date (3)	Billings Over Costs (4)	Costs Over Billings (5)	Estimated Cost to Complete (6)	Estimated Gross Profit (7)	Percent Complete (8)	Gross Profit Earned (9)	Billings Over Costs — Earned (10)	Billings Over Costs — Unearned (11)	Unbilled Costs and Earnings (12)
396	Newkirk School	$ 600,000	$ 326,000	$ 301,000	$ 25,000		$ 205,000	$ 94,000	59	$ 55,460	$ 25,000	$	$ 30,460
399	Planet Petroleum Co.	1,298,000	550,000	420,000	130,000		758,000	120,000	36	43,200	43,200	86,000	
402	Krimp Manufacturing Corp.	1,900,000	940,000	945,000		5,000	675,000	280,000	58	162,400			167,400
	Totals	$8,600,000	$3,750,000	$3,100,000	$700,000	$50,000	$4,468,000	$1,032,000	41	$625,000	$445,000	$255,000	$230,000

Figure 3-6

Exhibit C

CONTRACTOR'S CONSTRUCTION COMPANY
Statement of Income and Retained Earnings
Year Ended June 30, 19___

CONTRACT INCOME

Billings	$7,250,000	
Unbilled costs and earnings	230,000	
Less unearned billings over costs	(255,000)	$7,225,000
COST OF CONTRACTS		6,125,000
GROSS PROFIT FROM CONTRACTS		$1,100,000
GENERAL AND ADMINISTRATIVE EXPENSE (Schedule 5)		905,000
NET INCOME FROM OPERATIONS		$ 195,000
OTHER INCOME		
Discounts	$ 10,000	
Sale of assets	5,000	15,000
OTHER EXPENSE		
Interest expense		42,000
INCOME TAXES		
Federal	$ 51,000	
State	5,000	56,000
NET INCOME (PER SHARE $1.49)		$ 113,000
RETAINED EARNINGS, BEGINNING OF YEAR		394,000
RETAINED EARNINGS, END OF YEAR		$ 507,000

Figure 3–7

there can be a substitution of notes for schedules. For example, property and equipment can be analyzed by means of a note rather than a schedule.

Notes need not be as elaborate as those accompanying audited financial statements. However, it is a good practice to give note references to all items that might raise questions. Examples are:

- Accounting basis for recording income
- Depreciation policy
- Composition of notes payable
- Composition of income tax liability
- Composition of accrued expenses
- Contested liabilities

READY TO PLAN FOR FINANCIAL SUCCESS?

Having learned how to solve the percentage of completion problem and how to present construction in progress in financial statements, you can now help the contractor plan for financial success. The chapter that follows contains detailed instructions for the accountant and the contractor to use in putting together a successful financial game plan.

4

HOW TO BUDGET AND PREPARE A PRO-FORMA FINANCIAL GAME PLAN

The risks that the construction contractor faces daily are uniquely frustrating because he feels that he can exert little if any control over them. There are risks in the weather, the unions, the subcontractors, the architects, the engineers, the owners, the economy, the suppliers, the bankers, the surety underwriters, and the investors. He often views then as an uncooperative lot, seldom there when he needs them.

The typical contractor can easily find himself in a position where he is spending too much time either putting out fires or worrying about them breaking out. This is hardly the proper setting for the successful management of a business.

This chapter shows the contractor how to extricate himself from the clutches of the kind of uncertainty that is characteristic of the construction business. It will outline methodical planning techniques with financial success as the principal objective. It will illustrate how the accountant can help the contractor operate his business successfully.

MANAGEMENT OBJECTIVES IN THE CONSTRUCTION INDUSTRY

When the subject of management objectives comes up, the contractor will probably say that staying alive is his immediate and most important objective, and that he has little time for anything else. The fact is that the contractor *must* find time for something else. He must find time to ask himself, "What do I want to be? How big do I want to get? What does it take to get that big? And am I willing to pay the price?" The price consists of much thinking, careful planning, hard work, self-discipline, and perseverance.

HOW TO ORGANIZE THE CONTRACTOR'S MANAGEMENT OBJECTIVES

Objectives for the contractor will generally follow this pattern:

• I want to become a contractor with a yearly volume of $_____.
• I will allow myself five (or ten, or fifteen) years to reach this objective.
• I will accomplish this objective in an orderly manner, taking my time and avoiding wild gambles that will put me out of business if they don't pay off.
• I need facts and figures, a logical and attainable plan of action reduced to dollars and cents.
• I need a management information system that will measure progress toward the accomplishment of my objectives.

THE SECRET OF SUCCESS

The contractor must not allow himself to stop at volume objectives. He must attach to planned volume the appendages of job costs, gross profit, general and administrative expense, and income taxes. He must continue his planning through net income after taxes, right on through its effects on working capital. In the construction business, success is a function of working capital. Bonding capacity, bidding strategy, management practices, and the very survival of the business all depend on working capital.

THE PROBLEMS OF THE UNDERCAPITALIZED CONTRACTOR

So often the contractor will start his business "on a shoestring." As long as he remains in such an undercapitalized position, he will be beset by a steady stream of frustrating and dangerous risks. His anxiety will mount as he begins to realize that sooner or later these risks will become something more than he can cope with. The world of the undercapitalized contractor looks like this:

• He is constantly putting out fires as he struggles for survival.

• He has to bid every job that comes along, since he cannot afford to be without work while waiting for the good ones.

• Operating at a ruggedly competitive level, he has to take risks in order to get a job.

• When he does get a job, he has to worry about getting it bonded, often making unwise financial concessions to lure an idemnifier.

• He is constantly on the brink of disaster, and even if he survives the day-to-day crises of normal times, *he will not survive the hard times that are bound to come sooner or later*.

WORKING WITH THE STRONGLY CAPITALIZED CONTRACTOR

The contractor who has either started out in a strong working capital position, or who has managed to work his way into it, enjoys great advantages. Here is his situation:

• Free of financial crises, he can devote his full time to managing his company.

• He can afford to wait for the good jobs.

• Having moved up to a larger scale of operations, his competitors are fewer in number and his chances of getting profitable work are greatly improved.

• When he does get a job, bonding it is no problem.

• During hard times he trims overhead, watches his cash flow, *and waits for better times, which are bound to come sooner or later*.

Arriving at this point means more than reaching a volume objective. In fact, volume per se, without a healthy mix of other profit ingredients, can lull the contractor into a false feeling of success. Such euphoria will never produce the raw desire needed to make him extricate himself from the problems of the undercapitalized contractor.

HOW TO TRANSLATE VOLUME OBJECTIVES INTO FINANCIAL SUCCESS

The accountant can help in the formulation and execution of the contractor's plan of success by showing him how to translate volume objectives into favorable impacts on working capital. Working capital is not the bottom line, but it is very close to it, and this is what we must concentrate on if we are to help the contractor achieve financial success.

Let's assume that the contractor sets his objectives in this fashion:

- I am now doing a volume of $5 million a year.
- My objective is to reach a volume of $10 million in five years.

The accountant can translate volume objectives into a financial framework that will form the basis for ultimate financial success. A five-year master plan can be roughed out into the manner shown in Figure 4–1. One word of caution: The contractor is used to working with markups on his cost estimates. The accountant's plan relies on the use of gross profit, since this is the particular type of price-volume-profit technique employed in this chapter. Use Figure 4–2 to go back and forth between markup and gross profit. If you want to interpolate, use these equations:

$$\frac{\text{Gross Profit}}{\text{Sales Price} - \text{Gross Profit}} \times 100 = \text{Mark-Up Percentage}$$

$$\frac{\text{Mark-Up}}{\text{Cost} + \text{Markup}} \times 100 = \text{Gross Profit Percentage}$$

HOW THE CONTRACTOR VIEWS FINANCIAL PLANNING

The contractor will think that the accountant's five-year master plan is too simplistic. For one thing, he will not agree with all the linearity, although he might not use this term. He will simply state that the volume-profit relationship cannot be represented by a straight line. He knows that the base-year markup

CONTRACTOR CONSTRUCTION COMPANY
Five-Year Master Plan
$000

	Base Year	Year Number				
		One	Two	Three	Four	Five
Contract Revenue	5,000	6,000	7,000	8,000	9,000	10,000
Cost of Contracts	4,132	4,958	5,785	6,611	7,438	8,264
Gross Profit	868	1,042	1,215	1,389	1,562	1,736
Fixed Costs	500	500	600	700	800	800
Net Income Before Taxes	368	542	615	689	762	936

Figure 4–1

CONVERSION TABLE	
Percentage Mark-Up to Gross Profit Percentage	
5.00	4.76
5.25	5.00
6.00	5.66
6.38	6.00
7.00	6.54
7.53	7.00
8.00	7.41
8.70	8.00
9.00	8.25
9.89	9.00
10.00	9.09
11.00	9.91
11.11	10.00
12.00	10.71
12.36	11.00
13.00	11.50
13.64	12.00
14.00	12.28
14.94	13.00
15.00	13.04
16.00	13.79
16.27	14.00
17.00	14.53
17.65	15.00
18.00	15.25
19.00	15.97
19.05	16.00
20.00	16.67
20.48	17.00
21.00	17.36
21.95	18.00
22.00	18.03
23.00	18.70
23.46	19.00
24.00	19.35
25.00	20.00

Figure 4–2

of 10 percent overhead and 10 percent profit will not hold true for the higher volumes. He is no doubt right. Price, volume, job cost, and fixed costs all enter into the mix that produces the desired increase in working capital.

HOW TO MAKE A PRICE-VOLUME-PROFIT SLIDE CHART: A STEP-BY-STEP GUIDE

This section will show you how to make a price-volume-profit slide chart. You might want to turn over these instructions to your drafting department, or, if you don't have one, to a friend in an organization that has one. Or, if you have the time, you might try to do it yourself. One advantage of doing it yourself is that by the time you get through, you will have a thorough understanding of the price-volume-profit relationship, in addition to having a device that you can produce for your board of directors so that they will understand it.

1. The base of the price-volume-profit slide chart is a piece of white chart board 8½ by 14 inches—a handy size for photo-copying. Inside, draw a grid 17 cm wide by 32 cm long with the grid about 3.5 cm from the bottom and equidistant from each side. See Figure 4–3.

2. The next step is to construct the gross profit curves on the sliding plastic overlay (See Figure 4–4). An easy way to position the curves is to place the bottom of the plastic overlay at −$1,400 of the vertical scale. The −$1,400 represents general and administrative expense that must be recovered before any net income is generated. Now go to the $10 million contract revenue line. Follow it up to the point where it intersects the −$600 line. This is the second point of the 8 percent gross profit curve.

Proof: $10 million × 8% = $800,000 − $1,400,000 = −$600,000

Note that as you continue to move up 1 cm on the $10 million contract revenue line, the gross profit goes up one point. Check this out by consulting Figure 4–4. Draw curves from 9 percent to 20 percent. Use India ink for permanency. There is no problem if the 20 percent curve does not register on the higher volumes. In our planning, we are not going above $10 million, and if we were, it is very unlikely that the 20 percent curve would be operative.

3. The final step is to dress up your chart with a square, U-shaped paneling made out of the same material as the base, so that the inside dimensions are the same as the grid—16 cm by 32 cm. See Figure 4–5.

How to Use the PVP Slide Chart

Suppose that fixed costs are $1 million. Slide the plastic sheet so that the point of origin on the left bottom part of the plastic sheet lines up with the −$1 million mark. Now you can read profit contributions for any indicated sales volume and gross profit percentage.

You can draw your own curve on the plastic sheet, using a felt-tip pen filled with washable ink. Suppose that your gross profit on contract revenue is 15.5 percent. Set the point of origin on the plastic sheet at some convenient point—for example, −$1 million on the vertical scale. Now, use any convenient sales volume, say $10 million. At that volume, gross profit will be $1.55 million. Of this amount, $1 million must be used to take care of the fixed costs. The

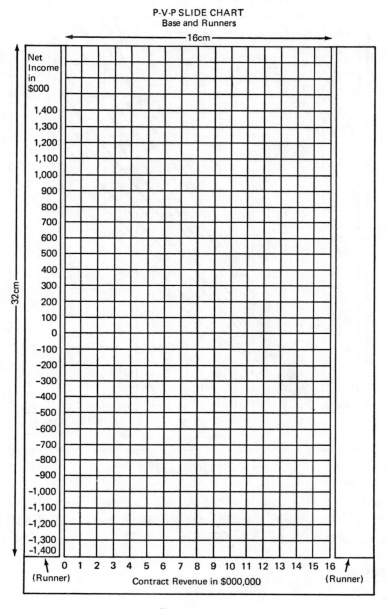

P-V-P SLIDE CHART
Base and Runners

Figure 4–3

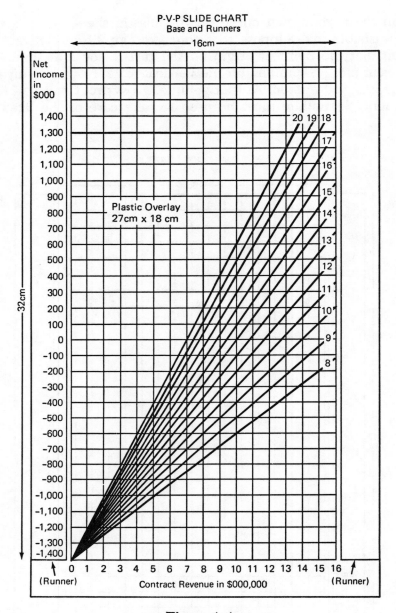

Figure 4–4

remaining $550,000 represents net income. Locate your point where the net income of $550,000 coincides with sales (contract revenue) of $10 million.

Breakeven can be figured as follows:

$$\frac{\text{Fixed costs}}{\text{Gross profit}} = \%\ \text{Breakeven Point}$$

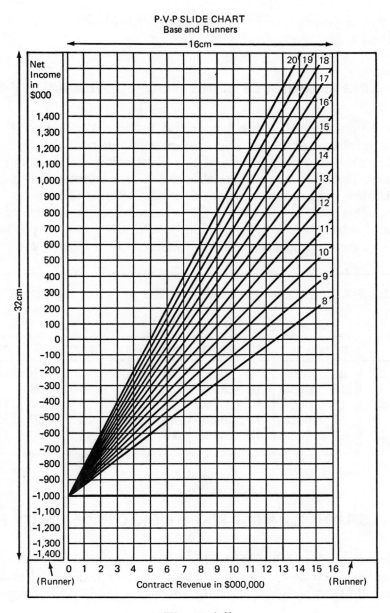

Figure 4–5

Advantages of Using the PVP Slide Chart

Very quickly, here are the advantages:

• Different mixes of volume, gross profit, and fixed costs can be quickly evaluated to arrive at the most desirable objective.

• Actual performance can be annualized and quickly charted to compare with the planned objectives.

PROFIT PLANNING TECHNIQUES USING WEIGHED PROBABILITY FACTORS

Using the hypothesis that the larger the volume the lower the markup, the contractor might want to organize his plan along probability factors such as shown in Figure 4–6. For the sake of this illustration, the factors chosen are strictly arbitrary. The contractor must choose his own factors. This is important. He can use intuition, experience, an analysis of past bidding failures and successes, probabilistic models such as the Monte Carlo simulation, or whatever capability is at hand. Once he has chosen the probability factors, the next step is to compute weighed markup percentages, such as has been done in Figure 4–6.

		WEIGHED MARKUP FOR INDICATED ANNUAL VOLUME								

Year Volume		*One* $6,000,000		*Two* $7,000,000		*Three* $8,000,000		*Four* $9,000,000		*Five* $10,000,000	
Probability of Success	.10	.20	.0200	.19	.0190	.18	.0180	.17	.0170	.16	.0160
	.15	.19	.0285	.18	.2070	.17	.0255	.16	.0240	.15	.0225
	.20	.18	.0360	.17	.0340	.16	.0320	.15	.0300	.14	.0280
	.25	.17	.0425	.16	.0400	.15	.0375	.14	.0350	.13	.0325
	.30	.17	.0480	.15	.0450	.14	.0420	.13	.0390	.12	.0360

Figure 4–6

HOW THE CONTRACTOR CAN ADJUST WEIGHED PROBABILITY FACTORS

The contractor will not be satisfied with the first computation of weighed markup percentages. However, let's assume that after much trial and error, he arrived at the following weighed markup and gross profit percentages:

Year	Mark-Up %	Gross Profit %
One	18.00	15.25
Two	17.00	14.53
Three	16.00	13.79
Four	15.00	13.04
Five	14.00	12.28

In arriving at these factors, the contractor has taken a close look at job costs. He has considered economies of scale—such factors as volume buying, purchase discounts, shop fabrication techniques, and other factors not easily quantified such as training, job incentives, and employee benefit plans.

HOW TO DEAL WITH FIXED COSTS IN PROFIT PROJECTIONS

Having arrived at the gross profit percentages for each of the five years of his plan, the contractor can now concentrate on fixed costs. A word about fixed costs: perhaps a better term might be nonvariable costs. The use of the PVP slide chart eliminates the worry of exact isolation of fixed costs. Movements caused by the presence of semivariable costs will cause no problem since the sliding plastic overlay can be moved up and down to accommodate these movements.

HOW THE PVP CHART WILL PUT IT ALL TOGETHER

By using the PVP slide chart, the contractor can evaluate net profit for different mixes of volume, gross profit, and fixed costs. Appraisal of the various net profit situations will result in adjustments to the ingredients making up the total plan. This process of feedback and adjustment is a continuous process and is the very essence of a successful planning system. Its presence will be felt at the formulation stage, and will continue through the execution and evaluation stages.

HOW TAXES AFFECT PROFIT PLANNING

As he approaches the final stages of the profit-planning process, the contractor will keep in mind the trade-off between the need for working capital buildup and the hazards of the Internal Revenue Code. He knows, from talking to his accountant and his auditor, that unreasonable accumulation of retained earnings will trigger penalty taxes reaching confiscatory proportions. Chapter 12 will deal with the special tax problems of the construction industry. In the meantime, the contractor has planned to avoid the penalty by projecting an increase in:

- Salaries for his nonunion personnel, including himself.
- Employee benefits in the form of pension and profit-sharing plans.

The solution is not quite that simple. Salary increases have to be reasonable, and there is a limit as to how much can be put into employee benefit plans. Besides, a certain amount of exposure to the penalty cannot be avoided if the desirable buildup in working capital is to be carried out. Ultimately, the buildup can be justified, provided the contractor is ready with specific plans for its utilization.

HOW TO USE THE FIVE-YEAR MASTER PLAN

Let us assume that after much hard work, analysis, and soul-searching, the contractor, with the help of his accountant, arrives at the five-year master plan shown in Figure 4–7. He is now off to a good start, knowing where he wants to go and how to get there.

The finishing touches to the five-year plan consists of converting planned net income after taxes to a figure representing the working capital situation as it progresses from year one to year five. This is an important but an easy step to overlook. In the construction business, the translation of planned net income into planned working capital is an absolute necessity. As previously stated, success in the construction business is a function of working capital. Bonding capacity, bidding strategy, management practices, and the very survival of the business all depend on the working capital strength of the business.

	Base Year	One	Two	Three	Four	Five
CONTRACTOR CONSTRUCTION COMPANY Five-Year Master Plan Revised ____ $000						
Contract Revenue	5,000	6,000	7,000	8,000	9,000	10,000
Cost of Contracts	4,132	5,085	5,983	6,897	7,826	8,772
Gross Profit	868	915	1,017	1,103	1,174	1,228
Percent Gross Profit	(17.36)	(15.25)	(14.53)	(13.79)	(13.04)	(12.28)
Fixed Cost	500	550	650	700	750	800
Net Income Before Taxes	368	365	367	403	424	428
Income Taxes	170	169	170	189	199	201
Net Income After Taxes	198	196	197	214	225	227

Figure 4–7

CONTRACTOR CONSTRUCTION COMPANY
Pro Forma Statement of Changes in Financial Condition
$000

	Base Year	Year Number				
		One	Two	Three	Four	Five
Funds Provided by:						
Net Income from Operations	198	196	197	214	225	227
Non-Working Capital:						
Depreciation	20	25	25	25	25	25
Amortization	1	1				
	219	222	222	239	250	252
Funds Applied to:						
Reduction of Long-Term Debt	60	60	60	60	60	60
Replacement of Equipment	20	25	25	25	25	25
Payment of Dividends	5	5	5	10	15	15
	85	90	90	95	100	100
Increase in Working Capital						
Each Year	134	132	132	144	150	152
Cumulative	134	266	398	542	692	844
Summary of Changes in Working Capital						
Current Assets:						
Cash	10	36	100	180	280	385
Receivables	230	271	350	403	453	500
Inventories	95	120	130	160	180	200
Prepaid Expenses	10	11	11	13	14	15
	345	438	591	756	927	1,100
Current Liabilities:						
Accounts Payable	90	60	70	80	90	100
Notes Payable	50	40	50	60	70	80
Accrued Expenses	11	12	13	14	15	16
Current Maturities, Long-Term Debt	60	60	60	60	60	60
	211	172	193	214	235	256
Increase in Working Capital	134	266	398	542	692	844

Figure 4–8

Converting the bottom line of the contractor's five-year plan into a working capital bottom line can be accomplished by following the familiar format of the statement of changes in financial position (See Figure 4–8). Doing this focuses attention on the wise use of funds generated by the business. Old timers will often say, "it isn't what you make, it's what you keep that counts." A steady increase in working capital is a good measure of what the contractor is able to keep.

HOW TO PROJECT AND CONTROL CASH FLOW

Financial success in the long run depends on successful management of working capital. For the short run, cash flow is the immediate problem. Day-to-day problems will not wait for the contractor to convert improved working capital, consisting of accounts receivable and inventory, into improved cash flow.

After solving his working capital problems, the contractor should immediately become concerned with moving current assets up the liquidity ladder—from inventories to receivables, and from receivables to cash. Improvement of the cash flow will help the contractor improve the quality of his working capital. The use of long-term borrowing can therefore be avoided, together with the oppressive monthly payments consisting mostly of high interest rates that go along with this type of financing.

HOW TO INSTALL A CASH FLOW SYSTEM

A cash flow projection and control system is easy to install. The accountant should begin by preparing weekly cash flow reports such as shown in Figure 4–9. At the end of each four- or five-week period, as close to the end of the month as possible, the accountant will want to prepare a report such as shown in Figure 4–10 to cover the four- or five-week period that will fit closest to the end of the month. This should be done for two or three months before attempting a projection for a similar time span.

The next step is to prepare a cash-flow projection for a four- or five-week period. As with the actual reports, the final week should coincide as closely as possible with the end of the month, as shown in Figure 4–11.

The final phase is the preparation of the inevitable control report where planned cash flow is compared to actual cash flow. See Figure 4–12.

CONTRACTOR CONSTRUCTION COMPANY
Cash Flow Statement
Week Ending _____ 19___

	Total	Operating Account	Payroll Account
Receipts:			
Accounts Receivable	_____	_____	_____
Other Income	_____	_____	_____
Fund Transfers			
(Eliminate from			
Total)	_____	_____	_____
	_____	_____	_____
Total Receipts	_____	_____	_____
Disbursements:			
Payroll	_____	_____	_____
Payroll Withholding	_____	_____	_____
Other Taxes	_____	_____	_____
Insurance	_____	_____	_____
Rent	_____	_____	_____
Utilities	_____	_____	_____
Other Operating			
Expense	_____	_____	_____
Accounts Payable:			
Current	_____	_____	_____
Past Due	_____	_____	_____
Notes Payable	_____	_____	_____
	_____	_____	_____
	_____	_____	_____
Fund Transfers			
(Eliminate from			
Total)	_____	_____	_____
	_____	_____	_____
Total Disbursements	_____	_____	_____
(Over) Under Receipts	_____	_____	_____
Bank Balance Beginning			
* of Week*	_____	_____	_____
Balance (Deficit)			
* End of Week*	_____	_____	_____

Figure 4–9

CONTRACTOR CONSTRUCTION COMPANY

Cash Flow Statement

_____ Weeks Ending _____ 19__

	Total	Week Ending
Receipts:		
Accounts Receivable		
Other Income		
Fund Transfers (Eliminate from Total)		
Total Receipts		
Disbursements:		
Payroll		
Payroll Withholding		
Other Taxes		
Insurance		
Rent		
Utilities		
Other Operating Expense		
Accounts Payable:		
Current		
Past Due		
Notes Payable		

Fund Transfers
(Eliminate from Total)

Total Disbursements

(Over) Under Receipts

Bank Balance Beginning of Period

Balance (Deficit) End of Period

Figure 4-10

CONTRACTOR CONSTRUCTION COMPANY
Cash Flow Projection
___ Weeks Ending _____ 19___

Week Ending

Total

Receipts:

Accounts Receivable

Other Income

Fund Transfers (Eliminate from Total)

Total Receipts

Disbursements:

Payroll

Payroll Withholding

Other Taxes

Insurance

Rent

Utilities

Other Operating Expense

Accounts Payable:

Current

Past Due

Notes Payable

Fund Transfers
(Eliminate from
Total) ___ ___ ___ ___

Total Disbursements ___ ___ ___ ___

(Over) Under Receipts ___ ___ ___ ___

*Bank Balance Beginning
of Period* ___ ___ ___ ___

*Balance (Deficit) End
of Period* ___ ___ ___ ___

Figure 4-11

CONTRACTOR CONSTRUCTION COMPANY
Cash Flow Control Report
__ Weeks Ending _____ 19__

	Planned	*Actual*	*(Over)* *Under Plan*
Receipts:			
Accounts Receivable	_____	_____	_____
Other Income	_____	_____	_____
	_____	_____	_____
Total Receipts	_____	_____	_____
Disbursements:			
Payroll	_____	_____	_____
Payroll Withholding	_____	_____	_____
Other Taxes	_____	_____	_____
Insurance	_____	_____	_____
Rent	_____	_____	_____
Utilities	_____	_____	_____
Other Operating Expense	_____	_____	_____
Accounts Payable: Current	_____	_____	_____
Past Due	_____	_____	_____
Notes Payable	_____	_____	_____
	_____	_____	_____
	_____	_____	_____
Total Disbursements	_____	_____	_____
(Over) Under Receipts	_____	_____	_____
Bank Balance Beginning of Period	_____	_____	_____
Balance (Deficit) End of Period	_____	_____	_____

Figure 4–12

HOW TO IMPROVE THE CASH FLOW SYSTEM

As with any sound planning system, the cash flow projection and control system will improve with age, the secret being the constant feedback and adjustment process previously discussed in this chapter.

Working papers backing each of the line items of the plan will also improve with experience. For example, projecting collections on accounts receivable will require careful analysis of the progress billings affecting each job. Job-cost requirements, flowing through accounts payable, will likewise require a careful analysis of purchase orders, delivery schedules, subcontracts, payment schedules, and related discount deadlines. The main thing to keep in mind is that in planning and controlling your cash flow, there is no substitute for experience. The sooner you get started the better.

CAPITAL INVESTMENT DECISIONS

There are any number of excellent texts and articles dealing with the subject of capital improvement decisions. As a result, coverage in this chapter will be confined to the highlights. The accountant should know that bad decisions in this area can wreck the contractor's working capital improvement program. He should therefore prepare himself to offer solid guidance in this area.

THE CASE OF THE ASSET-HAPPY CONTRACTOR

The temptation to buy equipment is an ego factor that most contractors simply cannot resist. As usual, it falls on the accountant to play the role of the devil's advocate, showing the contractor the harsh economic consequences of tying up good money in inert assets. It's up to the accountant to show that the major risk lies in the long-range nature of the decision and the adverse effect it will have on cash flow for the entire payout period.

THE CHAIN OF EVENTS LEADING TO ASSET ACQUISITION

• The contractor decides to buy a piece of equipment.
• He is convinced that it will save time and that it will enable him to improve on the quality of his work.
• He goes to his banker armed with brochures and obtains a long-term loan to purchase the equipment.
• He is overjoyed when the equipment performs admirably on a specific job, the same job he had in mind when he first began to consider the investment.
• Eventually the job is finished, and other work in process or new jobs obtained for some reason or other cannot make use of the piece of equipment.
• The equipment sits idle in the contractor's yard while the monthly payments become a drag on the cash flow of the company.

HOW TO PUT A PENCIL TO THAT INVESTMENT DECISION

Suppose that instead of proceeding on his own, the contractor had consulted with his accountant about the investment. Suppose that he sets forth factors. The piece of equipment will cost $100,000. The bank loan will run for five years, with add-on interest of 8 percent, a total of $40,000. Monthly installments are $2,333.33, or $28,000 a year. The contractor figures the machine will save him $50,000 a year. "It will pay for itself in two years," he tells you, ignoring several offsetting factors.

THE NET PRESENT VALUE EQUATION

A simple net present value evaluation of the savings will help dispel the foggy thinking. Let's start with the equation,

$$NPV_i = \sum_{t=1}^{n} \frac{P_{it}}{(1 + k_i)^t} - C_i,$$

where NPV_i equals the NPV of the ith project, P_{it} equals the expected profits (or savings) of the ith project in the tth year, k_i is the risk-adjusted discount rate applicable to the ith project, and C_i is the project's cost.

HOW TO CONSTRUCT THE NET PRESENT VALUE TABLE

Example 1. Assuming a risk-adjusted discount rate of 10 percent, the NPV of the proposed investment can be calculated as follows:

Year	P	PV Factor at 10%	PV of P	C	NPV
1	$50,000	.909	$ 45,450	$ 28,000	$17,450
2	50,000	.826	41,300	28,000	13,300
3	50,000	.751	37,550	28,000	9,550
4	50,000	.683	34,150	28,000	6,150
5	50,000	.621	31,050	28,000	3,050
			$189,500	$140,000	$49,500

Example 2. Please note that the NPV of $49,000 depends on a yearly savings of $50,000 for the entire five-year term of the equipment loan. Suppose, as

often happens, that the contractor had in mind a particular job to be completed two years hence. Utility could easily be cut in half for years three, four, and five. The picture might change in this way:

Year	P	PV Factor at 10%	PV of P	C	NPV
1	$50,000	.909	$ 45,450	$ 28,000	$ 17,450
2	50,000	.826	41,300	28,000	13,300
3	25,000	.751	18,755	28,000	(9,225)
4	25,000	.683	17,075	28,000	(10,925)
5	25,000	.621	15,525	28,000	(12,475)
			$138,105	$140,000	$ (1,875)

HOW TO EVALUATE THE INVESTMENT DECISION

Even with the adjustment reflected in the second table, there are still many unknowns. For example:

- How good is the $50,000 profit projection?
- Is a 50 percent utility probability factor for years three, four, and five reasonable? Is a 50–50 chance of continued success too optimistic?
- Is the 10 percent risk factor adequate, or should it be higher?
- Will the piece of equipment last five years, or will it wear out sooner?

The questions are on the pessimistic side because experienced planners will tell you that realistically, this is the way things usually turn out.

The problem here seems to be that the five-year cash outflow is not compatible with the foreseeable short-term benefits. Obviously, long-term cash outflow commitments should not be made in the hope that "something will happen" to create future benefits. In this case, the equipment could perform profitably on one job, with the contractors having no way of knowing whether other jobs would be obtained in which it could be used advantageously. Discounted cash flow projections, based on knowns and adjusted for unknowns, revealed the negative aspects of the investment.

LEASING VERSUS BUYING

A solution to the problem might have been accomplished by considering leasing rather than buying. Short-term discounted cash-flow benefits would not have been as great as under a purchase plan, but the long-range drag on the cash flow would have been avoided. Also, the total net benefits from leasing versus buying would at least have been positive rather than negative.

Caution. The contractor should avoid reaching the conclusion that leasing is always better than buying. Obviously, leasing will be more expensive. The point to consider is the trade-off between risk-avoidance afforded by leasing versus its higher cost. This means that the long-range commitment of a purchase plan must be carefully priced-out, to make sure that the benefits will last throughout the duration of the commitment.

OTHER WAYS TO EVALUATE INVESTMENT DECISIONS

Finance courses and texts will cover other evaluation methods such as:

- internal rate of return
- payback
- average rate of return
- profitability index.

NPV is presented here because it is theoretically the best and affords a logical take-off for meaningful refinements of the factors used in the equation.

HOW A STRONG WORKING CAPITAL POSITION HELPS IN DEALING WITH OUTSIDERS

The accountant can make a great contribution in helping the contractor deal with outsiders by lending support, encouragement, and assistance in launching him on the working capital improvement program outlined in this chapter. Problems of dealing with outsiders for the undercapitalized contractor previously described in this chapter are almost insurmountable, whereas the strongly capitalized contractor will find outsiders falling all over themselves trying to make him even more successful than he already is.

The Bonding People. Working capital will receive close scrutiny by the bonding people. The portion comprising construction in progress will receive the closest attention. The accountant must be thoroughly familiar with the percentage of completion problem discussed in Chapter 3. His presentation of construction in progress, regardless of the format prescribed by the surety company, must be based on the solid estimating factors and analytical techniques presented in Chapter 3.

The Banker. The contractor's plan for improving his working capital position will please the banker. He will be even happier with the cash flow projection and control system, since he will appreciate the healthy effect such a system will have on the liquidity of the working capital.

The Supplier. A contractor who knows how to manage his cash flow, and who can take quantity and payment discounts, makes a good impression on suppliers. A little bit of help here and there on the part of suppliers might often make the difference in coming up with the lowest bid.

The Investor. Investors, like bankers, are seldom there when you really need them. The strongly capitalized contractor, on the other hand, if he has solid plans for expansion and shows a good track record and sound cash-flow management, will have no difficulty attracting investment capital. A continuation of the good management practices that gave him financial strength will also tend to keep the investor happy and cooperative.

Architects, Engineers, and Others. This group worries mostly about the ability of the contractor to see the job through to its successful completion. The concern of this group is not unlike that of the surety company. Technical competence is assumed. Not always clear to this group is the financial stability of the contractor. Sensitivity to such danger signals as overbilling and a bad pay record will cause:

1. Close scrutiny of progress billings and
2. Overreaction to complaints of suppliers and subcontractors.

Working capital improvement and cash-flow techniques outlined in this chapter are the best guarantees of establishing a happy relationship with this group.

DESIGNING THE CONTRACTOR'S ACCOUNTING SYSTEM

Up to this point, we have covered key aspects of the contractor's way of doing things, and how this affects his accounting system. We have learned how to solve the percentage of completion problem, and how to use all this knowledge for financial planning.

The quantum leap was deliberate. We wanted to establish one point early in the game: The best accounting system in the world is of little use unless something important can be done with it. Financial planning is probably the most important thing that can be done with an accounting system. But there are other things, closer to day-to-day routine, such as controlling operations and preparing interim financial statements.

It is necessary to get into the nuts and bolts of operating the accounting system. But before we do this, we must delve into details underlying the contractor's accounting system. Why must it operate in such and such a manner? The chapter that follows answers this question, thereby establishing criteria for actually designing the system itself.

5

DESIGNING AND INSTALLING THE CONTRACTOR'S ACCOUNTING SYSTEM

A good accounting system is basic to the successful application of accounting and auditing methods and controls prescribed in this book. This chapter will show the practitioner how to design and install such a system. Techniques of systems analysis and form design will be covered in detail. Also described are the basics of mechanical aids available for the operation of the accounting system, ranging from manually operated systems to the more sophisticated in-house computers.

The main objective of this chapter is to prepare the accountant to perform with confidence in the design, installation, and modification of construction accounting systems. This is creative work of the highest order. The intelligent, imaginative, and energetic accountant will find this work satisfying and rewarding.

DESIGN CRITERIA FOR THE CHART OF ACCOUNTS

The chart of accounts is the beginning of order and logic in the design of any accounting system. It is the framework that helps to mold the flow, processing, and presentation of financial data.

In designing a chart of accounts certain criteria must be observed. For example, a good chart of accounts must be:

- Logical
- Flexible
- Adaptable to both manual and data processing.

85

The chart of accounts should faithfully follow the logic of the general ledger, which in turn should always follow the structure of the financial reports.

The chart of accounts must meet the needs of the small contractor, while at the same time offering expansion capabilities consistent with the needs of the larger contractor.

The account-numbering system must be so arranged that sequential listing will produce desired reporting formats, whether it be through manual processing, the use of large computers, or systems in between.

HOW THE CHART OF ACCOUNTS ANCHORS THE ACCOUNTING SYSTEM

While the chart of accounts serves the purpose of assuring order and compatibility in the presentation of data, the accountant must look beyond, to the very source of such data, in order to assure its orderly flow into the various established accounts. Here is where the accountant will find the input elements that blend with design criteria established for the whole system.

To illustrate this point, let us begin with the most important account from the contractor's point of view—cost of contracts. Although shown as one line in the chart of accounts, most contractors will break it out to at least include the cost elements described below.

The chart of accounts presented in Figure 5-1 is designed to satisfy the requirements of logic, flexibility, and adaptability.

THE JOB COST SYSTEM BEGINS WITH THE LABOR COST-PAYROLL SYSTEM

In the construction business, the design and installation of a good labor-cost payroll system is the natural point of departure for the design of the total job-cost system. This subsystem is the most meaningful of all those making up the total job-cost system because labor costs are subject to greater variations, and therefore greater control, than any other job costs. Whether a contractor makes a profit or incurs a loss on a particular job depends almost entirely on his ability to hold labor costs within estimated amounts. This, of course, assumes that estimated amounts are free of major errors.

TAILORING THE LABOR-COST PAYROLL SYSTEM TO THE CONTRACTOR'S NEEDS

As discussed in Chapter 2, the guidance of the contractor becomes important in designing the labor-cost payroll system because it is he who must ultimately determine the depth and range of the labor costing process. For example, as a

CHART OF ACCOUNTS

Balance Sheet Accounts

100 Assets

101 *Current Assets*
102 Cash in bank—general
103   —payroll
104   —savings
105 Petty cash
___ _____
120 Accounts receivable
125 Cost and earnings over billings
130 Inventory
135 Prepaid expenses

150 *Investments*

200 *Property and Equipment*
201 Land
205 Building
210 Office furniture and equipment
215 Automobiles and trucks
220 Tools and equipment
245 Accumulated depreciation

280 *Other Assets*
285 Due from officers
287 Deposits
289 Advances to employees

300 Liabilities and Net Worth

301 *Current Liabilities*
302 Notes payable
312 Accounts payable
314 Billings over costs and earnings
320 FICA
322 Federal withholding
326 State withholding
330 Apprenticeship program
332 Industry promotion fund
334 Medical insurance
336 Employee savings
___ _____
340 *Other Liabilities*
345 Long-term
346 Equipment mortgages
400 *Net Worth*
405 Common stock
410 Contributions for common stock
     over par
420 Retained earnings

Income Statement Accounts

500 Income

502 *Contract Income*

604 *Cost of Contracts*

700 *General and Administrative Expenses*
702 Officer salaries
704 Other salaries
710 Auto and truck expense
720 Bad debts
725 Company meetings
730 Contributions
735 Depreciation
740 Dues and subscriptions
750 Entertainment and travel
755 Equipment rental
760 Freight
765 Miscellaneous
770 Insurance
775 Interest
780 Legal and accounting
790 Licenses and permits
800 Maintenance
810 Office expense
820 Outside services
830 Repairs
840 Taxes, other than income
850 Telephone
855 Tool expense
860 Utilities

870 *Other Income*
872 Discounts
874 Interest
876 Sale of assets

880 *Other Expense*
___ _____
890 *Income Taxes*
895 State
896 City
897 Federal

Figure 5–1

home builder or a small subcontractor, he might be able to get along quite well with a breakout of labor costs by jobs. For the large general contractor and major subcontractors, a more elaborate labor costing system might be required. Such a system might call for detailed functional breakouts to be fed into a computer for evaluation under a Critical Path Method, or as input for the refinement of probabilistic models, or for elaborate comparison and evaluation with respect to planned costs of functions contained in the job takeoff.

CRITERIA FOR DESIGN OF THE LABOR COST-PAYROLL SYSTEM

The degree of detail to be built into the labor-cost payroll system ultimately depends on the preference of the contractor. However, the accountant, in discussing this matter either with a new client or a new boss, should be prepared to offer the following criteria as guidance:

• Time sheets should be prepared by the workers themselves and submitted not less than weekly.
• If an elaborate functional breakout is part of the job-cost system, daily time sheets might be desirable.
• Even if time sheets are submitted weekly, they must be filled out each day.
• For any system going beyond a simple costing by job, additional detail must conform to the following guidelines:
  • As a minimum it must agree with the major functional groupings of the takeoff sheets.
  • As a maximum it must agree with each functional line item of the takeoff sheets.
• Time sheets must be so designed as to be compatible with both the job-cost system and the payroll system.
• The system must provide for weekly reporting of estimated versus actual labor costs, at least by job and preferably by phase within each job.
• Estimated labor costs will be taken directly from the takeoff sheets.

HOW TO MAKE THE TIME SHEET DO DOUBLE WORK

Once criteria has been determined in the manner outlined above, it should be incorporated into a set of instructions to assure compliance. Figure 5-2 shows how to fill out time sheets to be used in a simple job-cost system utilizing a minimum of functional codes. If a more elaborate set of breakouts is required to satisfy a demand for greater detail by management, the instructions could remain essentially unchanged, with the expansion effort being directed to the coding structure rather than to the instructions or the time sheet itself. It is important to keep the instructions simple and concise so that they can be easily followed by the workers, and so that they can be printed on the back of the time sheet.

HOW TO FILL IN YOUR TIME SHEET

Be sure to fill in all blank spaces above the first double line. The information you furnish is used to figure your paycheck and for various reports.

Turn in your time sheet to your foreman at quitting time each Wednesday. You will be paid on Friday for time worked through Wednesday.

Time must be entered each day.

Use the upper square of the job block for regular time, the bottom square for overtime.

In addition to job number, account for all your time by using the following functional codes:

01	Fabrication
02	Rough-in
03	Installation
04	Finishing
05	Cleanup
06	Punch list
07	Call-back
08	Travel time
09	Miscellaneous

Figure 5–2

Since time sheets are to be used both for labor costing and payroll computations, a reconciliation must be performed, either on the time sheet itself or on a worksheet. The section in this chapter on designing forms will show you how a time sheet can be constructed to provide input for both job costing and payroll purposes, while at the same time containing the elements needed for a reconciliation of the two systems.

LABOR COST-CONTROL ILLUSTRATED

The design criteria for the labor-cost payroll system stressed the need for the presentation of estimated versus actual costs. Figure 5–3 shows the labor portion of the job-cost analysis report. Note that the report satisfies this criterion:

JOB-COST ANALYSIS REPORT:
Labor

Date _____

No.	Description	Estimated-Actual		Balance			
		Hours	Cost	Hours	%	Cost	%
323	Consolidated School						
01	Fabrication	500 00	6,000 00				
01	Fabrication	-250 00	-3,320 00	250 00	50 00	2,680 00	44 67
02	Rough-in	700 00	10,500 00				
02	Rough-in	-710 00	-10,615 00	-10 00	-1 43	-115 00	-1 10
03	Installation	1,200 00	18,624 00				
03	Installation	720 00	10,728 00	480 00	40 00	7,896 00	42 40
29	Total Labor	5,000 00	75,500 00				
29	Total Labor	-2,160 00	-33,510 00	2,840 00	56 80	41,990 00	55 61
Etc.							

Figure 5-3

The system must must provide for weekly reporting of estimated versus actual labor costs, at least by job and preferably by phases within each job.

HOW TO ESTABLISH CRITERIA FOR MATERIAL COSTING

The design of the new accounting system can now move on to the next element of cost of contracts—material costs. Here again the accountant should be prepared to discuss with the contractor the basic criteria for the design and installation of the material costing system. For example:

• Purchase orders must agree with the takeoff sheets, which in turn are based on price quotations furnished by suppliers at the time the job was bid.
• Purchase orders must follow the same functional breakdown as the job takeoff.
• Normally, a purchase order will cover only one job, although the home builder might conveniently group purchase requirements for several homes on one purchase order.
• Suppliers must be required to cite purchase order numbers on all invoices, and those not bearing such references must be returned for correction.
• Invoices will not be costed until matched and reconciled to purchase orders and receiving reports.
• Invoices will be posted to job costs and to accounts payable as part of the same operation.
• A breakdown of material costs within jobs will be undertaken only when it follows a natural subdivision of material items on the takeoff sheet or when required as part of the billing instructions in the contract.
• Weekly reports will be prepared comparing estimated to actual material costs.

Material Cost-Control Illustrated

Since a criterion for material costing calls for a breakdown by line item rather than the functional codes of the labor costing format, the columnar headings shown in Figure 5–4 will differ from those shown in Figure 5–3. Please note that in Figure 5–4 we have line item within the job, rather than the format of function within the job shown in Figure 5–3.

Line items coincide with billing specifications of the contract, and may or may not coincide with the functional breakout of the labor report. In fact, it is sometimes necessary for the functional codes of the labor report to be changed for a specific job, in order to agree with the line-item structure of the contract, which in turn will probably establish the breakout requirements of the progress

JOB-COST ANALYSIS REPORT:
Material

Date____

No.	Description	Estimated-Actual		Balance	
		Take-off Sheet No.	Cost	Cost	%
323	Consolidated School				
31	Rough-in	1 to 5	11,000 00		
31	Rough-in		-11,090 00	-90 00	- 82
32	Wiring Devices	6 to 8	7,500 00		
32	Wiring Devices		-6,320 00	1,180 00	15 73
33	Light Fixtures	9 to 13	15,500 00		
33	Light Fixtures		-11,300 00	4,200 00	27 09
49	Total Material		65,000 00		
49	Total Material		-29,300 00	35,700 00	54 92
Etc.					

Figure 5–4

billings. Such a change is logical, since it makes sense to cost the job, both for labor and material, to agree with the way it was bid and the way it is going to be billed.

Equipment Cost-Control Illustrated

Some contractors will cost equipment costs separately from other material costs. This is particularly true of mechanical and electrical contractors, for whom equipment costs come in large amounts and often relate to complex delivery and installation problems.

From an accountant's point of view, system design criteria can be the same as for material costing, with special emphasis on the matching of invoices with purchase orders. Thus the report comparing estimated versus actual costs will not only match invoices with purchase orders, line-item by line-item, but will also show what has been delivered and what has not. See Figure 5–5 for an example of an equipment delivery status report.

Subcontractor Cost-Control Illustrated

The next element to consider in designing the cost of contract system is the cost of subcontracts. The following criteria need to be considered in the design of the system:

• Subcontracts (or purchase orders if used in lieu of subcontracts) must agree with the takeoff sheets, which in turn are based on bids furnished by the subcontractors at the time the job was bid.

• Subcontracts (or purchase orders) must contain specific instructions for progress billing, including requirements for functional or other line-item breakouts.

• Progress billings will be matched with subcontracts or purchase orders before posting.

• Progress billings will be posted to job costs and to accounts payable as part of the same operation.

• Weekly reports will be prepared, comparing estimated versus actual subcontractor costs with the amount remaining to be billed shown both in terms of dollars and percent of total subcontract.

Figure 5–6 shows a typical subcontractor breakout of the cost analysis report. The example shown here is for a general contractor with a large number of subcontracts. It is conceivable that a further breakout might be required for each of the subcontracts, for example, in order to control progress billing requirements by line-items if called for in the contract.

JOB-COST ANALYSIS REPORT:
Equipment Delivery Status Report

Date _____

No.	Description	P.O.	Ordered-Delivered			Undelivered	
			Qty	Cost		Qty	Cost
323	<u>Consolidated School</u>						
51	Control Panels	764	10	10,000	00		
51	Control Panels	763	-2	-1,875	00		
51	Control Panels	761	-1	-1,500	00		
51	Control Panels	762	-5	-5,025	00	2	1,600	00
51	Control Panels						
52	Electric Heaters	781	2	25,000	00		
52	Electric Heaters	781	-1	12,500	00	1	12,500	00
52	Electric Heaters						
69	Total Equipment		30	150,000	00	9	51,250	00
69	Total Equipment		21	98,750	00		
	Etc.						

Figure 5-5

JOB-COST ANALYSIS REPORT:
Subcontractors

No.	Description	Est. No.	Subcontract - Payments	Balance Amount	Balance %
323	Consolidated School				
81	Site Preparation		30,250 00		
81	Site Preparation	1	-10,500 00		
81	Site Preparation	2	-19,750 00		
81	Site Preparation			-0-	-0-
85	Mechanical		570,000 00		
85	Mechanical	1	-57,000 00		
85	Mechanical	2	-76,000 00		
85	Mechanical	3	-125,000 00		
85	Mechanical	4	-108,000 00	204,000 00	35 79
86	Electrical		490,000 00		
86	Electrical	1	-50,000 00		
86	Electrical	2	-110,000 00		
86	Electrical	3	-100,000 00		
86	Electrical	4	-90,000 00	140,000 00	28 57
99	Total		2,325,000 00		
99	Total		856,000 00	1,469,000 00	63 18

Figure 5-6

Control of Miscellaneous Job Costs

Miscellaneous job costs may or may not develop as envisioned on the take-off sheets. The job-cost system, however, must make use of estimated amounts as the basis for comparing and evaluating actual miscellaneous costs as these develop. Documentation in the form of subcontracts and purchase orders will not always agree with takeoff amounts, since orders are placed as needed, and will more than likely differ from the estimated amounts. Nevertheless, the accounting system must prescribe criteria similar to those required for the costing of subcontracts, except that strict adherence to takeoff amounts will not always be possible.

DESIGN BASICS FOR THE WEEKLY JOB-COST-ANALYSIS REPORT

The accounting system, whether it be a manual system or fully mechanized, must provide for a weekly comparison of estimated versus actual costs, by job and by cost element within each job. The accountant must realize that, to the contractor, this report is the most meaningful of all other reports produced by the system. Since this is the report he will use more than any other, the degree of detail and variations in the format must conform to his mode of management. The accountant must use his ingenuity to satisfy the needs of the contractor, without creating a monster that defies orderly processing and compatibility with the rest of the system.

Figure 5–7 shows a job-cost analysis report that should be easily adaptable to any cost system. The format is quite sparse. Breakouts within this reporting structure can be left up to the desires of management and the capabilities of the accounting system.

HOW TO HANDLE GENERAL AND ADMINISTRATIVE EXPENSES

General and administrative (G and A) expenses are basically the same in the construction industry as in other businesses. Here, as in other businesses, one might expect management habits to vary from contractor to contractor. Some believe in full absorption accounting, and will demand total allocation of G and A expenses to job costs. Others will establish an elaborate 600-series breakout in their chart of accounts (see Figure 5–1) to assign to job costs all possible expenditures that can be directly related to the jobs. They prefer to bring together under the G and A category only those costs and expenses that are not directly related to the jobs.

JOB-COST ANALYSIS REPORT

Date _____

No.	Description	Contract		Cost to Date		Balance		%	
323	Consolidated School	3,125,000	00	1,754,600	00	1,370,400	00	43	85
357	Krueger Manufacturing Co.	10,600,000	00	7,360,500	00	3,239,500	00	30	56
362	WXY Shopping Center	7,900,000	00	3,806,000	00	4,094,000	00	51	82
	Total	50,380,000	00	22,096,000	00	28,284,000	00	56	14

Figure 5–7

Most contractors will use a worksheet allocation of G and A expense. They will avoid a formal scattering of these expenses via the accounting system, for fear of dilution and loss of control. The general feeling is that control of G and A expenses is better accomplished by keeping them all together. Budgetary control can be used more effectively if totals rather than fragments are being considered. But even so, certain G and A expense elements will present budgeting problems because they tend to be more variable or semivariable than fixed. For example, automobile and truck expense, bad debts, equipment rental, freight, and licenses and permits will tend to vary with work volume. A budgetary control system for G and A expenses must take this characteristic into account.

CONSTRUCTION IN PROGRESS AS A BALANCE SHEET ITEM

Balance sheet items will present no problems in the design and installation of the accounting system. An exception is construction in progress. This account has ramifications in other parts of the balance sheet as well as the income statement. It poses a problem of such magnitude that it deserves separate, in-depth treatment. This is done in Chapter 3. However, basic to the solution of this problem are the design criteria specified in preceding paragraphs that dealt with the cost of contracts. In fact, without close attention to the system design methodology contained in this chapter, as it pertains to cost of contracts, the percentage of completion problem cannot be solved.

HOW TO USE FLOWCHARTING TECHNIQUES

Flowcharting techniques used by industrial engineers and data processing specialists can be used effectively by designers of accounting systems. By their use, the accountant can quickly and conveniently analyze, isolate, and resolve problems involving the flow of data into and through the accounting system. An immediate advantage of flowcharting is that it gives the accountant an overview of the system, including compatibility with feeder systems and integrity with the accounting system as a whole.

Flowcharting to Evaluate Internal Control

In designing the system of internal control, the accountant can use flowcharting techniques to reveal potential weak spots. He should be aware of the fact that outside auditors are turning more and more to the use of flowcharts in the evaluation of the system of internal control. The use of internal control questionnaires is beginning to lose the great appeal it once had. This is due primarily to perfunctory use by some auditors. At the same time, written descriptions are also becoming less popular because they are time-consuming, and often are so loaded with detail that they hamper the spotting of significant weaknesses in the system.

Flowcharting in Systems Design

The accountant can use flowcharting techniques to good advantage in systems design. Not only are weaknesses in the system of internal control highlighted, but so are other trouble spots and inconsistencies. By going through an actual flowcharting application, we will quickly learn how to use this simple technique and at the same time begin to appreciate the fact that it is indispensable to good systems design.

Flowcharting Illustrated

For the sake of illustration, let us assume that you are designing a labor-cost payroll system to function within criteria set forth in the previous section of this chapter. You begin by charting the flow of the time sheets in a very general way, starting with its preparation by the workers on the job site or the shop, and going through to its final processing and storage in the accounting department.

The preliminary sketch will be rough, the objective being to make sure that the general flow, together with each of its principal steps and ramifications, has been considered. Figure 5–8 shows such a sketch.

The next step is to begin the refining process. Reference to design criteria outlined in the preceding section will be helpful. The system should take in good internal control practices. When the best possible flow of data has been roughed out, the next step is to put it in final form. The accountant should use standard systems flowcharting symbols adopted by the American National Standards Institute. These are shown in Figure 5–9. Templates with these symbols are available in some office supply stores and in most architect-engineering supply houses.

With the aid of template and typewriter, the rough sketches can be converted into a respectable product. This method was followed in preparing Figure 5–10. The back and forth meandering shown here is not typical of most flowcharts. Most will flow generally from top to bottom, with plenty of room to permit branching out to left or right. However, the process presented in Figure 5–10 was a simple one, and it was felt that the weaving would not prove too distracting.

TIME SHEET PROCESSING

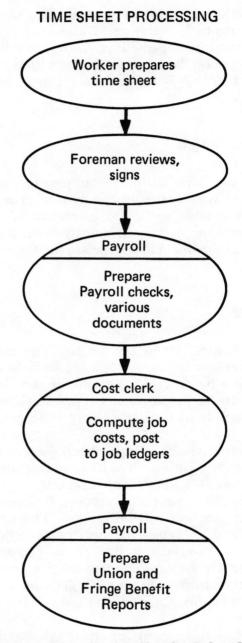

Figure 5–8.   Preliminary Flowcharting Sketch—Labor-Cost Payroll System.

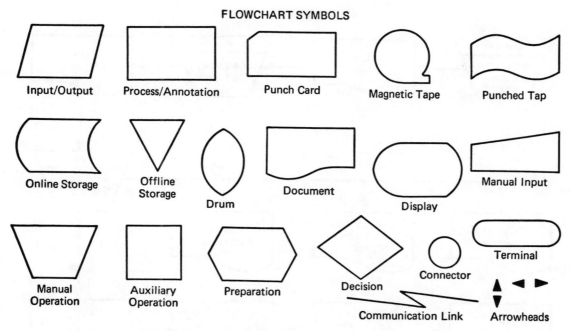

Figure 5–9

WHY SYSTEMS DESIGN NEVER ENDS

Although the term "final form" has been used in describing Figure 5–10, in actual practice such a stage is never reached. Debugging of the newly designed or modified system will dictate a certain number of changes. Others will come from review and updating of the accounting manual. Accounting department personnel will invariably come up with improvements. Several changes will come from the workers, the foreman, the contractor, and the estimators. Finally, changes in Federal, state, and local regulations will require accommodation within the accounting system. In systems work there is no such a thing as a final "final form."

HOW TO DESIGN FORMS

Several contractor associations have developed forms for use by their members. Among these are the following:

- Associated General Contractors of America, Inc.
- National Electrical Contractors Association, Inc.

TIME SHEET PROCESSING

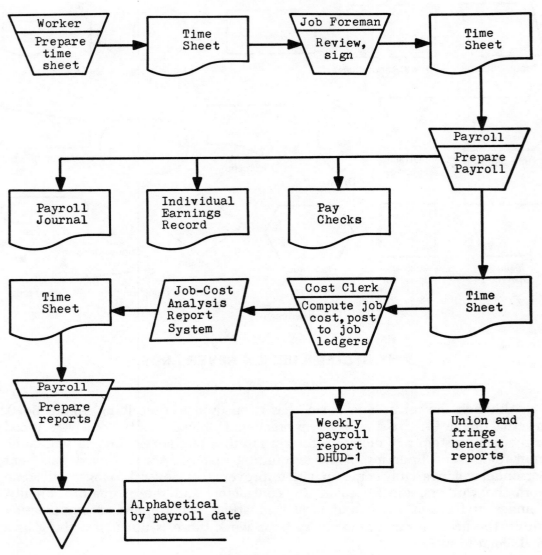

Figure 5–10

- National Association of Plumbing-Heating-Cooling Contractors, Inc.
- Sheet Metal and Air Conditioning Contractors National Association, Inc.
- National Association of Home Builders

Some contractors are able to use association-developed forms successfully. However, most contractors prefer to tailor their forms to serve the needs of their own particular accounting systems, which in turn reflect their own type of management. The feeling is that forms are first, a function of systems design criteria, and second, must fit the specifics of the flowchart. For example, if we were to design a time sheet that is compatible with instructions shown in Figure 5–2, and can accomplish the tasks assigned to it through the flowchart depicted in Figure 5–10, we would come up with a time sheet with a shape and form that has almost been predetermined.

TIME-SHEET DESIGN CRITERIA ILLUSTRATED

An examination of the time sheet illustrated in Figure 5–11 will show that it is designed to serve the needs of two subsystems—job costs and payroll. The design of the form facilitates conversion of job costs to gross pay. This is the beginning figure for the payroll process, the number-one task as highlighted by the flowchart in Figure 5–10. After payroll checks are on their way to the job sites, the time sheets can then proceed to the cost clerk, where they can be used to satisfy the various requirements of the job-cost system as depicted in the flowchart. Now the time sheets can come back to the payroll clerk, where they can be used to prepare the many reports to government and union entities.

This rather simple example has been given in order to provide a taste of the very important function of form design. Please keep in mind the sequence of events. The design of the form pretty well takes care of itself if design objectives, as specified by the flowchart, have first been carefully worked out. The form will get the job done only after its job specifications have been determined and the form is then designed to follow these specifications.

HOW MUCH AUTOMATION?

Designing the accounting system provides a good idea as to *how* the system is going to operate. The next step is to determine *who* or *what* is going to operate it; that is, whether it will be operated by people or machines, or a combination of both.

The choice is not an easy one because, as often happens in systems designs, the rules are never the same, even when it appears that they should be. As it turns out, there is more than one way to operate an accounting system. However, in order to avoid unnecessary trail-blazing, we can first review the various manual-machine options, and second, find through such a review a combination that will fit the particular situation the systems designer has in mind. If nothing else, such a review might provide generalized rules for the proper manual-machine mix under different sets of conditions.

TIME SHEET

Name _____ Week Ending _____ 19__

Address _____ Zip _____

Married ( )　Single ( )　Payroll Exemptions _____　Social Security No. _____

Job No.	Functional Code	Thu	Fri	Sat	Sun	Mon	Tue	Wed	Total Hours	Rate	Amount	Fireman's Signature
SHOP												
TOTAL JOB COST												

REMARKS:			
	Less nontaxable fringe benefits		
	Total gross pay		
	Deduct:		
	FICA		
	Fed. Wh. Tax		
	State Wh. Tax		
	City Wh. Tax		
	Vacation Pay		
	Group Ins.		
	Total Deductions		
	Net Pay		
	Other Compensation		
	Total Amount of Check		

Figure 5–11

THE ACCOUNTING SYSTEM COMPARED TO MANUFACTURING

All processing systems have in common the transformation of input into useful output. We think of the raw data as proceeding from input to processing, to output to action, with information feedback keeping the system under control. Conceptually, the system operates as shown in Figure 5–12. One might note the similarity between the accounting process and the manufacturing operation. For example:

• In accounting, raw data consisting of check stubs, time sheets, invoices, etc., is processed to satisfy the objective of conversion to information packages,

MANAGEMENT INFORMATION SYSTEMS

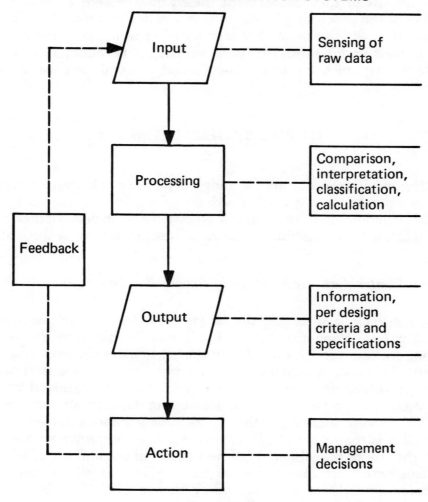

Figure 5–12

in accordance with management criteria and the specifications of the systems designer.

• In manufacturing, raw material input is processed to satisfy the objective of conversion to finished products, in accordance with management criteria and specifications of the engineer.

• As in manufacturing, any portion of the accounting system can be automated. In fact, a completely automatic system is theoretically possible, but at least in accounting, such a system is not economically feasible. As an example, sensing information for input is usually better done by people, although increasingly efficient input devices are gradually taking over this task completely. Automation of the sensing function is already here for many nonaccounting operations, and is close to practicality in certain accounting processes.

Older models of the management information system invariably showed intervention of the processing function by a monitor or controller. Fortunately for accountants, even the smallest of automated or semiautomated systems will keep the process under control without human intervention. This is a far cry from the early days of automation, when constant monitoring was an essential part of the system.

MANUAL SYSTEMS DEFINED

Strictly speaking, there is no such thing as a purely manually operated system. Even the one-person operation will make use of mechanical aids such as adding machines, calculators, slide rules, and a typewriter. Our definition of a manual system will assume this minimum amount of mechanization, at the least.

Why Many Contractors Prefer Manual Accounting Systems

Many contractors, including the larger ones, are able to get along quite well by using only a manual system. Production problems in the accounting department are resolved by a division of duties. For the one-person accounting department, this means additional personnel, but since such a person can handle a surprisingly voluminous amount of work under a well-organized system, the addition of one or two persons to the accounting department can take care of a 100 or 200 percent increase in the contractor's volume, and even more. The reason for this is that a growth in volume for the contractor usually means a growth in the size of the jobs, and not necessarily in the number of jobs. Economies of scale enter into the picture, so that a $200,000 job becomes 60 to 70 percent more administratively demanding than a $100,000 job, and not 100 percent as demanding as one might expect.

WHY CONTRACTORS HATE TO CHANGE FROM ONE-PERSON ACCOUNTING SYSTEMS

Contractors who enjoy the services of an efficient one-person accounting department are reluctant to automate, even when their volume doubles and triples. They enjoy the efficiency and flexibility of the manual operation. They are delighted when, in the face of significant expansion, they can continue to enjoy these advantages by the economic and painless addition of one or two people. This, to many contractors, seems a happier solution than the upheaval that can sometimes accompany conversion to an automated system.

HOW TO ACCOMPLISH DIVISION OF DUTIES IN A MANUALLY OPERATED SYSTEM

When the division of duties in a manually operated system becomes inevitable, the first function to be set aside is usually the payroll function. Posting of invoices and subcontractor's billings, as well as the related paying function, can be stacked up for a few days until an economic run can be made. But the processing of paychecks cannot be put off, for the simple reason that union contracts call for the payment of premium pay for any time spent waiting for a paycheck after quitting time on payday. Even in nonunion shops, a contractor who fails to deliver paychecks on time will have trouble getting people to work for him.

A growth in volume, whether it results from more jobs or bigger jobs, means hiring more workers. The impact in the accounting department is immediate. When it can no longer be absorbed, it usually means setting the payroll function apart from the rest of the accounting work, and designating one full-time person to take care of it.

WRITE-IT-ONCE SYSTEMS DESCRIBED

Figure 5–13 shows the organization of the accounting department in a contracting company with a total of approximately 100 employees. In addition to conventional mechanical aids such as printing calculators and typewriters, the department uses a sliding, write-it-once mechanical aid for payroll and accounts payable. Specially designed journals, individual earning records, and accounts payable ledgers are printed on NCR (no carbon required) paper. The contractor-owner, young, capable, and ambitious, has no plans to automate the accounting department.

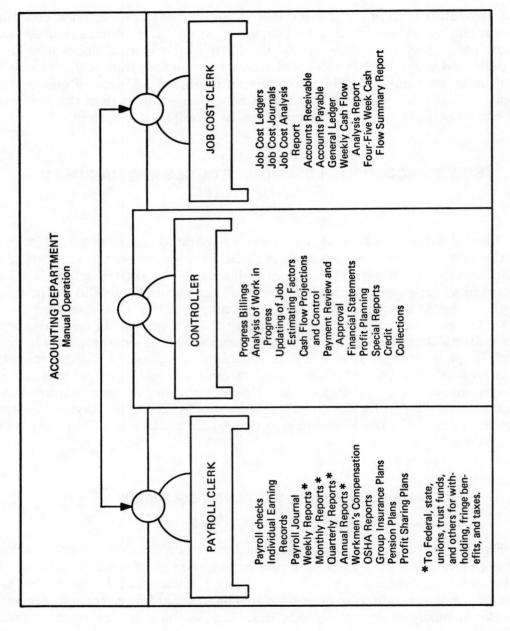

ACCOUNTING DEPARTMENT
Manual Operation

PAYROLL CLERK

Payroll checks
Individual Earning
  Records
Payroll Journal
Weekly Reports *
Monthly Reports *
Quarterly Reports *
Annual Reports *
Workmen's Compensation
OSHA Reports
Group Insurance Plans
Pension Plans
Profit Sharing Plans

*To Federal, state,
  unions, trust funds,
  and others for with-
  holding, fringe ben-
  efits, and taxes.

CONTROLLER

Progress Billings
Analysis of Work in
  Progress
Updating of Job
  Estimating Factors
Cash Flow Projections
  and Control
Payment Review and
  Approval
Financial Statements
Profit Planning
Special Reports
Credit
Collections

JOB COST CLERK

Job Cost Ledgers
Job Cost Journals
Job Cost Analysis
  Report
Accounts Receivable
Accounts Payable
General Ledger
Weekly Cash Flow
  Analysis Report
Four-Five Week Cash
  Flow Summary Report

Figure 5-13

Write-it-once systems can be expanded beyond the examples given above to include the operation of a job-cost system. Posting invoices and subcontractor's monthly estimates to the job ledger can be done concurrent with accounts payable processing. This is not so with respect to labor costs. The structure of job-cost breakdowns will vary greatly from that of the payroll system, thereby requiring separate processing of time sheets for cost purposes. In the time sheet processing flowchart shown in Figure 5–10, job costing takes place only after paychecks have been prepared.

WHY MICROCOMPUTERS WILL BEAT ANY MANUAL SYSTEMS

As a super-efficient bookkeeping machine, the microcomputer cannot be outdone. Even the most dyed-in-the wool advocate of manual accounting, if he gives the microcomputer a fair trial, will say, "How did we ever get along without it?"

How the Microcomputer Cycle Works

Input can be from check stubs, invoices, or journals. The journals can be cut down to three—the cash receipts and disbursement journal, the payroll journal, and the purchases journal. Columnar spread can be kept to a minimum. A miscellaneous section, consisting of account number, debit and credit, will catch all but the most common transactions. And there is no need to recap miscellaneous transactions. Input is made into the microcomputer, item by item. A detailed printout of entries is produced.

When journalization is completed, including adjusting entries, the microcomputer will sort transactions internally and will post, also internally, to general ledger accounts. The general ledger printout will show, for each account, beginning balance, current period postings and ending balance. The microcomputer will produce financial statements consisting of the balance sheet, the income statement, and the statement of changes in financial position after the operator has input the date of the balance sheet and the number of months, running from the beginning of the fiscal year, for the benefit of the income statement and statement of changes in the financial position. Programs are available that will compare income statement items with either budgeted amounts or last year's figures.

Limitations of the Microcomputer

This is a bookkeeping machine and its primary products are financial statements. It has several programs that are not tied in to the general ledger such as accounts receivable, depreciation, and Accelerated Cost Recovery System accounting. It does not operate a fully integrated data base type of system. Payroll systems with changing pay scales will swamp it. And there is no labor cost distribution spin-off.

HOW MINICOMPUTERS INFLUENCE THE ACCOUNTING FUNCTION

Compared with microcomputers, minicomputers are real heavyweights capable of fully integrated data base operations. They can quickly convert raw data into unlimited variations of finished products. Figure 5–14 shows the organization of the accounting department of a contracting firm using a minicomputer. Comparing this illustration with Figure 5–13 will show that all routine functions have been taken over by the computer. The Controller's functions have been left the same, as shown in Figure 5–13, mostly to depict unchanged responsibilities. Computer printouts specified by the controller become financial statements, special reports, and analytical studies. Note that no attempt has been made to automate administrative work relating to workmen's compensation, OSHA, group insurance plans, pension plans, and profit sharing plans, although such programs will exist in outside organizations involved with these functions. However, reporting requirements to these outside organizations is greatly eased by computer printout of payroll and other data.

HOW THE MINICOMPUTER INTEGRATES ACCOUNTING, ESTIMATING, AND ENGINEERING

In addition to putting the computer to work in the accounting department, many contractors are also using it in their estimating and engineering departments. In fact, in more than one case, the computer was used for estimating and engineering work, prior to taking over in the accounting department.

Broadening the Use of the Data Base. Whether the minicomputer reaches the accounting department directly or through prior interest on the part of estimating and engineering personnel, the accountant should welcome the event as a unique opportunity to broaden the use of the accounting data base. Without getting into the complexity and sophistication characteristic of large computer installations, the accountant can organize that portion of the data processing effort dealing with dollars and manhours, so that it assures integrated input into all of the contractor's primary functions. This thought has been uppermost in the presentation of the design criteria approach used in this chapter. The idea is valid even for manual systems. The computer simply makes it easier to carry out.

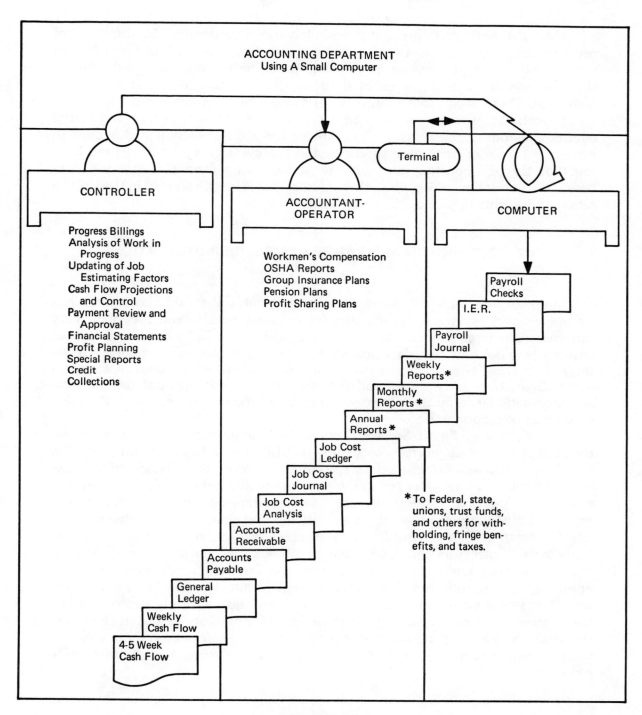

ACCOUNTING DEPARTMENT
Using A Small Computer

CONTROLLER

Progress Billings
Analysis of Work in
  Progress
Updating of Job
  Estimating Factors
Cash Flow Projections
  and Control
Payment Review and
  Approval
Financial Statements
Profit Planning
Special Reports
Credit
Collections

ACCOUNTANT-
OPERATOR

Workmen's Compensation
OSHA Reports
Group Insurance Plans
Pension Plans
Profit Sharing Plans

Terminal

COMPUTER

Payroll
Checks
I.E.R.
Payroll
Journal
Weekly
Reports *
Monthly
Reports *
Annual
Reports *
Job Cost
Ledger
Job Cost
Journal
Job Cost
Analysis
Accounts
Receivable
Accounts
Payable
General
Ledger
Weekly
Cash Flow
4-5 Week
Cash Flow

* To Federal, state,
unions, trust funds,
and others for with-
holding, fringe ben-
efits, and taxes.

Figure 5–14

How Estimating, Engineering and Accounting Interact. In this type of organization, the series of events, starting with the taking off of the job, and proceeding to the preparation of the bid, obtaining the contract, and running the job, become a cohesive effort held together by the computer's common data base. There is constant interaction between the contractor and his departments—estimating, engineering, and accounting. A series of sixteen sequential events, illustrating the sharing of computer-based information, is depicted in Figure 5–15. From beginning to end in the life cycle of a job, events are held together through constant dipping into and drawing from the common data base. The interaction taking place throughout this cycle is illustrated in the sixteen sequential events depicted in Figure 5–15.

THE CONTRACTOR AND LARGE COMPUTER INSTALLATIONS

Minicomputers are getting so cheap and versatile that large computers can no longer offer economic justification for in-house installation, except in very rare cases. The large service companies, recognizing the ability of their traditional customers to do their own data processing by using minicomputers, have turned their marketing efforts toward the super-giant clientele. Through a series of acquisitions, they have developed the capability of putting together national and international computer networks. In terms of speed and capability, the minicomputers are no match.

The Future of Small Service Companies. Acquisition characteristics also mean that the small service companies will become a thing of the past. The trend is already well established for the computer setup to be either an in-house minicomputer, doing a very respectable job in satisfying data processing requirements of all functions of the contractor, or a large computer installation, performing sophisticated applications through national and international networks.

Contracting Firms Using Large Computer Installations. For the great majority of the contractors, the minicomputer will be capable of satisfying all estimating, engineering, and accounting requirements. Only the supergiant contractor operating on a multibranch, international level, requires the use of large computers. The typical arrangement is characterized by the use of elaborate terminal hook-ups on a time-sharing basis to form part of a network operated by one of the giant service companies. Processing of input takes place at a remote location. Output response, in any medium, takes place at widespread location in milliseconds.

HOW TO PREPARE THE ACCOUNTING MANUAL

The secret of operating the contractor's accounting department in an efficient manner is to routinize as many transactions as possible. A situation where

USING THE DATA BASE

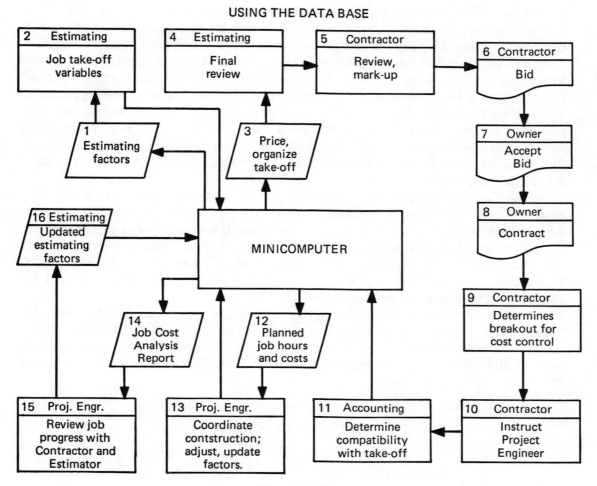

Figure 5–15

only one person knows how to put out the payroll or prepare the financial statements is dangerous. It is much better to put accounting procedures in writing, even for the one-person accounting department; in fact, this is true especially for the one-person accounting department. The ability to keep complex accounting procedures in one's head is no longer considered a great achievement. The human memory is no match for that of a computer program, a written procedure, or a flowchart.

The Chart of Accounts. This is the beginning. Immediately following it will be instructions on how to use it. Actually, the chart of accounts should be largely self-explanatory. Accounts requiring special instructions will consist of those in which there might be some doubt as to the content such as 810, office expense, or 820, outside services; or, where special handling might be required such as the 890 series dealing with income taxes. See Figure 5–1.

Payroll and Job Costing Functions. Routine payroll and job costing functions will be next. These will roughly parallel those assigned to the computer, as shown in Figure 5–14. Assuming that the contractor has a manual operation, the accountant can begin by writing procedures for the preparation of payroll checks, for example. Then he can go on to procedures for posting pay and deductions to the individual earnings records. As he writes these procedures he should look ahead. For example, what will he be using the individual earnings record for—quarterly Federal and state reports for withholding and unemployment taxes? If so, he should plan procedures and formats so that the individual earnings records can provide basic input for all of these reports. He then proceeds to the various weekly payroll reports and uses common basis data out of the individual earnings records, supplemented by weekly time sheets, as the source data for all of these reports.

One Procedure at a Time. The accountant should complete one procedure or one family of procedures, including backup flowcharts, before going to the next series. After routine functions have been taken care of, the accountant should proceed to the nonroutine functions, including those reserved for his personal attention. These are the controller functions and responsibilities shown in Figures 5–13 and 5–14, as well as those special responsibilities retained by the accountant operator in Figure 5–14.

Coordination with Other Departments. All procedures must be carefully coordinated before final inclusion in the accounting manual. Enough copies should be made to take care of each person in the accounting department as well as the contractor, the estimating department, the project engineers, and the general superintendent.

TABLE OF CONTENTS

	Page
Introduction	iii
Chart of Accounts	1
Using the Chart of Accounts	2
Preparing Payroll Checks	5
Individual Earnings Records	
Design	8
Use	10
Payroll Journal Entries and Recap	12
The Job Cost Analysis Report	25
Accounts Receivable Procedures	29
Etc.	

Figure 5–16

The table of contents will look somewhat similar to the example shown in Figure 5–16. It might be necessary to go into several subdivisions of the main topics shown in this example. Note that material for some of the content has already been developed in this chapter.

Include Operating Instructions.   The accounting manual is not exclusively related to systems design work. In fact, techniques for the successful operation of the accounting system, the subject of the next chapter, will receive ample illustration through the medium of procedures and flowcharts that can be readily included in the accounting manual.

PUTTING THE ACCOUNTING SYSTEM TO WORK

Now that you have designed and installed the contractor's accounting system, we have to put it to work. The next chapter demonstrates how to operate the contractor's accounting system.

6

OPERATING THE ACCOUNTING SYSTEM

Chapter 5 was heavy on the "why." Emphasis was on design criteria based on research and experience as to what the contractor needs to run his business successfully. This chapter is heavy on the "how." It assumes acceptance of the "why" chapter as the basis for a model that will assure a successful accounting system. Text and illustrations will be anchored on the "how to" theme, but in the background will be the all-important "why" of Chapter 5.

THE PRACTICAL VALUE OF INTERIM REPORTS

Year-end financial statements, usually audited by a CPA firm, and, for the bigger companies, made a part of the annual report to the stockholders, are carefully put together, require several months to produce, and really are in a different league from the monthly interim reports. Nevertheless, for the contractor as well as for key outside users such as bankers, surety underwriters, and credit managers, interim reports provide a valuable and somewhat uninhibited insight into the workings of the construction firm.

Why the Contractor Needs Timely Interim Reports

For the interim report, timeliness is more essential than completeness. The contractor needs to know as soon as possible whether financial objectives are being met. A financial statement less than 100 percent complete but on time will give the contractor a chance to take corrective action. Financial statements that are 100 percent complete, but coming to him four or five weeks after the end of the month, are really too late to do any good.

Interim Reports Alert the Outsider to Danger Signals

To the outsider, a timely report, even if not containing all disclosures expected in an audited report, will prove invaluable in detecting danger signals. For example, even over-optimistic estimates of gross profit, hidden away in the analysis of work in process, will not obscure danger signals from the trained eye of the banker, the surety underwriter, and the credit manager. Almost instinctively they will compare the current statement to the one for the previous month. The statement of changes in financial position from month to month will be used to evaluate the contractor's progress in building up his working capital. Mental or even mathematical adjustments to the percentage of working capital, represented by optimism in unbilled costs and earnings, will be made. The outside user will have his own discount factor. Generally, it will be based on the percentage of optimism for the past year that failed to survive the acid test of the year-end auditing report.

Computer-Produced Interim Reports

To the contractor fortunate enough to have the use of a minicomputer, timely interim reports are no problem. Interacting amounts flowing from a common data bank will create a flow of interim reports, either in the form of hard copy printouts, or as charts, or graphs glowing from the cathode ray tube (CRT). And all of this occurs in only a matter of seconds after the last input. The microcomputer will do almost as well, except that more time will be needed for internal posting to the general ledger after the last input.

Successful Production of Interim Reports via the Contractor's Manual Accounting System

Since the computer resolves the problem of timely interim reporting, we will deal principally with manual systems. Successful production of timely financial statements is simply a matter of planning for them to happen. It boils down to establishing get-ready steps, testing them, refining them, and finally, sticking with them. The accountant must be ready to move quickly. But he cannot do so unless he begins getting ready for the next cycle as soon as the current report has gone to press. This, then, is the secret of success. And success means putting out reports by not later than the tenth of the month following the monthly reporting period.

THE CASE OF THE DISORGANIZED CONTRACTOR

The importance of being organized to move ahead quickly and efficiently cannot be overemphasized. A specific case comes to mind, in which a contractor (let's call him Contractor X) was plagued with many problems in his accounting department. He envied his friend, Contractor Y, who, by contrast, enjoyed the advantages of a smoothly operated accounting system.

Contractor X knew that efficient operations, whether in the accounting department or on the job site, have to be made to happen. The principle of cause and effect prevails both in the office and out in the field. He discussed the matter with his accountant, who agreed that something had to be done. However, being new on the job and somewhat inexperienced although strong academically, the accountant felt that he needed to spend some time observing actual operations of a successful accounting department. Contractor X took care of this matter by arranging to have his accountant spend a few hours in the accounting department of Contractor Y.

Accounting Basis of the Contractor's Disorganization

When he got back to his office the accountant began to analyze his own situation, putting down his ideas in a cause and effect format. In a couple of hours, he had the following diagnosis:

- Chart of accounts fragmented, inconsistent, illogical and unstable
- Prefixes and suffixes inserted to meet monthly special reporting requirements
- No accounting manual.

How Accounting Disorganization Affected Operation of the System

The accountant went on with his analysis, listing the following bad effects inside and out of the accounting department:

- Bulky, complex journals are hard to post to and hard to balance.
- A bulky, fragmented general ledger is hard to post to and hard to balance.
- The illogical structure of general ledger accounts causes much extra work in the preparation of monthly financial statements.
- Blank financial statements ready to be roughed out cannot be prepared beforehand because the format is unstable.
- In spite of much overtime, financial statements are always late.
- Financial statements are so bad that financial projections cannot be prepared from them.

• Without financial projections, the banker will not increase our line of credit.

• Without an increased line of credit, we cannot pay our bills by discount time or take purchase discounts.

• While prefixes and suffixes facilitate the preparation of monthly special reports, they impede the routine processing of many transactions.

• Special handling requirements of these transactions produce a bunching up of month-end journal entries.

• The unusual number of month-end journal entries become a drag on the entire accounting system.

Financial Effects of the Contractor's Disorganization

The accountant next put a pencil to the whole matter, and came up with the following estimate of unnecessary costs produced by the disorganized accounting system:

Overtime	$ 2,500
Lost discounts:	
Cash	15,000
Purchase	45,000
Gross profit of jobs lost because discounts could not be considered in preparing bids	150,000
	$212,500

What if the Contract Had Not Been Disorganized?

When the accountant presented the analysis to the contractor, he pointed out that only tangible financial effects had been considered. However, several "what if" situations were readily apparent. For example, what if Contractor X had been in a position to anticipate discounts in his bids, and had succeeded in adding the $150,000 to his net worth? What could he do with an additional $1.5 million in bonding capacity? Would this have moved him into a smaller group of competitors? How much would this be worth in the long run?

HOW THE ACCOUNTANT CAN OVERCOME DISORGANIZATION

It took the accountant two months to change the chart of accounts and write the accounting manual. The timing was good because it coincided with the end of the fiscal year. By the end of the first quarter of the new fiscal year, the accounting department was operating smoothly. Overtime became a rarity, reports were out by the tenth of the month, and the accountant was able to prepare pro forma financial statements covering the remaining nine months of the fiscal year.

HOW TO GET THE OPERATOR TO WORK WITH THE ACCOUNTANT

A well-designed and tightly operated accounting system cannot exist for long without the continuing cooperation and goodwill of the operator. Who is the operator? Anybody outside of the accounting department. The contractor, the estimator, the purchasing agent, the general superintendent, the job foreman, the journeymen, the apprentices, and the laborers—all of these are operators. The importance to the accountant lies in the fact that they are all producers of input. Without this input, the accountant cannot operate the accounting system.

The Contractor Sets the Pace. The person who can make or break the accounting system is the contractor. In previous chapters, we discussed the prominent role the contractor plays in both policy making and design criteria. His continued involvement becomes an essential element of the accounting system as the accountant turns to him for help when judgment and experience are most needed. For example, without the contractor's personal review, the analysis of work in progress, with its impact on stated income and working capital, becomes too much of a responsibility for the accountant to tackle all by himself. Even after soliciting the help of the estimator, the project engineer, the job foreman, and others, the impact is so great that the contractor should have the final say about what will be presented on the financial statements.

Getting the contractor involved has another good effect. By participating in the production of financial statements, the contractor will know what is contained in them and most certainly will know how to use them.

Getting the Estimator Involved. In the larger firms, the estimator will do much of the leg work in determining estimated cost to complete a job. In addition, the estimator must be brought into the very important process of updating and refining that portion of the data base containing estimating factors. This valuable contribution, shown as Step 16 in Figure 5–15 of Chapter 5, makes the estimator an indispensable part of the system. Whether the data base consists of 3″ x 5″ cards, ledger sheets, punched cards and paper tape, magnetic tape, magnetic disks, magnetic drums, data cells, or core memory, the idea is the same: the estimator has certain knowledge that will improve the quality of the data bank. You must solicit that knowledge. You must show him that by working with you, you can, in turn, do a better job for him and the contractor. You must show him how this will improve your performance in the other functions having their roots deep in the data bank such as estimating, bidding, and controlling job costs.

Working with the Purchasing Agent. Most contracting firms will place the responsibility for administering purchase orders and subcontracts with the purchasing agent, although authority for approving, adjusting, and paying will be lodged elsewhere. In many firms, this authority will be retained by the contractor himself.

Since the purchasing agent is the administrator of purchase orders and subcontracts, he plays a vital role in shaping the input for the material, equipment, and subcontractor portions of the job-cost analysis reporting system. Examples of such reports are illustrated in Figures 5–4, 5–5, and 5–6 of Chapter 5.

The accountant seldom has problems getting the purchasing agent to work with him. Careful handling of details is second nature to him. As a result, a high degree of reliability can be placed on his input. In turn he will expect timely and accurate accounting reports. Not only will he know how to use them; he can easily be encouraged to offer suggestions for improving them.

Working with the General Superintendent. Firms having a good number of jobs going at the same time will find it useful to employ a general superintendent. His job is to help the contractor allocate resources to the different jobs and keep job costs under control.

The job-cost analysis report is the general superintendent's most important management tool. It is this report that will flag jobs that are in trouble or are about to have problems. With the aid of this report, he can establish priorities for his job-inspection program.

The accountant can get the general superintendent to work with him by:

- Soliciting his help in improving the job-cost analysis report
- Working closely with him and the job foreman in the effective use of the report to keep job costs under control.

  The job-cost analysis report is as good as the two elements that make it up:

  - Estimated hours and costs
  - Actual hours and costs

The contractor and the estimator, together with the project engineer if one is used, can pretty well assure the validity of Element 1—estimated hours and costs. The general superintendent, working with the job foremen, can do a great deal to assure the validity of Element 2—actual hours and costs. In the process of showing him how to use the job-cost analysis report, the accountant can stress the fact that the report is only as good as the input. Without valid actual data, the comparison to estimates becomes a meaningless exercise. The general superintendent will be quick to grasp the vital role he plays in helping with the validity of such data.

Working with the Job Foreman.   Bringing a job "in the money" is the principal role of the job foreman. If a job is in the money, it is also:

- a trouble-free job
- finished on time
- with a minimum of callbacks
- and, therefore, a good job.

The job foreman plays such a key role in bringing a job in the money that contractors will take this into account in bidding the job. Since the estimated job costs in a real sense represent the personal attributes of the job foreman, it is not only a matter of fairness but a powerful incentive to let him know what is expected of him, and how he is doing in meeting job objectives that have been set out for him.

The accountant must see to it that the job foreman is furnished a complete job-cost analysis report for his job as soon as possible after the close of the weekly pay period. The labor portion of the report will be of particular interest to him. The accountant can work with the general superintendent to show the foreman how to use the report. If there is no general superintendent, the accountant will work directly with the job foreman.

As in the case of the general superintendent, the job foreman will be quick to grasp the significance of valid input. His most valuable input will be accurate and complete time sheets. The job foreman must be helped in making sure that company instructions for the preparation of time sheets are carefully followed by all the men under his supervision.

Journeymen, Apprentices, Laborers and the Accountant.   A good job foreman will share accountability for bringing a job in the money with his men. The accountant can help enhance the team effort by making sure that the job foreman knows how to use the job-cost analysis report, and that he puts across to his men the importance of their performance in fulfilling the contractor's expectations. If the men know they are being monitored through the reporting system, they will usually cooperate in assuring a valid measurement of their performance. Sometimes there is too much cooperating. Sometimes the men will take it upon themselves to doctor up the input so as to make the job look good. The foreman's review of documents, with the accountant looking over his shoulder, is designed to stop this.

How the Accountant Depends on the Operator for Input.   The dependence of the accountant on the operator for input, and the operator's dependence on the accountant for output sums up the principal idea contained in this section. It is further illustrated in Figure 6–1.

OPERATOR — ACCOUNTING INTERACTION

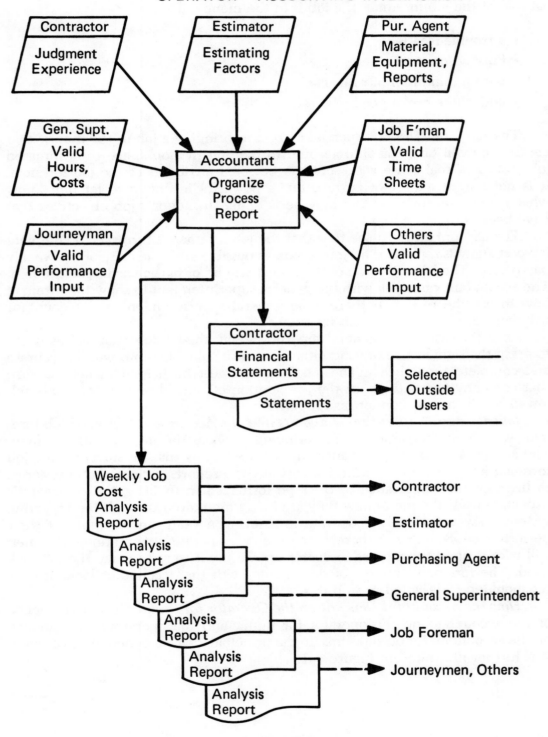

Figure 6–1

INTERNAL CONTROLS THAT WILL WORK FOR MANAGEMENT AND THE ACCOUNTANT

Internal control is present in all of the techniques presented in this book. For example, in Chapter 5, certain internal control basics were introduced in the design of the contractor's accounting system. Among these you will recall the following:

- A clean and logical chart of accounts
- The use of an accounting manual
- Budgetary control of costs and expenses
- Establishment of a cost accounting system

What is Internal Control?   It is a system that encompasses all steps taken by management to:

- Safeguard assets
- Produce accurate and reliable reports
- Assure compliance with company policy
- Measure efficiency of operations.

In this section, we will learn how to design and install a system of internal control that will not only accomplish these objectives, but by so doing, will help the accountant and the contractor do a better job.

The Role of Cash in Internal Control.   The principal rule of internal control is that no one person should handle all phases of a transaction from beginning to end. For the larger firms, a subdivision of duties can satisfy this maxim. For the small contractor, subdivision of duties is often impossible. However, even among the small contractors, there are certain minimum measures that can be taken to safeguard cash and conform with other good internal control practices.

Seventeen Steps That Assure Good Internal Control over Cash

Here, for example, are seventeen steps that can be taken even by the smallest of contractors to assure good internal control over cash:

1. Prepare a list of all mail remittances immediately.
2. Compare these with deposit slips and entries in the cash journal.
3. Deposit all cash receipts daily and intact.
4. Use serially numbered checks for all disbursements except petty cash.

5. Do not let the accountant sign checks. In a small company, the contractor himself should sign all checks.

6. Use an imprest petty cash fund, entrusted to a single custodian, preferably someone other than the accountant.

7. Use petty cash vouchers, coded for proper account number of the expenditure, that are signed by the recepient of the cash.

8. Review all petty cash vouchers when replenishing the fund.

9. Reconcile bank accounts monthly, this preferably done by someone other than the person recording the cash transactions.

10. Use serially numbered, properly approved purchase orders, for all but the smallest of purchase transactions.

11. Verify deliveries of material by using serially numbered receiving reports.

12. Pay only from invoices that have been matched with purchase orders and receiving reports.

13. Pay subcontractors only after verifying compliance with conditions of the subcontract or purchase order (whichever was used) and concurrence of the job foreman.

14. Mail work in progress requests for payment (estimates) monthly; mail statements for small jobs promptly upon their completion.

15. At the end of each month, reconcile subsidiary accounts receivable and accounts payable ledgers with control accounts.

16. Prepare comparative cash-flow control reports, in order to disclose significant variations in receipts and disbursements versus planned amounts. See Figure 4–12.

17. Utilize the services of a public accountant or a certified public accountant for the year-end audit.

Internal Control Needs the Contractor's Participation

For the small firm, there is no way that these precautionary measures can be installed without the active participation of the contractor himself. For example, if the secretary is also the bookkeeper, it might even be necessary for the contractor himself to make a list of all remittances, and to verify agreement with the deposit slip and entries in the cash journal.

Warning: Many a contractor has suffered large losses because he refused to concern himself with the details of an internal control system designed to safeguard his cash.

Please note that compliance with the measures listed above not only helps the contractor safeguard his cash, but provides the accountant with reliable input into the accounting system. This is because the input:

- benefits from proper review and authorization, and

• is processed in such a way as to assure accuracy and reliability by a system of checks and balances, reconciliations, and serial-number control.

The accountant produces accurate and reliable reports that measure the efficiency of operations. The contractor's assets are safeguarded, and compliance with his policy is assured.

Internal Control of Other Current Assets. Since cash is in and out of all current asset transactions, the steps listed above, with reference to the internal control of cash, take care of the internal control affecting other assets in this category. Inventory, however, might require additional steps, since certain transactions, flowing through the stockroom bins, are indifferent to controls affecting cash transactions.

Internal Control of Inventories. This requires more than the detection of defalcation. For example, excessive stockpiling, leading to obsolescence and erroneous costing of material requisitions, resulting in erroneous job costs, will cause the contractor more serious losses than inventory thefts.

Excessive stockpiling has a direct impact on holding costs. Taxes, insurance, warehousing space, and opportunity costs all enter into these costs. The contractor should know that all of these costs can add up to as much as 20 percent a year of the inventory value.

The first step in preventing excessive stockpiling is proper authorization and documentation of material purchases, as listed in the steps shown above. In addition, there should be a requirement for a quarterly usage report, broken down by major categories of material.

If perpetual inventory records are kept, the report can be prepared from the inventory ledgers. If such records are not kept, it will be necessary to prepare the report from an analysis of purchase orders and material requisitions. The objective of the report is to highlight slow moving items so that the contractor, armed with this information, can take remedial action.

Weakness related to job costing can be taken care of by bringing the purchasing agent and the estimator into the act. The purchasing agent should do the pricing, and the estimator should review the need for the material requisition. Significant amounts of material requisitions going into a particular job reflect on the completeness of the job estimate. The estimator should know about it, either as a means of detecting wasteful practices or of correcting his estimating factors.

Techniques for Internal Control of Noncurrent Assets. Capital investment procedures described in Chapter 4 are the principal techniques used in the internal control of noncurrent assets. Because of the large amounts involved, and the long-term consequence of the expenditure, initial control provided by capital investment procedures is of the utmost importance. After the initial step, there are two other control measures to be considered:

• A depreciation strategy consistent with profit objectives and a tax tradeoff between depreciation and the investment credit

- Subsidiary ledgers for each piece of equipment showing cost, salvage value, depreciation method and rate; and, for the more expensive pieces of equipment, usage information such as dates and hours used.

HOW TO USE EFFECTIVE PROCESSING TECHNIQUES

Ideally, the contractor's accounting system should be so designed that input flows in, is processed, and is converted into output, with a minimum of effort. The secret of achieving this type of an operation is to make routine as many transactions as possible, and to reduce the nonroutine transactions to some form of organized processing. Checklists and the accounting manual can be used effectively to assure consistent processing of nonroutine transactions.

Job Costs. Procedures designed to assure routine handling of job costs, discussed in previous chapters, will work effectively in most cases. There are four exceptions:

- Small jobs
- Joint ventures
- Cost-plus contracts
- Home builders.

How to Handle Processing for Small Jobs. The main difference from routine processing associated with the normal job-cost procedure is the fact that the cost elements are charged to a composite small-job ledger, rather than to individual job ledgers. Because of the large number of jobs involved, the usual job number identification is not used. Instead, a work order number or an invoice number becomes the mustering point for the accumulation of job costs.

In a manual system, a single small job worksheet, subdivided into the cost elements of labor, material, equipment, miscellaneous, and subcontractors, is used to record all costs applicable to small jobs.

The small jobs worksheet provides not only the totals for work in process inventory, but also the cost figures to be used in determining gross profit. Figure 6–2 shows how the small jobs worksheet is put together, and how its various elements flow into the income statement and the balance sheet.

You will note that the end-of-the-month recap, by work order number or invoice number, will bring together all job costs into two categories:

- Completed jobs, including balance forward from the previous month, and
- Uncompleted jobs carried forward to the next month.

Completed small jobs are recapped and billed as soon as completed. Most contractors do not wait until the end of the month to bill them.

CONTRACTOR'S CONSTRUCTION COMPANY				
Small Jobs Worksheet				
Month Ending _____ 19__				

Date		Reference	Total	*Various Cost Elements*
	(1) Uncompleted small jobs from previous month (ONE LINE TOTALS)			
	(2) Current month charges (DETAIL)			
	(3) Total			
	(4) Less completed small jobs (RECAP)			
	(5) Uncompleted jobs at end of month (RECAP)			

	Flow to Financial Statements	
	Balance Sheet	*Income Statement*
(1) REVERSE	Cr unbilled costs and earnings	Dr contract income
(2)	Cr cash or payables	Dr job cost
(4)	Dr accounts receivable	Cr contract income
(5) ACCRUE	Dr unbilled costs and earnings	Cr contract income

Figure 6–2

Handling Joint Ventures. For tax purposes, a joint venture is treated as a partnership. In addition to the normal job-costing techniques previously discussed, other precautions must be taken to assure an accounting of each participant's account. This information is needed for the preparation of the K-1 report at the end of the year, and the reconciliation of the participants' accounts.

For interim reporting purposes, joint ventures can be handled as if they were separate work orders. They can take their place in the analysis of work in process and in the spin-off from it to the balance sheet and income statement.

Cost Plus Contracts Require Special Attention. Processing of cost-plus work can follow established procedures, but both data input and output must receive special attention.

Input

- Be sure that cost-plus work orders *stand out*.
- Use different-colored work orders, or a distinctive set of job numbers.
- Impress upon your men that failure to report work performed on cost-plus jobs means money out of your pocket.
- Insist on separate purchase orders, careful physical segregation of material and equipment, and separate invoicing.

Output

- Study billing requirements and be prepared, either by modifying your accounting system or by worksheet analysis, for costs to flow into the various billing slots.
- Get ready for end-of-month billing by preparing a blank worksheet with line items that follow the billing requirements of the cost-plus contract. See Figure 6–3 for an illustration of a worksheet used successfully by various contractors in organizing the information needed for billing cost-plus work.

Handling Processing for Home Builders. Instead of a job number, the home builder will use either an address or a lot number for reference. The horizontal cost element breakdown is not needed in home building. The flow of financial data stems from either direct expenditures or subcontracting. Therefore, the whole cost system can be run with the use of only one column for all of the cost categories.

The vertical cost structure in home building, however, can become quite elaborate. Within the single cost column various subdivisions of the total cost of construction can be listed. This breakdown is facilitated by the fact that the normal cost components of home building will flow to specific tasks to be performed separately.

Since the home builder finishes his jobs in a relatively short period of time, he keeps his payables fairly current. As a result, he can probably go directly from a monthly recap of the check stubs to the job-cost sheet illustrated in Figure 6–4, leaving the total column open until the house is finished.

CONTRACTOR'S CONSTRUCTION COMPANY
Cost-Plus Worksheet

Project _____

Month Ending _____ 19___

Description	Line Item	Total	Labor	Material	Equip.	Misc.	Subcontractors
Exhaust System:	1019						
	1020						
	1022						
	1026						
Total							
Etc.							
Etc.							
Total Cost This Month							
Mark-up:							
%							
%							
%							
%							
Total Billed This Month							

Figure 6-3

HORIZON HOMES, INC.
Job-Cost Sheet

Lot _____ Block _____ Section _____

Beginning Date _____ Completion Date _____

Address _____

Costs Incurred During the Month of

	Budget	*Total Cost*	
Lot			
Taxes			
Architect			
Loan expense			
Insurance			
Permits			
Sitework			
Footing:			
Concrete			
Labor			
Masonry			
Material			
Labor			
Lumber			
Carpentry			
Plumbing			
Electrical			
Heat & air			
Etc.			
Etc.			
Total			

Figure 6–4

INTERIM CLOSING TECHNIQUES ILLUSTRATED

When it comes to a discussion of interim closing techniques, there will be those who will advocate short-cuts; others will tend to be more conservative.

Experience both in internal and external operations will cause most accountants to be cautious. Short-cuts such as those you often read about in accounting literature will tend to break down when exposed to accounting systems beyond those serving the smaller operations.

Radical processing techniques that will do away with work-sheets, adjusting, entries, journals, and the general ledger will not stand up beyond the most elementary accounting systems, which after all can be developed right off the check stubs.

By the same token, the conservative approach might tend to honor such niceties of accounting as keeping the books open until everything is collected into a neat package. It could tend to ignore such practical considerations as producing useful financial statements as soon as possible after the end of the month, which is more important than completeness that sacrifices timeliness. The contractor can better use data that is 90 percent complete when presented to him on the 10th of the month, than data that is 99.9 percent complete but not available to him until the 25th of the month.

What Holds Up Interim Closings? Mostly, it's a failure to get ready. When certain things happen over and over again at the end of each month, it is foolish not to start getting ready as soon as possible.

Ordinarily, journals take care of themselves. Column totals posted to the general ledger can be part of a routine procedure that any one can take care of.

For the contractor there is a set of special adjusting entries related to the analysis of work in process that must be considered. Once these are out of the way, other adjusting entries can be taken care of quickly and routinely.

HOW TO PREPARE A TIMELY ANALYSIS OF WORK IN PROCESS

Chapter 3 deals in depth with the problem of percentage of completion. In this chapter, we are concerned with the prompt presentation of the analysis so that journal entries depending on it will not be delayed.

To prepare the analysis of work in process as soon as possible, begin putting together the amounts making up the elements of work in process. Some are constants or almost so; others can be determined shortly before or right at the end of the month; still others require end-of-month computations.

Elements of the Work in Process Analysis

Let's list the elements that make up the work in process analysis, with a comment as to when the figures can be put together.

1. *Contract amount.* Practically a constant, except for contract changes that are usually available well before the end of the month.

2. *Billings to date.* Most billings have to be in before the 20th of the month *for that month.* The subcontractor's billing has to be in even earlier. As a result, there is no problem in accumulating totals for billing to date well before the end of the month.

3. *Cost to date.* Prompt processing of invoices and subcontractors' progress billing will mean that payroll costs will constitute the only problem. Payrolls cover weekly periods, whereas interim financial statements will be done on a monthly basis. Most contractors will cost whatever payrolls have ended within the month. Others will take into account the fact that there are eight months with four weekly paydays and four months with five. If strict accrual of labor costs is desired, for each month with only four pay periods, labor costs amounting to .3333 per week must be accrued $\left(\frac{52 \text{ weeks}}{12 \text{ months}} = 4.333 \text{ weeks per month} \right)$. For the four months containing five weekly pay periods, labor costs amounting to .6667 per week must be deferred, or $5.0000 - 4.3333 = .6667$.

4. *Billings over costs.* The greater of 2 over 3.

5. *Cost over billings.* The greater of 3 over 2.

6. *Estimated cost to complete.* Task-cost analysis techniques are described in detail in Chapter 3. In this chapter, the secret of success lies in compiling actual labor hours and costs, plus other cost elements such as material, equipment, miscellaneous, and subcontractors for each job in progress as quickly as possible; comparing these to the cost estimates used to bid the job; then arriving at the balance remaining for each from the original job estimate. After this is done, the accountant needs to make the estimator and the contractor commit themselves to a cost element figure of estimated costs to complete each job. A bit of pressure on the part of the accountant will be necessary, because without this figure, the remainder of the work in process analysis cannot be completed. *As you will note, all of the remaining elements of the analysis are merely functions of step 6.*

7. *Estimated gross profit:* $1 - 3 - 6$.

8. *Percentage gross profit:* $7 \div 1 \times 100$.

9. *Percentage completion:* $\frac{3}{3 \times 6} \times 100$.

10. *Billings over costs, earned:* 7×9.

11. *Billings over costs, unearned:* if 10 is less than 4, enter difference in 11.

12. *Unbilled costs and earnings*: if 10 is more than 4, add difference to 5 and enter in 12.

Items 11 and 12 are totaled for each job.

Net unearned billings over costs, for all work in process, is the basis of the following adjusting entry:

> Dr Job income (contract revenue)
>   Cr Unearned billings over costs (a current liability).

Net unbilled costs and earnings, for all work in process, is the basis for the following adjusting entry.

> Dr Unbilled costs and earnings (a current asset)
>   Cr Contract revenue.

How to Prepare and Use Dummy Statements: A Time-Saver for Interim Closing

You must not overlook this time-saver for interim closing: the preparation of dummy statements.

It might take a few periods of trial and error to come up with the format that makes both you and the contractor happy, but eventually you will. As soon as you do, you should immediately prepare master dummy statements, ready to be reproduced for worksheets, showing everything that eventually will become the financial statements, minus the figures. All you have to do is to transfer the figures from the general ledger to your worksheets.

If you will turn to Figure 6–5, you will notice everything that could possibly be figured out in advance has been included in the balance sheet dummy. For example, the heading even shows a spacing count in parenthesis—a small point, but one that will save the typist a little time.

The format is pretty specific. For example, it calls for:

• Tight structure within each balance sheet category
• A space between each category
• A separate total for all liabilities to facilitate comparison with net worth or stockholders' equity
• Typing close to the bottom of each line, so that additional accounts can be inserted without disturbing the preplanned sequence.

The income statement dummy is also complete, except for the actual amounts. (See Figure 6–6.) Please note the use of a separate schedule for general and administrative expenses.

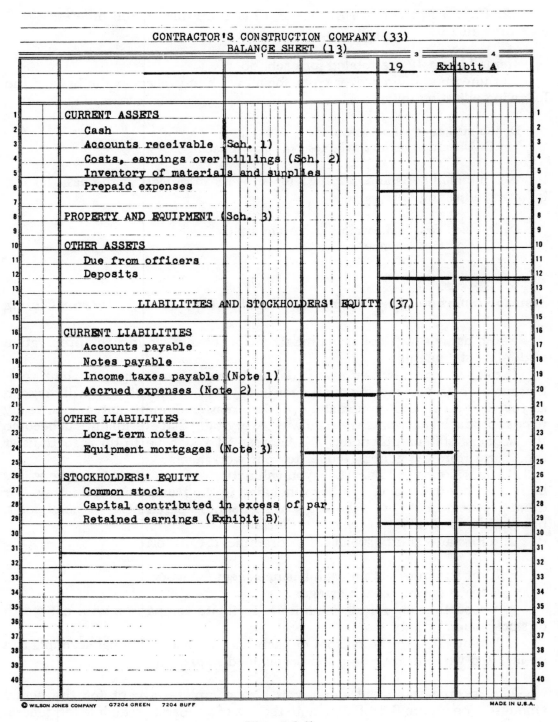

CONTRACTOR'S CONSTRUCTION COMPANY (33)
BALANCE SHEET (13)

19___   Exhibit A

1	**CURRENT ASSETS**
2	Cash
3	Accounts receivable (Sch. 1)
4	Costs, earnings over billings (Sch. 2)
5	Inventory of materials and supplies
6	Prepaid expenses
7	
8	**PROPERTY AND EQUIPMENT (Sch. 3)**
9	
10	**OTHER ASSETS**
11	Due from officers
12	Deposits
13	
14	LIABILITIES AND STOCKHOLDERS' EQUITY (37)
15	
16	**CURRENT LIABILITIES**
17	Accounts payable
18	Notes payable
19	Income taxes payable (Note 1)
20	Accrued expenses (Note 2)
21	
22	**OTHER LIABILITIES**
23	Long-term notes
24	Equipment mortgages (Note 3)
25	
26	**STOCKHOLDERS' EQUITY**
27	Common stock
28	Capital contributed in excess of par
29	Retained earnings (Exhibit B)

© WILSON JONES COMPANY   G7204 GREEN   7204 BUFF   MADE IN U.S.A.

Figure 6–5

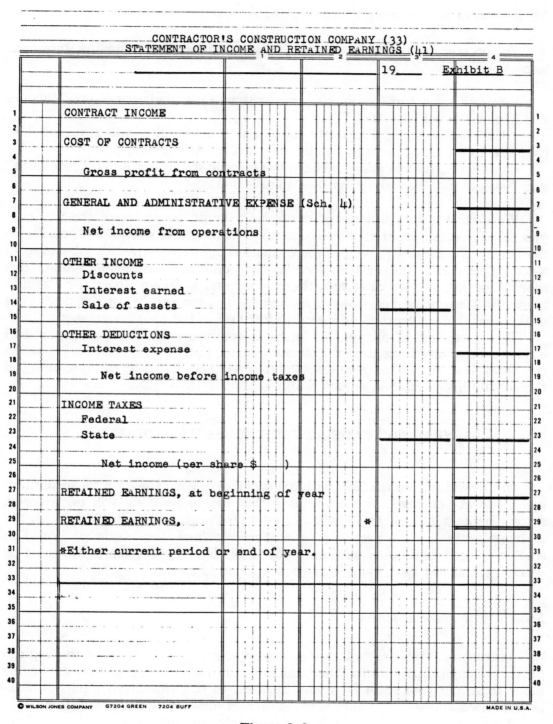

Figure 6–6

Variations in the Dummy Financial Statements

The accountant should be aware of three variations to the income statement format:

- Some contractors like to see a comparison of planned versus actual income and expenses. (See Figure 6–7.)
- Others like to see a separate statement of retained earnings, rather than having it as a part of the income statement. (See Figure 6–8.)
- Some contractors prefer to have the income statement show "this month" and "year to date" breakdowns. (See Figure 6–9.)

With the third variation, the contractor should be aware of the fact that precise measurement of month-by-month income is not possible, especially in the construction industry, where the estimated costs to complete a job can have a strong impact on income. As long as the contractor understands that "this month" figures can be distorted, there is no real problem. In fact, he should realize that even the year-to-date figures are not too reliable at the beginning of the year. However, they will tend to level off as the year progresses.

The statement of changes in financial condition can also be prepared in advance for everything except current figures. Indeed, the summary portion can show amounts for current assets and current liabilities at the beginning of the accounting year. (See Figure 6–10.)

YEAR-END CLOSING TECHNIQUES ILLUSTRATED

In this section, we will deal with the specifics of what the internal accountant has to do at year end. Not everything that has to be done will be covered, since Chapters 7 through 11 will extend year-end functions to fit in with the audit program and the particular *modus operandi* of the outside auditor. This section instead deals with minimum year-end closing procedures that must be carried out at any rate, even if there is no outside auditor.

Schedule of Prepaid Items

Year-end techniques will require the adjustments to expense of the expired portion of any prepaid items. The familiar examination of expenditures covering more than one year must be done, in order to determine what portion is to be expensed and what portion is to be carried forward as a prepaid item.

A simple technique, applicable to both interim and year-end closings, is to prepare a schedule similar to that shown in Figure 6–11, in which the prepaid

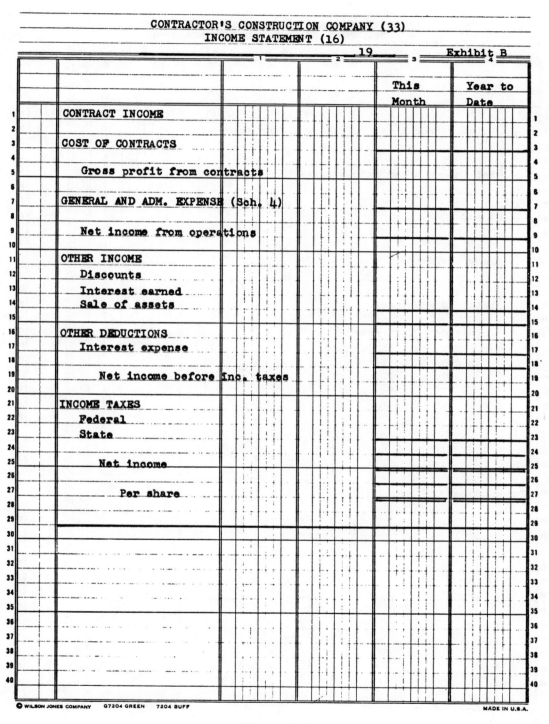

Figure 6–7

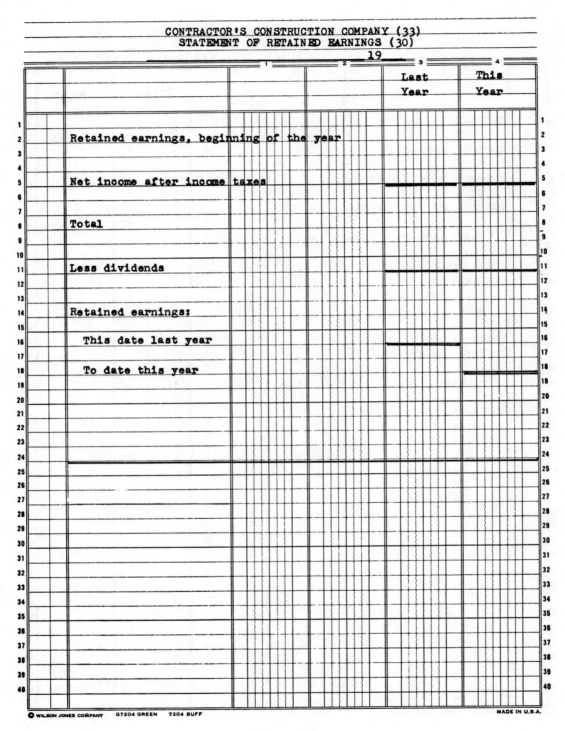

Figure 6–8

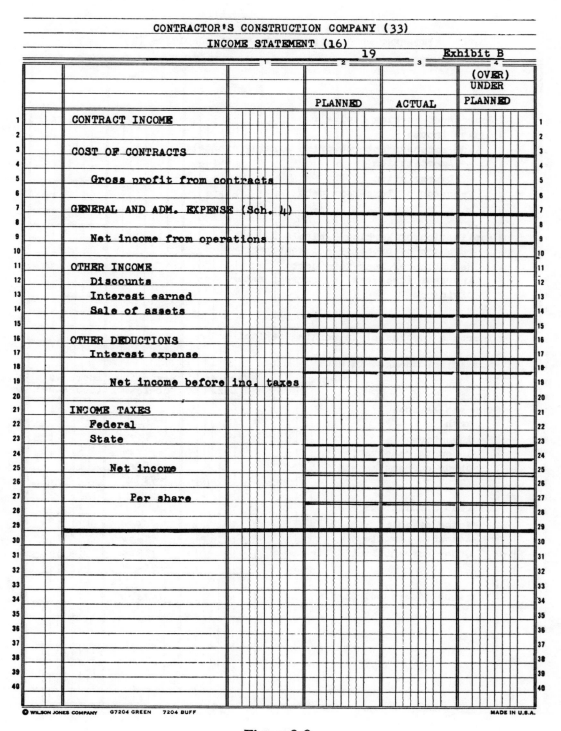

Figure 6–9

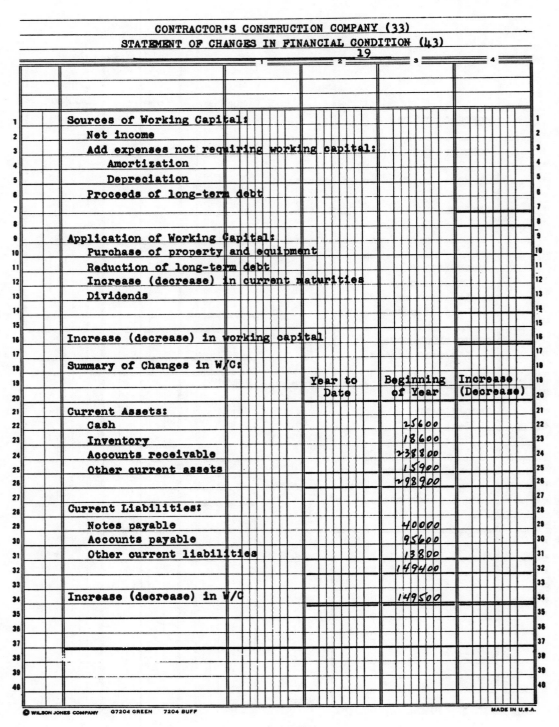

CONTRACTOR'S CONSTRUCTION COMPANY (33)

STATEMENT OF CHANGES IN FINANCIAL CONDITION (43)

19____

		1	2	3	4
1	Sources of Working Capital:				
2	Net income				
3	Add expenses not requiring working capital:				
4	Amortization				
5	Depreciation				
6	Proceeds of long-term debt				
7					
8					
9	Application of Working Capital:				
10	Purchase of property and equipment				
11	Reduction of long-term debt				
12	Increase (decrease) in current maturities				
13	Dividends				
14					
15					
16	Increase (decrease) in working capital				
17					
18	Summary of Changes in W/C:				
19			Year to Date	Beginning of Year	Increase (Decrease)
20					
21	Current Assets:				
22	Cash			25600	
23	Inventory			18600	
24	Accounts receivable			238800	
25	Other current assets			15900	
26				298900	
27					
28	Current Liabilities:				
29	Notes payable			40000	
30	Accounts payable			95600	
31	Other current liabilities			13800	
32				149400	
33					
34	Increase (decrease) in W/C			149500	

© WILSON JONES COMPANY   G7204 GREEN   7204 BUFF   MADE IN U.S.A.

Figure 6–10

CONTRACTOR'S CONSTRUCTION COMPANY
Schedule of Prepaid Items

EXPIRED

	Total	Jan	Feb	Mar	Apr	May	Jun	Jul	Aug	Sep	Oct	Nov	Dec
Prepaid Insurance:													
Total													
Prepaid Taxes:													
Total													
Etc.													

Figure 6–11

item can be set up initially as it is paid or billed, then written off periodically.

The Depreciation Schedule. This schedule can become a time-consuming project if left till year-end. A simple device to avoid the year-end hassle, and at the same time assure more accurate interim statements, is to prepare the depreciation schedule at the beginning of the year. Figure 6–12 will show you how to be ready to determine interim write-offs, while at the same time providing for year-end reconciliation.

Planning Inventory Taking. Fortunately for the contractor, year-end count of inventory is not a huge undertaking. Even for the plumbing and electrical contractors burdened with a great variety of stocked items, the year-end count is not a formidable task, provided that good housekeeping practices have prevailed throughout the year. This means good physical management of inventory, including orderly stocking in bins and clear identification of the parts in each bin.

Inventory taking should be done as close as possible to the end of the accounting year. However, if for the sake of convenience it becomes necessary to start the count several days before the end of the accounting year, by all means do so. Adjustments to year-end amounts can be accomplished from the records, with little fear of significant distortions. Since the time span between the actual count and the official year-end is relatively small, any distortions will not be too great.

Inventory count sheets, available at office supply firms, should be used. The secretary or bookkeeper can type up dummy sheets using the previous year's inventory listings as a guide.

Numerically controlled two-part tags can be used, in conjunction with the dummy sheets, to document the physical count. The top part of the tag is left in the bin or tied to the larger parts and assemblies. The lower part, together with revised and completed listings (the updated dummy sheets), are left for the usual verification by the internal or external auditor.

The Problem of Adjusting Entries. The problem boils down to this: The more you do, the less the outside auditor has to do. If there is no outside auditor, you should nevertheless record, document, and explain adjusting entries. Keep in mind that your work will be reviewed, either by an outside auditor or your successor. Do a complete, professional job, so that your work will stand up to the scrutiny of others.

Statement Preparation. If you have an outside auditor, the final make-up of the financial statements, schedules, and accompanying notes will be his responsibility. Suppose that you do not have an outside auditor. Then the burden for complete disclosure of significant facts falls on your shoulders.

If such is the case, here are three steps you can take to bring your work up to professional standards:

• Carefully prepare the analysis of work in progress. Be sure that you fully understand Chapter 3, where the problem of percentage of completion is treated in detail.

CONTRACTOR'S CONSTRUCTION COMPANY
Depreciation Schedule

| Description | Asset Accounts | | | | | | Depreciation Accounts | | |
	Beginning Balance	Additions (Deletions)	Ending Balance	Method	Life	Prior	Cancelled	Current	Balance

First Quarter
Second Quarter
Third Quarter
Fourth Quarter
Total

Figure 6–12

• Prepare separate schedules for accounts receivable, work in progress, property and equipment, and general and administrative expenses.

• Prepare a separate section for your notes. Put yourself in the place of the outside user of the financial statements. Try to anticipate his questions, and prepare notes that will clear them up. Clarity and simplicity are the marks of professional work. Keep this in mind while preparing your notes.

WHY THE ACCOUNTANT IS IN CHARGE OF AUDIT GET-READY PROCEDURES

After this chapter, the accountant should know how to operate the contractor's accounting system in a very professional way. He is now in the driver's seat when it comes to getting ready for the auditor. The next chapter will illustrate specifically what the contractor's accountant can do to get ready for the year-end audit.

7

PREPARING
FOR THE YEAR-END
AUDIT

The outside auditor, normally a CPA, is in such demand that anything the contractor's accountant can do to help him will not only make the CPA happy, but will save the contractor money. Most CPAs feel that they can justify a reasonable hourly rate if they succeed in holding to a minimum the time spent on an audit. This can be done only if the contractor's accountant and his staff are willing and able to take over the bulk of clerical and junior accountant functions associated with the year-end audit.

Needless to say, such arrangements not only allow the CPA to earn profitable fees, but will save the contractor from spending his money on outside skills that are already available in-house.

HOW THE CONTRACTOR AND THE CPA SHOULD APPROACH
PRE-AUDIT AGREEMENTS

Nothing disgusts the contractor more than to watch the CPA's highly paid personnel engaged in such routine tasks as scheduling, analyzing, summarizing, and flow-charting transactions—tasks that he knows his own people are quite capable of doing.

By the same token, nothing is more annoying to the CPA than to find himself bogged down in remedial bookkeeping and clerical details that the contractor should have taken care of, but perhaps felt that "this is what I'm paying the CPA to do."

The solution to the problem is to come to an understanding before the audit gets underway. The CPA should approach the problem with the idea that:

• He is going to charge a professional fee for the work he does.

• He cannot justify a professional fee if he gets involved in clerical and junior accountant tasks that the contractor himself is equipped to handle.

• He and the contractor will both be happy if, through careful preaudit planning, he permits the contractor to do as much as he is capable of doing.

HOW THE CONTRACTOR'S ACCOUNTANT SHOULD APPROACH PRE-AUDIT PREPARATIONS

The contractor's accountant should approach the problem with the idea that:

• No one knows the contractor's accounting system as well as he does.

• If the CPA will tell him what he wants in the way of schedules, analyses, summaries, and flow charts, he can do it a whole lot better and cheaper than can the CPA.

What the Contractor's Accountant Can Do to Get Ready

Of necessity, there are many things that can be done only after the end of the accounting year. For example, verification of balance sheet items such as cash, receivables, inventories, and payables cannot be carried out until year-end balances are determined. On the other hand, schedules and analyses that cover a time-frame, and slow-moving balance sheet items such as fixed assets, can usually be gotten ready long before the reporting period closes.

How to Get the Records Ready for the Auditor

If the contractor's accountant has taken a professional approach to his responsibilities, and has made good use of the methods and controls described in previous chapters of this book, his records should be in good shape. Records are considered in good shape when there are few if any mysteries. This means that transactions are consistently recorded in accordance with the chart of accounts and the accounting manual. The audit trail is clear, and the company accountant is confident that the auditor can trace transactions with relative ease from their documentation to their resting place in the financial statements.

Clarifying Obscurities Before the Auditor Arrives

Before the auditor arrives, the company accountant should give the records a final scanning in order to discover, clarify, and if necessary, properly document any remaining obscurities. These will usually consist of such transactions as:

- The purchase or sale of major pieces of equipment
- Unusual deviations from normal short-term financial arrangements
- Changes in stock ownership
- Changes in financial structure
- Changes in accounting policies.

Getting Non-Accounting Records Ready for the Auditor

The company accountant should also be aware of the fact that the auditor will look at records that are maintained mostly outside the accounting department. The accountant must take the lead in ascertaining that these records are correct, complete, and current. These are the records that the auditor will depend on to establish and/or update his permanent file. Among these are:

- Articles of incorporation and bylaws
- Minutes of meetings of stockholders, board of directors, the executive committee, and any other committees that the contractor might have established, whether temporary or permanent
- Documents pertaining to financial arrangements of whatever nature
- Organization charts
- Job descriptions
- Names of key personnel and brief outlines of their duties
- A description of accounting policies, unless these are reflected in the accounting manual
- Contracts, other than construction contracts, such as those involving:
  - Unions
  - Franchises
  - Stock options
  - Commission agreements
  - Pension or profit sharing plans
  - Buy-sell agreements
  - Leases
  - Joint ventures
  - Noncompetitive agreements.

Adjusting Entries That the Contractor's Accountant Should Handle

Routine adjusting entries, including those required to assure agreement of subsidiary records with control accounts, should be made before the auditor arrives. Old-time auditors used to take pride in producing a great number of adjusting entries to prove that they had looked at many things and had set them straight. The greater the number of adjusting entries, the better the job they were doing. Some of these ideas might have possibly rubbed off on the internal accountant to the extent that he might think, "This is something that the auditor will want to handle himself." It might be advisable to settle this matter before the audit begins. Today's CPAs normally feel that if they personally produce too many adjusting entries, they are in effect doing bookkeeping, and therefore cannot justify their high professional per diem rates.

Getting Ready for the Inventory Count of Parts and Supplies

Although the contractor's inventory of parts and supplies uncommitted to work in progress is normally not a major balance sheet item, auditing standards prescribed by the American Institute of CPAs require that the auditor observe the inventory process. The accountant should have established inventory count procedures, and should have reviewed them with the CPA before the year-end, so that there will be no last minute hang-ups to keep him from effectively carrying out his count observation and verification responsibilities.

Getting Ready for Confirmation Procedures

As soon as the eleventh month's financial statements are ready, the accountant and the auditor should agree precisely on what will be confirmed. In the construction industry, audits of the following accounts are subject to 100 percent outside confirmation:

• All bank accounts, using the AICPA and the Bank Administration Institute standard bank confirmation inquiry (See Figure 7–1.)
• Other holders of the contractor's notes such as insurance companies, suppliers, leasing companies, stockholders, officers, directors, and indemnifiers
  • Life insurance policies for which the company is beneficiary
  • Accounts receivable on all but the small jobs

The following accounts are confirmed, subject to the auditor's sampling methodology or any other selection process he might wish to follow:

• Accounts receivable from small jobs
• Accounts payable

The accountant should obtain exact commitments from the auditor regarding what is to be confirmed. In this manner, confirmations can be ready to be turned over to the auditor as soon as the year ends. Experience shows that the best response is obtained from bankers, creditors, and others when there is a minimum lag between the "as-of" date and the actual receipt of the request for confirmation.

THE AUDIT ENGAGEMENT

Essentially, the audit engagement is an agreement whereby the contractor in effect says, "I want or need an audit" and the independent auditor responds, "I can give you an audit." During the preliminary conference, the contractor and the auditor will hash out audit objectives, fees, and logistics. If this is a first engagement, agreement must be reached as to who does what and when; for example, what working papers the contractor's staff will prepare. (See the section in this chapter entitled, "Audit Working Papers the Company Accountant Can Prepare.") The agreement must also determine when the auditor will test the system of internal control, and when and how compliance with AICPA auditing standards will be carried out, such as observing the taking of inventories, and confirmation of receivables, investments, and payables.

Precautions when Taking Over from Another CPA

If the independent auditor is taking over from another CPA, it will be necessary for him to comply with AICPA requirements. Statements on Auditing Standards (SAS) are specific as to what must be done as the succeeding CPA. For example:

- He must not negotiate with the client of another CPA.
- He must be sure the contractor has discharged the preceding CPA.
- He must obtain the contractor's permission to consult with the preceding CPA.
- He must be sure to determine reason for change.
- If the contractor is a publicly held company, SEC regulations must be complied with, requiring reporting of the change and the reason for it.

Pointers on Fee Agreement

Agreement on the fee to be charged will probably depend on the results of the examination of the contractor's internal control. The usual practice is to establish a time budget, based on a breakdown by personnel to be used in the audit, such as clerical, juniors, seniors, and partners, and extend the hours for each by the prevailing billing rate. The contractor will want to know the "maximum, tentative, not-to-exceed" figure resulting from this budget.

The independent auditor should be aware of special audit problems of the construction industry before he determines his estimated fee. (See also the section in Chapter 8 entitled, "Audit Pitfalls Peculiar to the Construction Industry.")

STANDARD BANK CONFIRMATION INQUIRY
Approved by
AMERICAN INSTITUTE OF CERTIFIED PUBLIC ACCOUNTANTS
and
BANK ADMINISTRATION INSTITUTE (FORMERLY NABAC)

_____19____

Dear Sirs:

Your completion of the following report will be sincerely appreciated. **IF THE ANSWER TO ANY ITEM IS "NONE,"** PLEASE SO STATE. Kindly mail it in the enclosed stamped, addressed envelope _direct_ to the accountant named below.

Report from   Yours truly,

_____
(ACCOUNT NAME PER BANK RECORDS)

(Bank) _____   By _____
                                                              Authorized Signature

_____

Bank customer should check here if confirmation of bank balances only (item 1) is desired. ☐

_____

NOTE—If the space provided is inadequate, please enter totals hereon and attach a statement giving full details as called for by the columnar headings below.

Accountant

Dear Sirs:

1. At the close of business on_____19____our records showed the following balance(s) to the **credit** of the above named customer. In the event that we could readily ascertain whether there were any balances to the credit of the customer not designated in this request, the appropriate information is given below.

AMOUNT	ACCOUNT NAME	ACCOUNT NUMBER	Subject to Withdrawal by Check?	Interest Bearing? Give Rate
$				

2. The customer was directly liable to us in respect of loans, acceptances, etc., at the close of business on that date in the total amount of $_____, as follows:

AMOUNT	DATE OF LOAN OR DISCOUNT	DUE DATE	INTEREST Rate	INTEREST Paid to	DESCRIPTION OF LIABILITY, COLLATERAL, SECURITY INTERESTS, LIENS, ENDORSERS, ETC.
$					

3. The customer was contingently liable as endorser of notes discounted and/or as guarantor at the close of business on that date in the total amount of $_____, as below:

AMOUNT	NAME OF MAKER	DATE OF NOTE	DUE DATE	REMARKS
$				

4. Other direct or contingent liabilities, open letters of credit, and relative collateral, were

_____

5. Security agreements under the Uniform Commercial Code or any other agreements providing for restrictions, not noted above, were as follows (if officially recorded, indicate date and office in which filed):

_____

Yours truly, (Bank) _____

Date_____19____   By _____
                                                  Authorized Signature

Additional copies of this form are available from the American Institute of CPAs, 1211 Avenue of the Americas, New York, N. Y. 10036

Figure 7–1

STANDARD BANK CONFIRMATION INQUIRY
Approved by
AMERICAN INSTITUTE OF CERTIFIED PUBLIC ACCOUNTANTS
and
BANK ADMINISTRATION INSTITUTE (FORMERLY NABAC)

```
┌─────────────────────────┐
│ D U P L I C A T E       │
│ To be retained by Bank  │
└─────────────────────────┘
```

_____19_____

Dear Sirs:

Your completion of the following report will be sincerely appreciated. **IF THE ANSWER TO ANY ITEM IS "NONE," PLEASE SO STATE.** Kindly mail it in the enclosed stamped, addressed envelope *direct* to the accountant named below.

Report from

Yours truly,

_____
(ACCOUNT NAME PER BANK RECORDS)

(Bank) _____

By _____
Authorized Signature

_____

Bank customer should check here if confirmation of bank balances only (item 1) is desired. ☐

NOTE—If the space provided is inadequate, please enter totals hereon and attach a statement giving full details as called for by the columnar headings below.

Accountant

Dear Sirs:

1. At the close of business on_____19_____our records showed the following balance(s) to the **credit** of the above named customer. In the event that we could readily ascertain whether there were any balances to the credit of the customer not designated in this request, the appropriate information is given below.

AMOUNT	ACCOUNT NAME	ACCOUNT NUMBER	Subject to Withdrawal by Check?	Interest Bearing? Give Rate
$				

2. The customer was directly liable to us in respect of loans, acceptances, etc., at the close of business on that date in the total amount of $_____, as follows:

AMOUNT	DATE OF LOAN OR DISCOUNT	DUE DATE	INTEREST Rate	INTEREST Paid to	DESCRIPTION OF LIABILITY, COLLATERAL, SECURITY INTERESTS, LIENS, ENDORSERS, ETC.
$					

3. The customer was contingently liable as endorser of notes discounted and/or as guarantor at the close of business on that date in the total amount of $_____, as below:

AMOUNT	NAME OF MAKER	DATE OF NOTE	DUE DATE	REMARKS
$				

4. Other direct or contingent liabilities, open letters of credit, and relative collateral, were

_____

5. Security agreements under the Uniform Commercial Code or any other agreements providing for restrictions, not noted above, were as follows (if officially recorded, indicate date and office in which filed):

_____

Yours truly, (Bank) _____

Date_____19_____

By _____
Authorized Signature

Additional copies of this form are available from the American Institute of CPAs, 1211 Avenue of the Americas, New York, N. Y. 10036

Figure 7–1 (Cont'd.)

The Representation Letter in Preliminary Negotiations

A final step in the preliminary negotiations is to make the contractor aware of the fact that he will be asked to sign a representation letter. This is an AICPA requirement and is covered in SAS No. 19. Some auditors prefer to handle this announcement in their own way. Others will want to make use of the AICPA pamphlet entitled *The Representation Letter*.

How to Prepare an Engagement Letter

After verbal agreement with the contractor and compliance with SAS preliminaries, the independent auditor should prepare an engagement letter. The auditor will want to avoid unnecessary detail and complicated language. Please see Figure 7–2. You will note the following have been covered:

- What is to be done, when and why
- The preparation of federal and state tax returns
- The short-form report
- Recommended changes in internal control procedures
- Auditor's responsibility regarding fraud
- Basis for fees
- Schedule of client-prepared working papers
- Completion date

THE IMPORTANCE OF AUDIT OBJECTIVES

Let us assume that this is a first engagement for the auditor. He must first comply with the ethical and technical requirements of the AICPA discussed in the previous section, and then must ask himself, "Why does the contractor want an audit?" Although seeking an answer to this question is of particular importance in a first engagement, it is not to be overlooked even in repeat performances, since audit objectives often change from year to year.

How Outsiders' Expectations Affect Audit Objectives

Either the contractor or the outside parties who might have insisted on the audit such as bankers, security underwriters, and creditors, must have some predetermined results in mind. Before the auditor goes too far with his planning,

BENEDETTO & COMPANY, INC.
Certified Public Accountants

October 1, 19__

Mr. J. J. Johnson, Chairman of the Board
Contractor's Construction Company
6000 Geronimo Road
Oklahoma City, Oklahoma 73142

Dear Mr. Johnson:

This letter will confirm verbal agreements regarding our audit of financial statements of your company for the fiscal year ending October 31, 19__.

We will perform our audit in accordance with generally accepted auditing standards. We will use such tests and procedures as might be required to enable us to express an opinion on the fairness of the financial statements.

It is understood that the engagement will include the preparation of federal and state income tax returns. In addition to the usual short-form report we will also prepare the long-form report you requested for use by your banker and bonding company.

As part of our evaluation of your internal control system we will report changes to your procedures which we consider desirable.

Audit procedures are not designed to detect fraud and should not be relied upon to do so. Any irregularities that we discover will, of course, be brought to your attention.

Our fee will be based on time actually spent by our staff.

We understand that your staff will prepare a working trial balance by November 10, 19__. A schedule of other working papers to be prepared by your staff has been submitted to your Controller.

The audit will be completed by January 15, 19__.

Sincerely yours,
Anthony J. Benedetto
Benedetto & Company, Inc.

Accepted:

J. J. Johnson, Chairman of the Board

Date: _____

Figure 7–2

he should have a clear understanding of what he is supposed to accomplish: An examination of the records to enable expression of an opinion about the fairness of the financial statements? That's fine, but usually, there is an underlying objective. The auditor who disregards this point is asking for trouble.

Audit Objectives Checklist

The auditor cannot do a good job without a clear understanding of the audit objectives, since this knowledge determines the thrust of the work to be done. Here are a few questions he might ask himself in order to check himself on this important point:

• Is the audit being required by the banker to secure or increase a line of credit?

• Are the bonding people reluctant to increase bonding capacity, based on a growth in working capital resulting from an expanding and unverified growth in unbilled costs and earnings?

• Is there a buyer for the business?

• Is there a new investor who is relying on the opinion of the auditor before proceeding with negotiations?

• Is it possible that the contractor and interested outsiders expect results that the audit is not designed to accomplish?

• Are prospective new suppliers standing by, awaiting the audit report before granting the contractor credit?

• If the contractor is a subcontractor, is a general contractor hesitating to award a contract until seeing the audit report?

• Is the audit report needed to satisfy requirements for doing business in another state?

AUDIT WORKING PAPERS THE CONTRACTOR'S ACCOUNTANT CAN PREPARE

With the consent and guidance of the independent auditor, the contractor's accountant can prepare several working papers. Among these are the inventory analysis, the depreciation schedule, the investment schedule, the schedule of cash surrender value of life insurance, a preliminary analysis of work in progress, a schedule of receivables on contracts, the working papers for other assets, a schedule of accounts payable, and a schedule of notes payable.

How to Prepare the Inventory Analysis

A contractor's inventory will vary from minor to material. For example, a general contractor or a home builder, operating mostly through the use of subcontractors, will have a relatively low inventory of parts and supplies. On the other hand, the inventory of parts and supplies of mechanical and electrical contractors could comprise a substantial portion of current assets.

Note: It should be noted that the contractor's inventory of parts and supplies consists only of material in warehouse bins. The moment material is taken to the job site it becomes part of work in progress.

In addition to the usual inventory count sheets or bin tags, both of which are available at office supply stores, the independent auditor might want an analysis of inventory. Figure 7–3 illustrates a format designed to highlight slow-moving items. Variations of this format might call for other usage factors such as days in inventory or EOQ (economic order quantity).

A problem for contractors is the proper valuation of material excess from completed jobs. A special segregation of this material will help the auditor to focus attention on this problem. Figure 7–3 highlights the two-fold problem the auditor faces in dealing with excess material:

• Adjusting the job costs and
• Adjusting the inventory valuation.

If the inventory is significant, the auditor will want to test the pricing. This is a simple but somewhat tedious comparison of inventory versus invoice pricing. The company staff can save the auditor much time by scheduling selected items to be tested for pricing. Of course, the auditor will want to do the selecting. The final breakdown of Figure 7–3 suggests a format to help the auditor carry out this test.

How to Prepare the Depreciation Schedule

This schedule can be prepared early in the year from the previous year's audited schedule. Once the beginning balance is listed, updating for current year transactions is normally a minor task. Figure 6–12 in Chapter 6 is an example of a format that will satisfy most requirements, including the preparation of income tax returns. This assumes that financial and tax depreciation methods are the same. Such is not always the case. Some contractors will use one method such as straight line for financial purposes, and another such as double declining balance for tax purposes. The Accelerated Cost Recovery System (ACRS), introduced by the Economic Recovery Tax Act of 1981, has further complicated

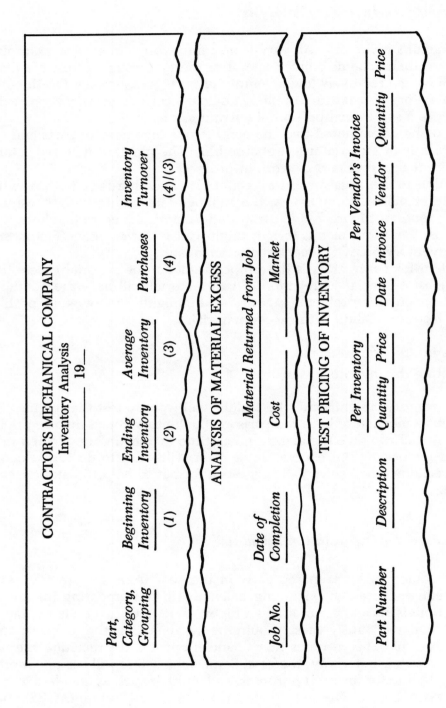

Figure 7-3

things. Some states have added to the confusion by refusing to recognize ACRS. Even the AICPA has feelers out concerning a depreciation system for financial reporting that will give a truer picture than ACRS. In summary, the contractor's accountant might find himself preparing several depreciation schedules for the auditor.

How to Prepare the Investment Schedule

The format of the schedule, as shown in Figure 7–4, provides for a reconciliation of audit date balances to previous year balances. There are columns to list the transactions that brought about the change in balances to scheduled investments.

Please note that it is quite possible to have investments listed both as current assets and other assets, in which case the auditor will want two separate schedules.

Short-term investments are listed under current assets. What are short-term investments? This is a matter of intent on the part of the contractor. If he is investing excess cash with the idea of converting the investment into actual cash as the need arises, this is a short-term investment and a current asset. Certificates of deposit of various kinds, short-term Treasury notes, and commercial paper all fall in this category. CDs may or may not be grouped into one cash category, depending on the deposit requirements of the banker.

Certificates of deposit should show the penalty requirements for premature liquidation. Usually, it means reducing interest paid by adjusting it to the passbook rate. Figure 7–4 shows the kind of detailed information that the auditor welcomes, since it facilitates his examination of investment documents.

How to Schedule Cash Surrender Value of Life Insurance

Many companies will have company-owned key man insurance programs, or buy and sell agreements funded by life insurance policies, also company owned, between or among the principal stockholders. The contractor's accountant is often asked to schedule these company-owned policies, using a format such as shown in Figure 7–5. In some cases, the accountant can compute the cash value by using tables and formulas contained in the policies. In other cases he might need the help of the insurance company.

In addition to scheduling the insurance policies, the auditor might also ask the accountant to prepare verification letters to the insurance companies.

How to Prepare a Preliminary Analysis of Work in Progress

The contractor's staff can take care of getting this important working paper prepared, at least through the portion that consists of data taken directly from

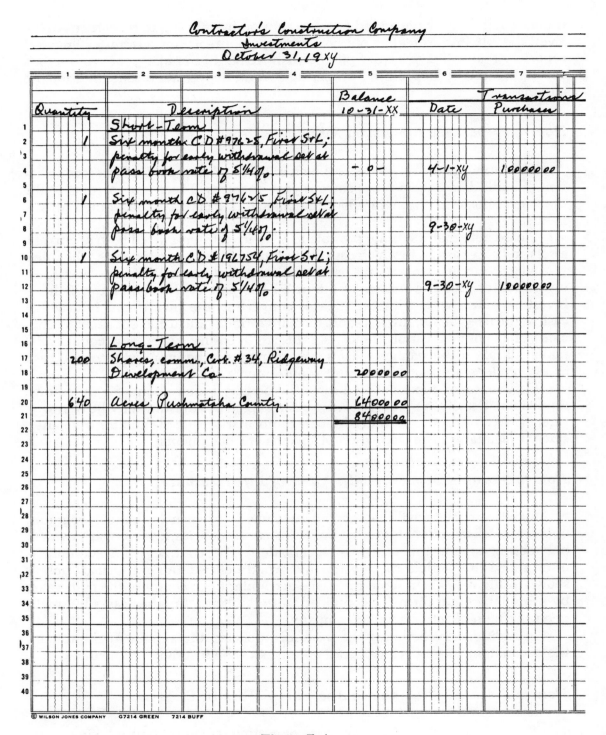

Contractor's Construction Company
Investments
October 31, 19XY

Quantity	Description	Balance 10-31-XX	Date	Transactions Purchases
	Short-Term			
1	Six month CD #97628, First S+L; penalty for early withdrawal set at pass book rate of 5¼%.	- 0 -	4-1-XY	10000000
1	Six month CD #97625, First S+L; penalty for early withdrawal set at pass book rate of 5¼%.		9-30-XY	
1	Six month CD #196754, First S+L; penalty for early withdrawal set at pass book rate of 5¼%.		9-30-XY	10000000
	Long-Term			
200	Shares, comm., Cert. #34, Ridgeway Development Co.	2000000		
640	Acres, Pushmataha County.	6400000		
		8400000		

© WILSON JONES COMPANY   G7214 GREEN   7214 BUFF

Figure 7–4

8 Sales	9 Balance 10-31-XY	10 Sales Proceeds	11 Gain (Loss) on Sale Acct. 876	12 Interest and Dividends Received	13 Market Value Per Share	14 Market Value 10-31-XY Total
	10000000			517500		
10000000	⟨1000000 00⟩	10000000				
	10000000					
	10000000			512500		
	2000000				108	2160000
	6400000					7000000
	8400000					9160000

MADE IN U.S.A.

CONTRACTOR'S CONSTRUCTION COMPANY
Insurance
_____ 19__

Policy No.	Insurance Company	Insured	Face Value	Cash Surrender Value
767–7766	Planet Life & Acc.	J. J. Johnson	500,000.00	7,960.78
767–7788	Planet Life & Acc.	W. W. Akins	500,000.00	7,960.78
767–8012	Planet Life & Acc.	R. J. Riley	500,000.00	5,472.95
			1,500,000.00	21,394.51

Figure 7–5

the company records. Figure 3–1 in Chapter 3 shows the recommended format. The accountant can list all long-term contracts in progress, showing the contract amount, billings to date, and costs to date. He can then compute Column 4, billings over costs, and Column 5, costs over billings. It is recommended that the auditor himself take care of computing Columns 6 through 12, in addition to testing amounts shown in Columns 1, 2, and 3. Procedures are detailed in Chapter 10.

How to Prepare the Schedule of Receivables on Contracts

The worksheet for receivables on contracts, an expansion of the format shown in Chapter 3, Figure 3–4, is illustrated in Figure 7–6. Some auditors might want to add an extra column to enter the control number assigned to confirmation requests. However, this practice is not prevalent in the construction industry, since receivables are not as numerous as in other industries. Also, in other industries, estimated uncollectibles are shown in a separate column. In the construction industry there is a separate worksheet for each job, since circumstances surrounding each case are usually complex and often involve litigation.

Please note that the aging schedule is reduced by the net payment received. For example, Job 546, Dawson Industries, Inc., was billed $46,350.00 in September. If the $41,715.00 had been received prior to October 31, 1980, the September billing on the worksheet would have been reduced by the amount paid to $4,635.00, this being the 10 percent retainage. Also, note that Job 563, Howard & Holmes Manufacturing, Inc., shows $29,700.00 due on completed contracts although the October billing was $33,000.00. The $3,300.00 difference is retainage, which together with the amounts of $7,250.00 and $8,250.00 remaining from the September and August billings, make up the total of $18,800.00 shown as retainage not currently due.

How to Schedule Other Assets

With the possible exception of amounts due from officers, the materiality of the contractor's other assets is usually not significant. Working papers can be kept to a simple format, with columnar headings as follows:

- Description
- Beginning balance
- Transactions
    - Date
    - Additions
    - Deletions
- Ending balance

How to Schedule Accounts Payable

Scheduling of accounts payable by the contractor's staff should not be attempted without the specific guidance of the auditor. The normal practice is to schedule vendor's billings in excess of a certain dollar base, say $500 for the smaller contractors and $1,000 for the larger ones. However, the auditor might have other criteria, or might want to make the specific selection himself.

Payables to subcontractors are scheduled 100 percent, since AICPA standards require extensive auditing procedures, including 100 percent verification by subcontractors.

Figure 7–7 illustrates the accounts payable worksheet. You will note that the total liability includes retainage to date. For example, the $30,000.00 retainage due Wooley Brothers Electrical Contractors, Inc., consists of $4,500.00 left over after $40,500.00 was paid on the $45,000.00 October billing, plus the retainage of $5,000.00, $6,400.00, and $14,100.00 left over from September, August, and prior months. The same is true of the $25,000.00 retainage due Wright Mechanical Contractors, Inc. It consists of $4,000.00 left over after $36,000.00 was paid on the October billing, plus the retainage of $6,000.00, $9,500.00, and $5,500.00 left over from September, August, and prior months.

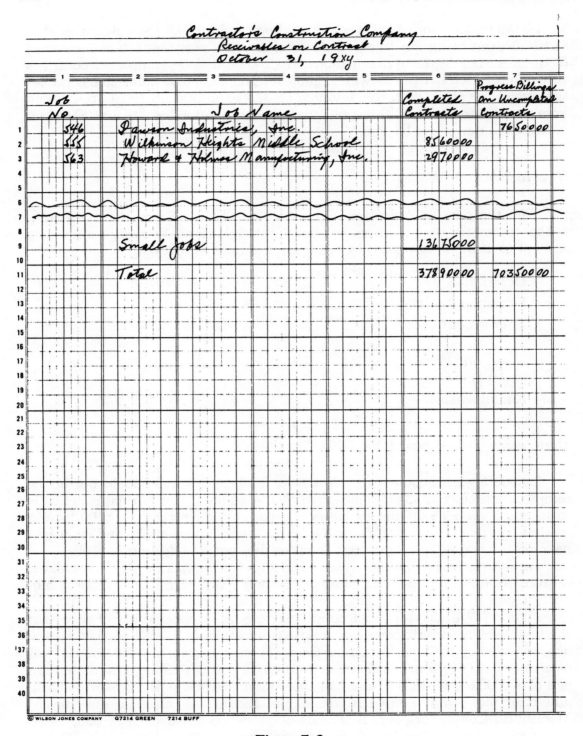

Contractor's Construction Company
Receivables on Contract
October 31, 19x4

Job No.	Job Name		Completed Contracts	Progress Billings on Uncompleted Contracts
546	Dawson Industries, Inc.			7650000
555	Wilkinson Heights Middle School		8560000	
563	Howard & Holmes Manufacturing, Inc.		2970000	
	Small Jobs		13675000	
	Total		37890000	70350000

© WILSON JONES COMPANY   G7214 GREEN   7214 BUFF

Figure 7–6

Retainage Not Currently Due	Total	October	Time of Billing September	August	Prior Months	Collections after 10-31-XY	
5400000	13000000	8415000	4635000			4171500	1
	8560000			8560000		8560000	2
1880000	4850000	3300000	725000	825000			3
							4
							5
							6
							7
							8
	13675000	12980000	320000		375000		9
							10
38980000	147220000	101000000	30200000	10500000	5520000	120120000	11

MADE IN U.S.A.

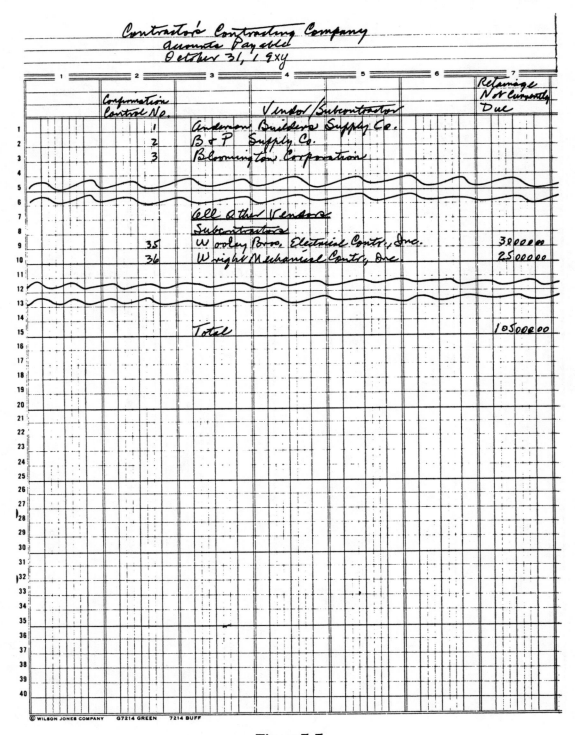

Contractor's Contracting Company
Accounts Payable
October 31, 19XY

	Confirmation Control No.	Vendor/Subcontractor				Retainage Not Currently Due
1	1	Anderson Builders Supply Co.				
2	2	B & P Supply Co.				
3	3	Bloomington Corporation				
7		All Other Vendors				
8		Subcontractors				
9	35	Wooley Bros., Electrical Contr., Inc.				3800000
10	36	Wright Mechanical Contr., Inc.				2500000
15		Total				10500000

© WILSON JONES COMPANY   G7214 GREEN   7214 BUFF

Figure 7–7

	Total	October	Time of Billing September	August	Prior	Paid after 10-31-XY	
1	2350 00	2350 00				2350 00	
2	30290 00	24500 01	5790 00			5790 00	
3	6300 00			6300 00			
4							
5							
6							
7	12650 00	11500 00	1150 00			10250 00	
8							
9	90500 00	65000 00	5000 00	6400 00	14100 00	40500 00	
10	101000 00	40000 00	6000 00	9500 00	45500 00	36000 00	
11							
12							
13							
14							
15	904750 00	750000 00	49750 00	40500 00	65000 00	803000 00	

CONTRACTOR'S CONSTRUCTION COMPANY
Notes Payable
October 31, 19xx

	Due in One Year	Due After One Year
Fifth National Bank: 30 day note, 10%, due November 4, 19xx	$100,000.00	$
Growth Mortgage Company: 20-year first mortgage on office and warehouse buildings and land located at 6001 Geronimo Road, dated November 1, 19yy, with interest at 6½%. Monthly payments $520.78, including interest.	3,120.00	65,735.00
Equipment mortgages (itemized); monthly payments of $1,926.00	21,690.00	12,500.00
	$130,790.00	$102,234.00

Figure 7–8

How to Prepare the Notes Payable Worksheet

The worksheet used to schedule notes payable includes all notes, whether long-term or otherwise. Figure 7–8 illustrates the separation of amounts due in one year, which are shown on the balance sheet as current liabilities and amounts due after one year, which are included under long-term debt.

HOW PAYROLL WITHHOLDING ACCOUNTS ARE AUDITED

A competent accountant will make use of the self-policing nature of payroll withholding accounts. For example, the payroll recap or computer printout must agree with or be reconciled to the various weekly, monthly, quarterly, and yearly reports to Federal, state, union, pension, and profit-sharing entities. The auditor will normally make use of operating worksheets and reports to test the fairness of these various amounts withheld from the employees' paychecks, rather than have the contractor's staff restate these transactions on additional worksheets.

If there is a weakness in this area or if amounts are not properly reconciled between actual and reported withholdings, the auditor will develop his own working papers as part of the process of examining the accounts and arriving at adjustments.

HOW STOCKHOLDERS' ACCOUNTS ARE AUDITED

The auditor can normally schedule, analyze, examine, and verify these accounts in quick order. If there is evidence of activity, he might have the contractor's staff prepare schedules for each class of stock, containing the following columnar headings:

- Description of the transaction
- Beginning balance
    - Date
    - Additions
    - Deletions
- Ending balance

HOW INCOME AND EXPENSE ACCOUNTS ARE AUDITED

Income determination being the principal problem relating to construction accounting, it is not possible to suggest a single set of working papers that the contractor's staff can prepare to help the auditor in this area. Most of the working papers already discussed in this chapter will be used to test and adjust job income and costs. For example, unbilled costs and earnings, and unearned billings over costs directly affect contract revenue. Adjustments to accounts receivable could also affect contract revenue. Adjustments to accounts payable could affect job costs. Such being the case, the only area remaining to be examined will be general and administrative expenses.

To audit accounts making up this group, the auditor will use testing procedures that in turn depend on various other portions of the auditing process. For example, the test and evaluation of internal control, and the existence or nonexistence of budgetary controls, will determine the nature and extent of tests, and therefore the context of the working papers.

It is possible that the auditor will call for assistance from the contractor's staff as he proceeds to audit the various accounts making up general and administrative expense. However, the many different twists that audit procedures can take in this area make it impractical to suggest a specific worksheet format.

WHAT THE CONTRACTOR CAN EXPECT FROM THE AUDIT

As the contractor completes preliminary arrangements with the auditor, he might ask himself this question: "In addition to complying with the request of the banker, the bonding company, the investor, and others who insisted on this audit, what am I getting out of it?" Both the auditor and the company accountant should take time to explain to the contractor that there are certain benefits he might expect. Some deal with outsiders. Others have to do with the contractor's own operations. Both are important.

HOW THE AUDIT BENEFITS OUTSIDERS

Audit objectives, which used to emphasize debt-paying ability and keeping the managers honest, now focus on fairness in the presentation of financial information. Boiled down to essentials, today's audit objectives are met by answering "yes" to the following questions:

• Can we rely on the fairness of amounts shown as assets and liabilities on the balance sheet?
• Can we rely on the fairness of profit or loss figures shown on the income statement?

For the contractor, "we" includes his banker, the bonding company, investors, creditors, labor unions, and governmental entities.

Improvements in dealing with outsiders brought about by the audit are easy to see. For example, if the contractor had been laboring under the burden of a credibility gap, the auditor has now lifted it. The contractor now has an independent, professional backer who is willing to proclaim to one and all that the contractor's financial position and the results of his operations, as stated in the financial statements, are *presented fairly*.

HOW THE AUDIT WILL BENEFIT THE CONTRACTOR

A more subtle benefit of the audit is the good that can come from the thorough going-over that is given to the contractor's accounting system. Since the auditor is required to test and evaluate the internal control system, the contractor might as well take advantage of this professional shake-down:

• By discussing freely with the auditor any suspected weakness in the accounting system, and

• By putting to good use the recommendations contained in the auditor's report on the internal control system.

WHAT INTERNAL CONTROL SHOULD MEAN TO THE CONTRACTOR

Internal control has to do with the safeguarding of assets and the reliability of the accounting records. Almost any contractor can see the need for internal controls that will safeguard assets. Not so easy to see are the in-house benefits of reliable accounting records. However, the contractor should realize that the techniques for planning and attaining financial success described in Chapter 4 cannot be carried out without a reliable set of records, nor can the design, installation, and operation of a good accounting system as described in Chapters 5 and 6.

ASSURING A GOOD BEGINNING TO THE AUDIT

Good preparation means good performance. If all of the get-ready measures contained in this chapter have been followed, then we are ready to begin the audit. A good beginning assures a good ending. The chapter that follows shows how to make sure that the audit gets off to a good start.

BEGINNING THE AUDIT

The cutoff between preliminaries and the actual start of the audit is not clear-cut, nor is the sequence of events subject to an even flow. Chapters that cover the auditing function are arranged in connected series to give this part of the book a sense of organization. Actually, there is considerable sifting and adjusting of procedures throughout the entire audit process.

Each section of this chapter depends on the previous one, but feedback and interplay are the common threads. For example, background information will help the auditor recognize pitfalls peculiar to the construction industry. This, in turn, affects audit plans. Evaluating internal control will feed changes back to the audit plans, in addition to fulfilling the basic function of determining the shape and scope of audit programs.

HOW TO FIND AND USE BACKGROUND INFORMATION

The auditor's permanent file is the depository of background information. It must be established for first engagements, or updated for repeat engagements, by examining several documents and other sources of information, most of which are outside the accounting department. What follows is a listing of sources of background information, what they are, where to find them, and what to do with them.

What to Do with Articles of Incorporation and Bylaws

Most contractors are incorporated, and therefore will have articles of incorporation and bylaws. The auditor will extract the following information for his permanent file:

- The exact and official name of the company
- Date of incorporation
- Names of incorporators
- Authorized stock by class
- Par value of stock
- Initial issue of stock by class
- Subscription agreements
- Section 1244 provisions[1]
- Subchapter S election[2]
- Authorization for unrelated business activities

How to Use the Minutes Book

The auditor must review the minutes book to establish or update his permanent file. Among the items he will want to extract for further testing and verification are:

- The currency of the minutes
- Names and titles of officers at audit date
- Composition of various standing committees
- Status of subscription contracts
- Currency of authorizations and resolutions regarding:
  - Changes in accounting policies
  - Union contracts
  - Capital investments
  - Long-term debt
  - Check-signing authorizations
  - Changes in capital structure
  - Appointment of an independent auditor
  - Executive bonuses
  - Joint ventures

Auditor's Review of Financing Agreements

All such documents must be examined. The contractor's staff can prepare working papers as illustrated in Chapter 7, Figure 7–8, but the auditor must review the documents themselves and verify outstanding balances independently. Other financial arrangements and agreements that might not be reflected in the financial records must also be examined such as indemnification agreements involving the contractor, other officers of the company and their spouses, and indemnification agreements with outsiders. These are often backed up by side agreements with surety banks, including escrow requirements and provisions for profit splitting on specified contracts.

How the Auditor Uses Organization Charts and Job Descriptions

The auditor must obtain copies or make extracts of organization charts and job descriptions, including names of key personnel. If not in existence, the auditor must at least rough out organization charts and functional statements to match the names of key personnel. This background information is essential in the subsequent testing and evaluation of internal control.

The auditor must go beyond the home office force in order to assure the inclusion of personnel on job sites. Contractors will have rather elaborate, semiautonomous organizations operating on the site of the larger contracts.

Review of Contracts Other than Construction Contracts

The contractor will also have other contracts that must be examined to make sure that the agreement is properly authorized, that the provisions are being complied with and properly reflected on the books, and that impending financial consequences are properly disclosed. For each of the following agreements, the auditor should seek answers to pertinent questions.

- Union contracts:
    - Expiration date?
    - Will there be a strike?
    - Pay scales being met?
    - Apprenticeship policies complied with?
    - Checkoff requirements being met?
    - Reporting and payment of fringe benefits current?
    - Evidence of contractor's input to contract negotiations?
- Franchises:
    - Provisions?
    - Compliance?
    - Contingent liabilities?
- Stock options:
    - Status?
    - Dilution potential?

- Commission Agreements:
  - Basis of computation?
  - Is formula valid?
  - Jobs affected?
  - Commissions current?
  - What is accrual?
- Pensions or Profit Sharing Plans:
  - ERISA reporting requirements being met?
  - Investments valid?
  - Investments tested?
  - Lump-sum distributions tested?
  - Amounts due plans accrued?
- Buy-Sell Agreements:
  - Description?
  - Funding agreement?
  - Documentation in order?
  - Agreements current?
  - Need for subsequent events disclosure?
- Leases:
  - Description?
  - Compliance with AICPA?
- Non-Competitive Agreements:
  - Description?
  - Compliance by buyer?
  - Compliance by seller?
  - Pending litigation?
- Joint Venture Agreements:
  - Capital contributions of participants?
  - Reimbursement and compensation methods?
  - Status of accounts receivable from joint venture?
  - Method of reporting income?

How to Use Interviews

Background information would not be complete without the auditor's interviewing the banker, the surety underwriters, and selected creditors, particularly subcontractors. The auditor should also contact the executive director of whatever association the contractor belongs to, as well as selected labor union personnel. Interviews should be informal. No note-taking. The auditor's objective should be to determine the contractor's reputation, reliability, and competence.

THE PITFALLS

Audit Pitfalls Peculiar to the Construction Industry

Income determination is the principal problem in construction accounting. The auditor must be alert to the many pitfalls generated by this single source of trouble. It is essential that this awareness come before the auditor begins to plan the audit, gets into internal control, and determines audit programs. Failure to recognize these pitfalls and think them through will get the auditor into trouble.

The Auditor's Approach to Percentage of Completion Contracts

Although this problem was covered in depth in Chapter 3, it will continue to command our attention as we proceed to discuss the audit process. Indeed, this theme will be emphasized repeatedly throughout this book, the idea being to remind the auditor that, unlike other industries where the estimated portion of income is limited to a relatively minor amount, in the construction industry, we have a situation where income resulting from improper use of analysis of work in progress can be quite significant.

Audit Pitfalls of the Completed-Contract Method

Income must be reported when a contract is substantially completed, or about 95 percent done, according to the AICPA.[3] The auditor should be on the alert for deliberate postponement of the reporting of income for whatever reason. Allocation of general and administrative expenses to contract costs rather than period costs is also required by the AICPA. Finally, ultimate losses on a contract in process should be reduced by the amount of income tax reductions of future periods.

Audit Pitfalls of Cost-Plus Contracts

The auditor should determine whether the contractor is an agent or a principal. For example, if the contractor is not responsible for material purchases and does not pick them up on his books as assets, he is an agent. He therefore reports only the fee paid to him for his services. However, if he is responsible for paying labor, material, subcontractor costs, and so on, he is a principal and will report reimbursable costs, together with his fee, as contract revenue. How does he report it? He uses a percentage of completion basis or the completed-contract method, depending on his choice.

Beware of These Audit Pitfalls in Reviewing Contract Costs

Regardless of what method the contractor uses, auditing of construction in progress requires special care to avoid common pitfalls, such as:

- Charges to cost-plus contracts that are not reimbursable
- Failure to pick up all time and material spent on cost-plus contracts, or charging such costs to nonreimbursable contracts
- Improper handling of leased equipment costs where there is an option to buy
- Improper allocation of equipment costs to jobs
- Improper allocation of overhead items

Audit Pitfalls of Job Sites

A dangerous pitfall is either to fail to include job sites in the audit process or to relegate the process to a lesser order of importance. Job sites are profit centers. The job site for a large construction contract is the focal point for profit determination, amounting to a significant portion of the contractor's bottom line. The auditor who expresses an opinion as to its fairness, based on home-office review of field reports, can hardly be said to have exercised due care as required by AICPA-prescribed auditing standards.

Audit Pitfalls of Inventory

Sometimes overlooked is the need to account properly for obsolete, excess, and allocated materials and supplies. The contractor's inventory of materials and supplies is usually not too significant. There are exceptions such as the larger electrical and mechanical contractors, where inventory amounts can be substantial. In such cases, failure to write off obsolete items can distort profits and inflate personal property taxes. For all contractors, failure to account for excess material that is later issued to other jobs can feed erroneous job-cost input to the estimator. Erroneously allocated material to jobs can have a chain reaction. It will affect the billing process and cash flow, and it will distort job costs, thereby distorting the percentage of completion, which in turn affects the amount of overbilling offset by earned gross profit. These problems are treated in detail in Chapter 10.

Audit Pitfalls of Accounts Receivable

The three principal pitfalls are:

- Inadequate control of and improper accounting for retainage
- Incomplete disclosure of disputed accounts
- "Robbing Peter to pay Paul," a form of lapping where the contractor will apply money collected on one job to pay the bills of another

Audit Pitfalls of Accounts Payable

There are four principal pitfalls:

- Failure to include retainage not currently due subcontractors
- Failure to report all subcontractor costs
- "Robbing Peter to pay Paul," as explained above
- Credit difficulties

Audit Pitfalls of Joint Ventures

The three principal pitfalls are:

- Less than clear agreement on capital contributions, reimbursement, and compensation of participants
- Improper accounting control of operations
- Improper disclosure

IMPORTANCE OF THE AUDIT PLAN

The audit will turn out to be what the auditor wants it to be if he plans it that way. This rather simple statement is true because auditing is a complex undertaking. Without a plan, it can get out of control. And therein lies an invitation to overlook something important, with disastrous consequences.

A plan not only tells the auditor where he has to go and what he has to do to get there, but also provides a point of reference to keep him on course.

AUDIT OBJECTIVES, PLANS, AND PROGRAMS DEFINED

Audit objectives tell the auditor what is to be accomplished by the audit.
Audit plans describe what is to be done.
Audit programs outline how these plans will be carried out.

CONTRACTOR'S CONSTRUCTION CO.
Audit Plan
FYE October 31, 19__

Item	Prepared By	Completion Date		
		Scheduled	Completed	Initials
Update background information	Rogers	10–06–__		
Test internal control	Rogers & Jones	10–13–__		
Prepare internal control report	R & J	10–16–__		
Prepare working papers	Client	10–10–__		
Review client-prepared working papers	R & J	11–10–__		
Obtain representation letter	Client	11–10–__		
Count cash, examine investments	R & J	10–31–__		
Select all accounts for confirmation	Jones	10–23–__		
Prepare confirmation letters	Client	10–31–__		
Review and mail confirmation letters	R & Staff	11–1–__ (Sat.)		
Test accounts receivable, contract revenue	R & J	11–13–__		
Approve inventory-taking procedures	Jones	10–27–__		
Observe and test inventory-taking	R & J	10–31–__		
Test inventory of depreciable assets	R & J	11–04–__		
Test job costs, payroll, and G & A	R & J	11–28–__		
Prepare rough draft of internal control report to management	Jones	12–12–__		
Prepare rough draft of financial statements and notes	Rogers	12–12–__		
Review W/P & rough drafts	Benedetto	12–31–__		
Type and reproduce audit report	Staff	01–15–__		
Plan reviewed and approved	Benedetto	10–3–__	10–3–__	A.J.B.

Figure 8–1

Objectives will affect plans, and plans will determine programs. One might say that plans are a function of objectives, and that programs are a function of plans. However, the relationship is not that mathematically precise. Interplay and feedback are everywhere.

Figure 8–1 illustrates an audit plan designed for Contractor's Construction Company. The emphasis is on coverage rather than detail. The audit programs and normal audit procedures will take care of the detail.

INTERNAL CONTROL PROBLEMS OF THE SMALL CONTRACTOR

The auditor will be dismayed on a first engagement as he examines the internal control of the small contractor. For example, he might find the complete cycle of income-deposits-payments, together with signature authority and bank reconciliation, in the hands of a trusted bookkeeper. He will rack his brain for a way to fit the division of duties formula into a one-man or a one-woman operation. Obviously, there is no book solution.

How the Contractor's Internal Control Can Fall Apart

The scenario stars the impatient and often harassed small contractor who looks upon accounting as a necessary evil, and is only too glad to turn everything over to the full-charge bookkeeper. Thus the contractor relinquishes basic management functions such as who gets paid and when.

By his action, the small contractor subjects the bookkeeper to pressures and temptations that detract from the accounting function and often lead to abuses of power. Construction industry auditors are only too familiar with cases where the small contractor has been taken for a cleaning because he refused to get himself involved in the handling of money under the erroneous assumption that this is "the job of the bookkeeper."

What to Do About Poor Internal Control

What can the auditor do if he comes face-to-face with the scene described above? Certainly, he cannot test internal control if there is nothing to test. Instead, he should refer to the section in Chapter 6 that deals with internal control that will work for management and the accountant. He should review the portion that lists steps the contractor can take to establish internal control. He should then discuss this problem with the contractor, and convince him of the need for immediate remedial action. If the contractor refuses to initiate such action, the auditor should seriously consider withdrawing from the engagement.

Procedures for Coping with a Poor Internal Control Situation

Most contractors will readily agree to the installation of internal controls, especially those needed to safeguard cash. Is that the end of the problem? No. The auditor must then proceed along these lines:

- Estimate the additional time needed to examine, extensively and simultaneously, all accounts affected by cash flow.
- Obtain the contractor's concurrence with the additional cost.
- Examine in detail all suspected irregularities.
- Be aware of the auditor's responsibilities.

THE AUDITOR'S RESPONSIBILITIES REGARDING IRREGULARITIES

The following are key responsibilities related to irregularities:

- If the irregularities are material, the auditor should qualify his opinion.
- He might even consider withdrawing from the engagement.
- If he withdraws, he may wish to consult with his legal counsel as to any responsibilities stemming from the engagement letter, since it consists of an offer and acceptance, and is therefore a contract.

Finally, there is the matter of being paid for work already done.

INTERNAL CONTROL AND THE LARGER CONTRACTOR

The internal control of the larger contractor will be more responsive to normal testing procedures. The auditor will face the problem of complex and fragmented operations. It will be necessary for him to understand the workings of the system in its entirety before deciding on tests and programs.

FRAMEWORK FOR INTERNAL CONTROL

Ideally, the contractor's internal control should rest on a framework consisting of the following parts:

- An organizational chart

- Clean-cut delineation of duties and responsibilities
- Job descriptions, or as a minimum, functional statements
- An accounting system based on principles and techniques described in previous chapters
- An accounting manual
- Budgetary control of costs and expenses
- Timely and dependable reports to the contractor and his operating staff
- Use of these reports to control operations and ask questions
- Competent accounting personnel

It is the duty of the auditor not only to point out missing parts in the internal control structure, but to guide the contractor and his staff in plugging the gaps.

HOW NOT TO USE INTERNAL CONTROL QUESTIONNAIRES

The biggest drawback in the use of internal control questionnaires is the tendency on the part of some auditors to use them as a substitute for thinking. Routine execution of internal control questionnaires accomplishes nothing *per se*. Actually, the questionnaire is nothing more than a rough indicator of trouble spots. It should be supplemented by flow charts and written descriptions.

What about "canned" questionnaires? Unfortunately, they seldom get the job done. They are a source of worry to the auditor who is quick to note that departmentalized questionnaires simply do not fit the situation at hand. For example, answering yes or no to the cash receipts questionnaire might bypass the source of the problem, which might lie in the contractor's failure to control progress billings.

SPECIALLY DESIGNED INTERNAL CONTROL QUESTIONNAIRES

The illustrated questionnaires that follow might cover some of the salient points found in textbooks and AICPA pronouncements. However, their structure is unique in that they are designed to test internal control as it relates to

- Audit pitfalls peculiar to the construction industry
- The function of interrelated accounts
- The size and type of operation

How to Design Internal Control Questionnaires

The specifications set forth above pretty well dictate the construction of a tailor-made questionnaire. For example, an examination of Figure 8–2 shows that we are dealing with a particular type of contractor with certain factors that must be taken into account, such as:

- An organization that is too small for the classic division of duties
- A contractor who generates a considerable amount of junk and excess material
- A contractor who even has some off-the-shelf sales

How to Use Internal Control Questionnaires

Obviously, the auditor in the situation depicted in Figure 8–2, cannot use a canned questionnaire. In fact, he cannot even design a suitable one until he has learned something about the contractor's operation by studying the background material carefully. Even if the auditor faces a situation that fits the questionnaire illustrated in Figure 8–2, he should not use it until he has subjected it to a very critical review. The auditor should look at each question and ask himself:

- What does it tell me?
- Is this what I want to test?
- If not, what do I want to test?
- Is anything missing?

Specifics of Reviewing the Internal Control Questionnaire

To further illustrate the critical review needed before using an internal control questionnaire, let's take Question 4 of Figure 8–2. The auditor might say to himself, "Bringing in the general superintendent is fine, but I also want to know if the estimator originated the billings, particularly billings of construction in progress. In addition, I'd like to know if the contractor and his accountant review the billings."

The auditor should give the same type of critical review to the questionnaire illustrated in Figure 8–3 before using it. For example, the auditor may not be happy with the coverage given to the payroll function and might want to separate and expand it. Job costing procedures at job sites might also call for a separate questionnaire, although flow charting and written descriptions might do a better job.

INTERNAL CONTROL QUESTIONNAIRE
Billings, Miscellaneous Sales, and Cash Receipts

	Y/N	Action
1. Written instructions for monthly billings?		
2. Good billing format?		
3. Task-cost procedures in use?		
4. Billings signed off by gen. superintendent?		
5. Retainage		
a. Adequately controlled?		
b. Properly accounted for?		
6. Consistent determination as to when contract is completed?		
7. Clear billing instructions for cost-plus contracts?		
8. Cost-plus billings current?		
9. Clear billing instructions for joint ventures?		
10. Joint venture billings current?		
11. Sale of excess material, junk, controlled by contractor?		
12. Cash from 11 turned over to contractor?		
13. Cash report of 11 sales to accounting?		
14. Off-the-shelf sales controlled by contractor?		
15. Such sales documented and reported to accounting?		
16. Written procedures for accrual of investment income?		
17. Accrued investment income reported to contractor?		
18. Does such report provide check-off for actual receipt?		
19. Written procedures for processing cash receipts?		

Figure 8–2

20. Does contractor or secretary receive all mail?		
21. Are checks received listed?		
22. Such list coded by account numbers?		
23. Such list forwarded to accounting?		
24. Such list used for posting to various affected accounts?		
25. Deposit slip prepared by a. Contractor?		
b. Secretary?		
26. If secretary, does contractor review?		
27. Is reviewed copy of deposit slip sent to accounting?		
28. Is deposit slip reconciled to list prepared in #21 above?		
29. Bank accounts reconciled by a. Contractor?		
b. Secretary?		
30. If secretary, does contractor review?		
31. Are reconciled bank accounts in agreement with general ledger?		
32. If not, are adjustments approved by contractor?		

Executed by: Date:

Figure 8–2 (Cont'd.)

Other questionnaires will most certainly be used; for example, there can be one to assure completeness in gathering background information. Review the first section of this chapter for help in designing questionnaires.

THE USE OF FLOW CHARTS ILLUSTRATED

Figure 8–4 illustrates how the flow chart can be used to highlight a troublesome job-site problem—the ordering of material by the job foreman. This practice

INTERNAL CONTROL QUESTIONNAIRE
Job Costs, Expenses, and Payables

	Y/N	Action
1. Time sheet format adequate?		
2. Job labor costs reconciled to payroll?		
3. Payroll reports current as to		
a. Federal government?		
b. State government?		
c. Union?		
d. Pension plan?		
e. Profit-sharing plan?		
4. Payroll withholding remittance/deposits current as to		
a. Federal government?		
b. State government?		
c. Union?		
d. Pension plan?		
e. Profit-sharing plan?		
f. Savings accounts?		
g. Medical insurance/reimbursement plans?		
5. Are there budgetary controls (job cost analysis report) for		
a. Labor?		
b. Material?		
c. Equipment?		
d. Miscellaneous job costs?		
e. Subcontractors?		
6. Such reports a. Timely?		

Figure 8–3

b. Used by management?		
7. Purchase-order system in use?		
8. Purchase orders generated by		
a. Estimator?		
b. General superintendent?		
9. If by general superindentent, does estimator review and approve?		
10. If by estimator, does contractor review and approve?		
11. Does accounting review purchase orders for agreement with supplier's quotation?		
12. Delivery tickets/receiving reports matched to invoices?		
13. Invoices checked-off against purchase orders?		
14. Report of undelivered items prepared?		
15. Subcontracts reviewed and signed by contractor?		
16. Retainage not currently due accrued as payable?		
17. Verified invoices and subcontractors' progress billings		
a. Attached to checks?		
b. Compared to check amounts by contractor before signing?		
18. Are bank debits properly authorized?		
Note: Questions 29–32 in Billings, Miscellaneous Sales, and Cash Receipts questionnaire cover reconciliation of bank accounts.		Executed by: ___ Date: _____

Figure 8–3 (Cont'd.)

is a problem mainly because it bypasses the normal material buying and using cycle. Briefly, the cycle can be described as follows:

- Estimating material requirements
- Obtaining quotations from suppliers

CONTRACTOR'S CONSTRUCTION CO.
Orders For Material Originating at Job Site
Fye 10-31- __
Prepared by Jones, 10-9-__

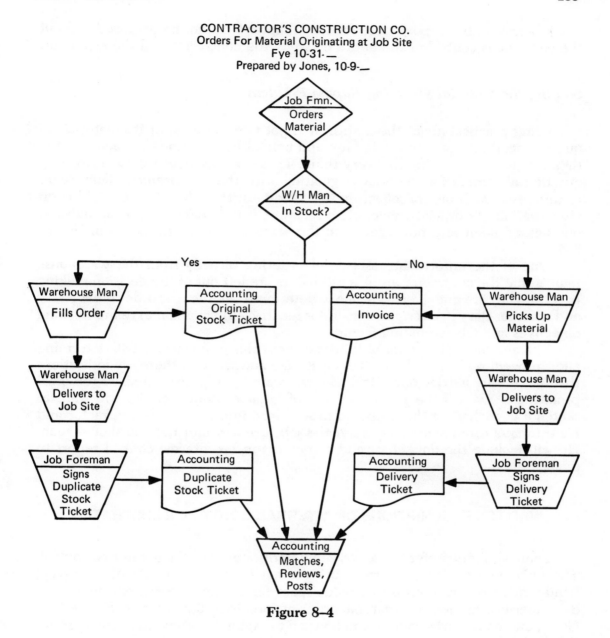

Figure 8–4

- Issuing purchase orders to buy from the low bidder
- Using the estimated requirements as the basis for controlling material costs
- Using control reports to refine estimating factors
- Using the purchase order to assure price compliance
- Using the purchase order to determine undelivered items

Job-cost control reports described in Chapter 5 cannot be prepared without the continuous control of the entire cycle by the contractor and the estimator.

Solving the Material Ordering Bypass Problem

Being practical about the matter, it is not possible to estimate material requirements right down to the last nut and bolt, although some contractors pride themselves in attempting this very thing. These are the ones that will severely question all orders for material originating with the job foreman. They seem to think that such orders reflect on the validity of the job estimates. And even after the job-site order survives close scrutiny, it is required to go through the purchasing agent and not directly to the warehouse man, as shown in Figure 8–4.

One of the unfortunate aspects of ordering directly from the warehouse man is that the contractor and his estimators are left out of the decision-making process. They are not given a chance to determine whether the order is necessary and whether the price is right. Also lost is feedback information to refine stocking objectives and job-estimating factors.

The auditor will do a lot of thinking about this problem. He will determine audit procedures to give him a feel for its size and scope. If there are indications that matters are getting out of hand, he will want to propose immediate remedial procedures. Even if the situation is not of great consequence, he will want to sketch a flow chart of the proposed procedures, interposing the contractor and his estimators somewhere between the job foreman and the warehouse man. He will include the flow chart and comments in his internal control report to management.

WRITTEN DESCRIPTIONS OF INTERNAL CONTROL ILLUSTRATED

Some auditors prefer to use written descriptions to evaluate internal control. The only suggested change from the normal textbook example of solid-page hand-written descriptions is to provide space for a running commentary. Figure 8–5 describes the job-site material-ordering problem illustrated in Figure 8–4. Note how the remarks column can be used to highlight problems as the description unfolds.

AUDIT PROGRAMS FOR THE CONSTRUCTION INDUSTRY

In addition to the normal testing, tracing, vouching, counting, confirming, comparing, reconciling, examining, and so forth required by any good audit program, the contractor's audit program should include steps designed to deal

Contractor's Construction Company
Orders for Material Originating at Job Site

FYE 10-31-XX
Prepared by Rogers 10-9-XX

Description	Remarks
Job foreman orders material from warehouse man, who determines whether material is in stock. If in stock he fills order, sending original copy of stock ticket to accounting. He delivers the material to the job site. Foreman checks it off against the duplicate of the stock ticket, signs the ticket, and sends it to accounting. If the material is not in stock, warehouse man picks it up at supplier, sends copy of invoice to accounting, delivers material to job foreman who checks it, signs delivery ticket and sends the ticket to accounting. Accounting matches, reviews, and posts documentation	No review by contractor or estimator. Consequences: By-passes normal material buying, using cycle, thereby negating benefit of control reporting system and feedback to stocking objectives and estimating factors. Check-off against purchase order not possible. Consequences: Could weaken validity of undelivered items report.

Figure 8–5

with the peculiarities of the industry. Examples that follow are designed to supplement normal audit programs in order to cope with these peculiarities.

Audit Program for Percentage of Completion Contracts

    1. Test the cost-to-date amounts for each job listed in the analysis of work in progress.

2. Verify validity of cut-off of transactions, documentation.

3. Reconcile cost elements to work in progress control accounts.

4. Examine billing documentation in detail.

5. Verify sign-off by contractor and/or estimators on progress billing documents.

6. Reconcile amounts billed as shown on the analysis of work in progress with billing documentation.

7. Perform task-cost analysis procedures on each contract listed in the analysis of work in progress. (See Chapter 10.)

8. Test mathematics of analysis of work in progress worksheet.

9. Trace unbilled costs and earnings to general ledger.

10. Trace unearned billings over costs to the general ledger.

Audit Program for the Completed Contract Method

1. Verify adequacy of provisions for ultimate losses for uncompleted contracts.

2. Determine proper reduction of ultimate losses by the amount of income tax reduction of future periods.

3. Examine uncompleted contracts substantially completed (95 percent) for evidence of deliberate postponing of income reporting.

4. Verify allocation of general and administrative expenses to contract costs rather than period costs.

Audit Program for Cost-Plus Contracts

1. Examine contract provisions for reimbursement and reporting.

2. Determine compliance with provisions.

3. Determine whether the contractor is an agent or principal.

4. If an agent, verify that only the fee is reported as income.

5. If a principal, verify that the fee and reimbursable costs are reported as income.

6. Isolate charges that are not reimbursable.

7. Test for completeness of charges for all time and material.

8. Test time sheets and invoices of adjacent, nonreimbursable contracts for evidence of charges belonging to cost-plus contracts.

Audit Program for Contract Costs

In addition to procedures dealing with contract costs already listed in this section, the auditor should do the following:

1. Determine proper handling of leased equipment costs when there is an option to buy.
2. Verify allocation of equipment costs to jobs.
3. Verify allocation of overhead items.

Audit Program for Job Sites

1. Select the larger contracts in progress and perform the following procedures at the job site.
2. Use copies of the latest time sheets to verify actual manning of the job.
3. Test time sheet preparation procedures.
4. Trace labor hours and costs to job-cost analysis reports.
5. Examine input to various labor reports prepared for outside agencies, or the reports themselves if prepared on the job site, for completeness, correctness, and timeliness.
6. Use copies of invoices and delivery tickets to test material ordering procedures.
7. Test for actual use of material ordered.
8. Obtain dates and dollar amounts of excess material returned from the job-site for the last three months.
9. Trace shipments of excess material for the last three months for proper accounting and recording.
10. Obtain or prepare estimates of excess material on hand, and be alert for the actual shipment to the warehouse, at which time you can verify proper control and accounting.
11. Use the latest progress billing to verify that material on the job site included in the billing is actually there.
12. Use analysis of work in progress worksheet to evaluate percentage of completion.
13. Reconcile petty cash and examine documentation.

Audit Program for Accounts Receivable

1. Verify proper control of and accounting for retainage.
2. Review all disputed accounts.
3. Test for prompt payment of principal suppliers and subcontractors on specific contracts following collection of amounts billed. Be alert for the use of proceeds from one contract to pay the bills of another.

Audit Program for Accounts Payable

1. Verify inclusion of retainage not currently due the subcontractors.
2. Test for inclusion of all subcontractor costs.

3. Test for prompt payment of principal suppliers and subcontractors on specific contracts following the collection of amounts billed. Be alert for the use of proceeds from one contract to pay the bills of another.

Audit Program for Joint Ventures

1. Review agreements for clarity regarding capital contributions, reimbursement, and compensation of participants.
2. Determine compliance with agreements.
3. Verify proper accounting.

FOLLOWING UP ON A GOOD BEGINNING

This chapter was intended to get the auditor off to a good start. Thoroughness in looking at audit objectives and audit programs, and technical aspects of getting things ready to actually conduct the audit have been emphasized to such a degree that the auditor might wonder if there is anything else left to do. There is. The next step involves the actual mechanics of conducting an audit—the subject of the next chapter.

Notes: Chapter 8

1. If stock is issued under the provisions of Section 1244 of the Internal Revenue Code, investors may have an ordinary loss rather than a capital loss.
2. Subchapter S of the Internal Revenue Code permits the corporation to escape practically all taxes. Gains and losses are passed on to the stockholders.
3. *Statement on Auditing Standards 16*, New York, American Institute of Certified Public Accountants, Inc., January 1977.

9

CONDUCTING
THE AUDIT

This chapter is devoted to the mechanics of conducting the audit. Here, we will get down to the details of carrying out the functions indicated by audit plans and audit objectives, refining and reshaping these functions as we seek answers to questions raised by the testing and evaluation of internal control. We will also develop subprograms on the spot whenever we feel that regular audit programs are not finding all the answers we need.

THE CONTRACTOR'S DOCUMENTARY NETWORK: THE PAYMENT FUNCTION

The contractor's operations are linked together by a documentary network that begins with the plans and specifications and ends with the financial statements. To function properly, the auditor must understand the grand scheme of the network and the specific role played by each of its links. The grand scheme is illustrated in Figure 9–1. The sections that follow will deal with the links.

THE LINK BETWEEN PLANS AND SPECS AND THE TAKEOFF

The network is firmly anchored to the plans and specifications. The plans are working drawings prepared by the architect and specialty engineers working with him. The specifications, or "specs," contain many requirements that cannot be conveniently shown on the drawings; for example, quality of workmanship, strength of material, make of equipment, and areas of responsibility for the various construction trades.

THE CONTRACTOR'S DOCUMENTARY CHAIN
The Paying Function

```
         Plans        Specs        Plans

                        │
                        ▼
                     Take-Off

                        │
                        ▼
                       Bid

                        │
                        ▼
                     Contract
                        │
          ┌─────────────┴─────────────┐
          ▼                           ▼
      Submittals                    Labor
          │                      Assignments
    ┌─────┴─────┐                     │
    ▼           ▼                     ▼
Purchase     Subcontracts        Time Sheets
  Order
    │           │                     │
    ▼           ▼                     ▼
Delivery     Progress             Payroll
Tickets      Billings
    │           │                     │
    ▼           │                     │
 Invoices       │                     │
    │           │                     │
    ▼           ▼                     ▼
Suppliers'   Accounting        Contractor-      Financial
  Stmts.   Review, Match,        Cashier          Stmts.
              Post,
            Summarize             Pay
```

Figure 9–1

Depending on how big an operator he is, the contractor himself, his estimator, or his engineering department will "take off" the job. This is a tedious function, complex and highly professional. By means of this function the plans and specs are converted into a carefully organized financial document. The document goes by such names as "cost summary sheets," "cost estimates," or simply "the takeoff."

Trouble Alert in Testing the Takeoff

Unless he is an architect, an engineer, or a skillful estimator, the auditor cannot be expected to determine that the takeoff is a completely valid financial expression of the plans and specs. However, he should be familiar with the principal requirements of the specs, and should be alert to two possible sources of trouble:

- Deviations between the specs and the takeoff
- Change orders

How Specs Are Put Together

Specs are written around a format developed by the Construction Specification Institute, Dupont Circle Building Washington, D.C. 20026.

The format consists of several divisions as follows:

Division 1   General Requirements
Division 2   Site Work
Division 3   Concrete
Division 4   Masonry
Division 5   Metals, Structure, and Miscellaneous
Division 6   Carpentry
Division 7   Moisture Protection
Division 8   Doors, Windows, and Glass
Division 9   Finishes
Division 10   Specialties
Division 11   Equipment
Division 12   Furnishings
Division 13   Special Construction
Division 14   Conveying Systems
Division 15   Mechanical
Division 16   Electrical

ILLUSTRATING THE USE OF SPECS IN THE AUDITING PROCESS

As part of his training, a construction industry auditor should read through an entire set of specs to become familiar with terminology and organization of the material within each division of the CSI format. For actual testing of the takeoff for compliance with the specs, he should select specific items affecting the contractor he is auditing. For example, if his client is a mechanical contractor, he will examine Division 15 and any portion of Division 1 affecting his client. He will select specific items for further examination. For instance, he might note the heating and air conditioning equipment specified, then track compliance with the specs right on through the takeoff sheets. Here is how he would actually do it.

- Note heating and air conditioning equipment specified.
- Examine suppliers' bids or "quotations"
  - for agreement with specs, and
  - to verify selection of the lowest bid.
- Trace selected supplier's quotation to the takeoff.
- Verify proper authorization for deviations from specs.
- Confirm the authorization by tracing it to the submittals.

How the Auditor Copes with Deviations from Specs

The last two steps shown above represent a real source of trouble. The auditor cannot be too careful in pinning down authorizations permitting differences between the specs quoted and those used. Many a contractor has succeeded in getting the low bid by obtaining verbal authority to deviate from the specs, only to find that the verbal authority will not pass the final test.

Here is what can happen. When a contractor is successful low bidder, he is asked to prepare "submittals" of material and equipment to be used on the job. The submittals consist of a package of technical literature furnished by the suppliers who came in with the low quotations. Submittals must be approved by the architect and his engineers.

If the contractor has deviated from the specs, he is not really sure whether he is on safe ground until the deviations, as reflected in the submittals, come back approved. This is the final test. If something goes wrong between verbal approval and submittal approval, the contractor, forced to stick with the specs, can sustain huge losses, sometimes big enough to put him out of business. What must the auditor do if he runs into this kind of a situation? He must, of course, disclose it fully, and in addition, must determine its financial impact.

How the Auditor Deals with Change Orders

As the work progresses, it often becomes necessary to have the contractor perform work not covered by the plans or specs. Here is another source of trouble. Too many contractors have sustained substantial losses, or needed to go to court to collect their money due to reliance on improperly authorized change orders. Subcontractors are particularly vulnerable. Too often, in a spirit of cooperation, the subcontractor will rely on the word of the general superintendent that the change order has been or will be approved by the owner.

On larger contracts in progress, the auditor should verify the proper authorization of every change order. Those not properly authorized should be discussed with the contractor, and if necessary, provisions made for possible losses.

The Link Between the Takeoff and the Bid. The auditor's test is simply to make sure that the takeoff does not contain mathematical errors and that amounts have been correctly transferred to the bid form.

The bid is prepared under tremendous pressure. Addenda to the plans and specs flow in a constant stream, often right up to the bid date. General contractors, subcontractors, and even sub-subcontractors could be affected. Changes can be made right up to the time the bid envelope is sealed and dropped in the bid depository. Suppliers and subcontractors will wait until the last minute to submit their bids in order to prevent bid "peddling," then finally will call in "cuts" in a frenzied attempt to "get low," meaning the lowest bid.

How the Auditor Tests the Bid

In addition to the normal testing of extensions, crossfooting and summarizations, the auditor should ascertain that changes brought about by addenda and the last minute flurry of bids and cuts to the bids are correctly reflected on the takeoffs. On jobs that are in the early stages, errors in the takeoff might require adjustments to the estimated profit. On jobs that are farther along, say over 30 percent complete, the analysis of work in progress should take care of adjustments to the original estimated profit. This, of course, assumes that the analysis of work in progress, and more particularly the key figure of estimated costs to complete the job, can be depended upon by the auditor. Chapter 10 contains in-depth techniques for testing figures contained in the analysis of work in progress.

THE AUDIT TRAIL FROM TAKEOFF TO PURCHASE ORDERS AND SUBCONTRACTS

The takeoff is not only the basis for the contractor's cost control and profit analysis reporting system; it is also the basis for issuing purchase orders and subcontracts. Recognizing this relationship, the auditor continues his testing of the documentary network by performing the following procedures:

• Verifying agreement of the amounts shown on the takeoff with those shown on the purchase orders and subcontracts.

• Examining conditions contained in suppliers' quotations and subcontractors' bids.

• Ascertaining that these conditions are correctly and completely reflected in purchase orders and subcontracts.

Why Accurate, Complete Purchase Orders Are Vital

The reason purchase orders must be accurate, complete and compatible with the takeoff and suppliers' and subcontractors' bids can be illustrated by the following example.

A contractor used a supplier who stated in his quotation that he would deliver a major piece of equipment fully assembled, and that delivery would be made by a specific date. Instead, the equipment came in eight different shipments. The first shipment beat the deadline by one day. The seven remaining shipments were anywhere from a week to three months late.

Fortunately, the contractor had carefully annotated on the purchase order the exact conditions of delivery. In addition, the contractor's attorney found several cases where purchase orders stood up as contracts, and conditions specified therein were treated as part of the contract agreement.

In this particular case, there was an out-of-court settlement, which considered losses incurred by the contractor for penalties imposed by the owner for late completion of the job, as well as for the extra time needed to assemble the equipment.

The Audit Trail from Subcontracts to Progress Billings. The auditor's main concern in testing this particular link is to make sure that terms of agreements with subcontractors are correctly reflected in the progress billings. For the small to medium contracts, the examination should be on a total basis. For the extraordinarily large contracts, testing on a scientific sampling basis will be necessary. Please note the special problems the auditor faces in this area because of the peculiarities of the construction industry. These are covered in the sections that follow.

SAMPLING TECHNIQUES AND PROBLEMS IN TESTING CONTRACTOR OPERATIONS

The methodical examination of transactions up and down the contractor's documentary chain will occasionally be interrupted by a proliferation of documents. Consider the material-intense contractors, such as those engaged in electrical, mechanical, sheet metal, concrete, structural, and paving activities. In such cases, it is not unusual for a single purchase order to contain several pages. Furthermore, these purchase orders will generate a volume of invoices that will end up in various pockets as they proceed to the payment cycle.

Tracing transactions generated by a single purchase order of the material-intense contractor can be a problem. The auditor will discover that deliveries are made to the job site on a sporadic basis, depending on availability. Delivery schedules are nonexistent. If available, the item is delivered; if not, it is back-ordered.

SAMPLING TECHNIQUES ILLUSTRATED

Let us suppose that the auditor is tracing a group of invoices issued by Cosco Supply Company, in response to a particular purchase order, and that he runs into the comingling situation illustrated in Figure 9–2. He notes that the group of invoices he is tracing matches only a part of the purchase order because of irregular deliveries. Furthermore, they have been grouped into one payment package with Cosco Supply invoices generated by several other purchase orders. Several jobs are involved, but payment has been made by one check.

The auditor decides that even a change in direction will not unscramble the transactions. For example, if he uses the payment function as a point of departure, thus reversing the flow shown in Figure 9–2, he encounters a diffusion to several purchase orders.

The auditor recognizes that in only a few areas of the contractor's operation will he be able to proceed from link to link, taking into account every single characteristic of every transaction. These are the exceptions. Perhaps this can be done for transactions involving subcontractors and the purchase of major pieces of equipment. But for the most part, the auditor must rely on scientific sampling techniques to test transactions, and thereby form conclusions about the condition of the accounting records as a whole.

The main objective of this section is to show the auditor how to cope with the problems he will encounter in applying sampling techniques to the contractor's operations. It is assumed that the auditor is not only familiar with the AICPA position on sampling, but also possesses formal training in this field. Therefore, sampling formulas, equations, and tables will not be presented here.

The Four Attribute Worksheets Illustrated

Let us suppose that in the process of testing cash disbursements, the auditor is dealing with a material-intense contractor and has determined confidence levels and precision, taking into account his evaluation of internal control. Let

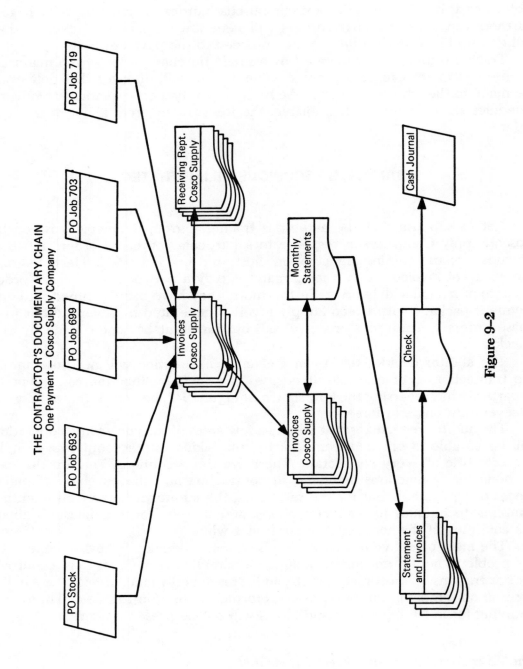

THE CONTRACTOR'S DOCUMENTARY CHAIN
One Payment – Cosco Supply Company

Figure 9–2

us further assume that by the use of tables, computations, and the indispensable elements of judgment and experience, the auditor has decided on a sample of 100 transactions.

The first thing he notices is that the use of a single attribute worksheet to test the payment function will not do the job, since the cash disbursements journal takes in all kinds of transactions. The contractor's functions are such that what is applicable to a routine purchase of office supplies, or the payment of rent, installment loans, or utility bills will differ greatly from payments to material suppliers. An entirely different set of attributes will apply to purchases of equipment as well as payments made to subcontractors.

The solution to this problem is to use four attribute worksheets. The first will test all of the 100 samples for the common attributes of the payment function. This worksheet is illustrated in Figure 9–3. The second, recognizing the scattering that takes place in the case of paying invoices for materials, uses different sampling criteria as well as a different attribute worksheet. This is illustrated in Figure 9–4. The third worksheet, dealing with the peculiar attributes related to the purchase of equipment, is illustrated in Figure 9–5. The fourth, illustrated in Figure 9–6, covers the peculiarities of payments made to subcontractors.

Common Attributes of the Payment Function

Figure 9–3 is an example of the worksheet the auditor will use to test the 100 samples for common attributes related to the payment function. However, before the samples could be listed, the auditor had to:

• Determine the total number of payments or population. In this case it was 5,000.
• Assign a number to each payment.
• Determine the sample size. The auditor had decided on a sample of 100 items, as previously explained.
• Select sample numbers through the use of random number tables or some similar device, so that all 5,000 items will have an even chance to be selected.

Since this was a manually operated accounting system, the auditor had to use a little ingenuity to assign numbers to the 5,000 transactions. He noted that journal pages contained a uniform 40 lines per page. The problem was quickly solved by assigning a cumulative beginning and ending number to each page, thereby establishing the range covered by each page. It was then an easy matter to locate the exact line listing of each sample.

The attributes highlighted on the worksheet are fairly common to the contractor's payment function, an exception being discounts, which of course are not offered in all cases.

Material Science Contractor, Inc.
Attribute Worksheet - Cash Disbursements
F/E October 31, 19__

PREPARED BY _____   DATE _____

Transaction Code: M=Materials; E=Equipment; S=Subcontractor; O=Other

Payee	1 Sample No	2 Check No / Date	3 Amount	4 Transaction Code	5 Agreement Statement-Inventory	Agreement Statement-Payment	7 Discount	8 Statement-Invoice Cancelled	9 Cancelled Check	Reviewed	Account Code
Tristate G & E Co.	12	1103 11-2	201.57	O	N.A.	√	√	√	√	√	√
City Supply, Inc.	94	1197 11-10	1097.74	M	√	√	√	√	√	√	√
B & R Equipment Co.	177	1280 11-10	1563.27	E	N.A.	N.A.	N.A.	√	√	√	√
Petty Cash	243	1346 11-25	190.29	O	N.A.	√	N.A.	√	√	√	√
Bryson Office Supply	263	1366 11-28	45.27	O	√	√	N.A.	√	√	√	√
First State Bank	345	1448 11-30	1025.00	O	N.A.	√	N.A.	N.A.	√	√	√
Kowalski Sheet Metal	4-8	1531 12-6	890.00	S	N.A.	N.A.	N.A.	√	√	√	√
Transfer to Payroll Acct.	447	1550 12-20	2500.00	O	N.A.	N.A.	N.A.	N.A.	√	√	√
Whistle Insurance Agency	493	1596 12-29	1750.00	O	N.A.	√	N.A.	√	√	√	Error
Porter Retailer, Inc.	4764	5867 9-30	52.875	O	N.A.	N.A.	N.A.	√	√	√	√
Petty Cash	4846	5949 10-4	187.48	O	N.A.	√	N.A.	√	√	√	√
The R. J. Poe Co.	4920	6033 10-10	963.27	E	√	√	√	√	√	√	√
Della Supply Co.	4951	6054 10-10	797.657	M	N.A.	N.A.	√	√	√	√	√
Bryson Office Supply	5017	6115 10-29	Error 116.67	O	N.A.	√	√	√	√	√	√
Total sample items			100	1	4	76	43	91	100	100	100
Occurrences			1	1	1	1	1	1	1	1	1
Reliability - 95%											
Actual occurrence rate			1.00%	100%		1.3% *		1.10% *	1.00%	1.00%	1.00%
Upper precision limits, table —			5%	5%		7% *		7% *	5%	5%	5%

* More samples needed.

Figure 9-3

Material Science Contractors, Inc.

Attribute Worksheet – Material Invoices

FYE October 31, 19__

PREPARED BY _____   DATE _____

Supplier	1 Inv. Gp.	Random No.	2 Date	3 Invoice No	4 Amount	5 Inventory	6 Purchased for Job No.	7 Receiving Report	8 Purchase Order	9 Submittals	10 Take Mo
Midwest Supply Co.	1	79	1-2-	123716	1714 67	✓	N.A.	✓	✓	✓	✓
Contractors Supply Co.	2	47	11-18-	37127	50271	N.A.	327	✓	✓	✓	✓
Thurman-Jones, Inc.	3	67	11-6-	7978	19767	N.A.	346	✓	✓	✓	✓
City Supply, Inc.	4	76	11-29-	N-169	98712	N.A.	349	✓	✓	✓	✓
Mott Specialties, Inc.	5	13	12-21-	13793	9726	N.A.	341	✓	✓	✓	✓
Delta Supply Co.	6	29	12-6-	323136	32123	N.A.	348	✓	✓	✓	✓
Ortega Bros, Inc.	7	85	12-17-	44731	75979	N.A.	351	✓	✓	✓	✓
Midwest Supply Co.	8	58	1-3-	169217	9112	N.A.	350	✓	✓	✓	✓
K & R Supply Co.	9	21	1-15-	6006	62712	N.A.	349	✓	✓	✓	✓
Lafayette Co.	10	1	1-5	989787	37976	N.A.	352	✓	✓	✓	✓
Union Supply Co.	11	81	2-14	57665	23279	N.A.	353	✓	✓	✓	✓
Delta Supply Co	29	64	8-7-	426676	87740	✓	N.A.	✓	✓	✓	✓
Mott Specialties, Inc.	30	33	8-6-	29776	45076	N.A.	389	✓	✓	✓	✓
City Supply, Inc.	31	3	8-17-	A-982	24135	N.A.	391	✓	✓	✓	✓
Midwest Supply Co	32	81	6-30-	389732	102617	✓	N.A.	✓	✓	✓	✓
Delta Supply Co.	33	28	9-1-	517276	22790	N.A.	451	✓	✓	✓	✓
K + R Supply Co.	34	4	10-5-	9746	52736	N.A.	456	✓	✓	✓	✓
Thurman-Jones, Inc.	35	19	10-30-	10716	71217	N.A.	457	✓	✓	✓	✓
Contractors Supply Co.	36	44	10-16	1298	47105	N.A.	458	✓	✓	✓	✓

Figure 9-4

Material Interior Contractor, Inc.
Attribute Worksheet – Equipment Invoices
FYE October 31, 19___

PREPARED BY _____ DATE _____

Supplier	Sample No.	Date	Invoice No.	Amount	JB No.	Receiving Report	Purchase Order	Low Quotation	Specs	Submittals
B+R Equipment Co.	6	11-3	1765	891.67	647	✓	✓	✓	✓	✓
Sorsin Equipment Co.	9	11-9	101010	1017627	656	✓	✓	✓	✓	✓
Ganison Corp.	17	11-26	65799	351.1076	617	✓	✓	✓	✓	✓
Boco Supply Inc.	37	12-2	1009	292.700	698	✓	✓	✓	✓	✓
Ferrara + Sons Inc.	45	12-9	9726	160029	701	✓	✓	✓	✓	✓
B+R Equipment Co.	67	12-18	3925	3r1040	79r	✓	✓	✓	✓	✓
Boco Supply Inc.	96	12-29	18719	100607	657	✓	✓	✓	✓	✓
The R.J. Poe Co.	133	1-6	41441	176109	701	✓	✓	✓	✓	✓
Sossin Equipment Inc.	204	1-9	6712	375-88	679	✓	✓	✓	✓	✓
	207	1-19	1766	190007	699	✓	✓	✓	✓	✓
Sorsin Equipment Co.	281	7-31	73071	11671.21	799	✓	✓	✓	✓	✓
Ferrara & Sons, Inc.	286	8-18	1406	36762	803	✓	✓	✓	✓	✓
Boco Supply Inc.	403	8-31	70000	1070017	796	✓	✓	✓	✓	✓
Ganison Corp.	405	9-1	19192	101301	811	✓	✓	✓	✓	✓
B+R Equipment Co.	411	9-2	67165	180016	798	✓	✓	✓	✓	✓
The R.J. Poe Co.	659	9-15	67121	912143	802	✓	✓	✓	✓	✓
Sossin Equipment Co.	679	10-22	1415	197113	800	✓	✓	✓	✓	✓
Ferrara & Sons, Inc.	698	10-26	387	27601	108	✓	✓	✓	✓	✓

Figure 9-5

Matwine Intense Contractor, Inc
Attribute Worksheet – Subcontractors
FYE October 31, 19___

PREPARED BY ___ DATE ___

Subcontractor	Sample No	Job No	Date	Estimate (Billing) No.	Gross Billing	Retention	No over-Billing	No over-Retention	Prompt Pay from Right Contract	Bid	Chg. Ord.	Take-off	Plans, Specs.
Donaldson Specialties Co.	7	327	11-√	7	517000	517000	√	√	√	√	N/A	√	√
Kowalski Sheet Metal	25	350	12-6	3	890000	89000	√	√	√	√	√	√	√
Velmo Controls, Inc.	35	349	1-√1	4	18000	18000 verify	√	√	No	√	N/A	√	√
The Gordon Co.	36	341	2-6	7	18000	18000	√	Error	√	√	N/A	√	√
Dauthines & Assoc, Inc.	55	348	3-19	10	2417000	Final (-0-	√	N/A	√	√	√	√	√
Kowalski Sheet Metal	60	351	4-15	9	189000	189000	√	√	√	√	√	√	√
Murdock Co.	67	353	6-30	11	375000	375000	√	√	√	√	√	√	√
Salinas-Brett Co.	77	389	8-√	2	190000	190000	√	√	√	√	√	√	√
Velmo Controls, Inc.	78	451	8-13	8	2970000	297000 verify	√	√	√	√	√	Error	√
The Gordon Co.	80	458	10-√8	13	1650000	165000	√	√	√	√	√	√	√

Figure 9-6

Please note that Column 4 shows a coding of transactions so that those subject to further examination can be picked out. Specifically, these are purchases of material, equipment, and subcontractor services.

Sampling Techniques for Testing Purchases of Material

In reviewing the purchases journal, the auditor noted that the contractor was doing business with ten major material suppliers. Assuming that each was paid on a monthly basis, that meant 120 payments for the year. However, only two such payments showed up in the attribute worksheet illustrated in Figure 9–3.

The auditor also noted that the payment packages contained an average of 30 invoices each. That meant there were 3,600 invoices in the population. Did all 3,600 have an equal chance of being pulled for further examination? No, because the first sample of 100 items produced only two payments, involving approximately 60 invoices. The remaining 3,540 were not able to be considered.

The auditor decided to give all 3,600 invoices an equal chance to be pulled. He further decided on a sample size of 36, after going through the usual steps of determining confidence levels, precision, and other factors. That meant that one out of every 100 invoices would be selected.

Keeping the payment packages intact, the auditor placed all 120 of them in a box. He then divided the entire file into groups of approximately 100 invoices, overlapping from one payment package to the next when necessary. Finally, by using a table of random numbers, he selected 36 numbers from 1 to 100, and assigned a number to each of the 36 groups of invoices as follows:

Invoice Group	Random Number	Invoice Group	Random Number	Invoice Group	Random Number
1	79	13	96	25	66
2	47	14	84	26	71
3	67	15	40	27	20
4	76	16	18	28	36
5	13	17	74	29	64
6	29	18	33	30	33
7	89	19	77	31	3
8	58	20	49	32	81
9	21	21	76	33	28
10	1	22	93	34	4
11	81	23	39	35	19
12	41	24	18	36	44

Selecting one sample from each of the invoice groups was merely a matter of counting until the indicated number was reached. Invoices thus selected were listed on a worksheet as illustrated in Figure 9–4.

You will note that purchases for stock or inventory are in the minority. The frequency of such purchases depends on the takeoff habits of the contractor. Some, as pointed out in Chapter 8, will estimate material requirements down to the last nut and bolt. Others use a more general measure of material requirements. What the auditor will have to be on the alert for is the situation illustrated in Figure 8–4, in which ordering material from the job site has gotten out of control, leaving the contractor and his estimators out of the decision-making process.

Sampling Techniques for Testing Purchases of Equipment

Since there were two payments to equipment suppliers listed on the worksheet illustrated in Figure 9–3, the auditor recognized the problem as being similar to the one involving material purchases. The need to go behind and beyond these two payments was obvious.

By scanning the cash disbursements journal, the auditor noted six major equipment suppliers. Each payment package contained an average of ten invoices. There had been 70 payments during the year, so the equipment invoice population amounted to 700.

The auditor decided on a different approach from that normally used in selecting his samples. Strictly speaking, statistical sampling criteria such as tolerance limits and precision would have been satisfied by taking a rather small sample, say 2 percent. But the auditor realized that each invoice for the purchase of equipment represented significantly large expenditures. He therefore decided to use judgment rather than mathematics, and ended up selecting 35 invoices at random, a good 5 percent of the total.

The attribute worksheet for testing equipment purchases was similar to that used for testing material purchases. However, certain tests were performed that were relevant only to the purchase of equipment. For example, there are tests checking the agreement of the purchase order with the supplier's quotation, with the low quotation, and with the plans and specs. The worksheet is illustrated in Figure 9–5.

Sampling Techniques for Testing Payments to Subcontractors

Figure 9–6 illustrates the attribute testing worksheet for payments involving subcontractors. Here again, the auditor had to amend his basic sampling program to consider the realities of the situation.

The contractor was doing business with seven subcontractors. Each had 12 payments for the year, with a total of 84. The auditor decided on a sample total of ten payments.

Payments of the subcontractors' billings revealed attributes that were different than those previously examined. For example, the auditor saw a need to test the following characteristics peculiar only to subcontractors:

- Agreement of the subcontract with the:
    - Subcontractor's bid
    - Change orders
    - Takeoff
    - Plans and specs
- Propriety of progress billing—no overbilling
- Proper recording of retention
- Prompt payment of subcontractors from the properly related contract revenue

These attributes are the basis for the construction of the worksheet illustrated in Figure 9–6.

Keeping an Open Mind About Other Sampling Techniques

The auditor will encounter a great variety of situations, some of which will not exactly fit the sampling techniques described in this section. In such cases, the imaginative auditor will improvise while using the basic ideas presented in this section. Since these have been developed through years of experience and have been thoroughly field-tested, the auditor can be sure that they will stand up.

One last precaution: examples and illustrations in this section, particularly those concerning sample size, are just that. They are not rules. The auditor should already possess a basic knowledge of statistical sampling. This section is not a substitute for that knowledge.

THE CONTRACTOR'S DOCUMENTARY NETWORK: THE INCOME FUNCTION

The contractor's documentary chain is easier to follow in the income function than in the paying function. The reason is that the integrity by contract is maintained throughout the entire cycle. Therefore, the events progress within the confines of a specific contract or work order, which is the equivalent of a contract for a small job. As you trace these events in Figure 9–7, imagine the contract structure within which they are taking place, as follows:

- Billings are prepared in accordance with the terms of the contract.
- If the contractor is actually a subcontractor, the billings go to the next-up contractor, continuing up the ladder to the general contractor.
- The general contractor incorporates subcontractor billings, and dealing directly with the architect, submits them for approval.
- The architect coordinates portions of the billing with the appropriate engineer—electrical, mechanical, and so on.
- The approved billing goes to the owner, who pays the contractor.

An Audit Alert: Maintain Integrity by Contract

If the billing refers to a specific job, say the Live Oak Elementary School, the last check to the lowest echelon sub-subcontractor will also cite the Live Oak Elementary School. The auditor's chief concern is to make sure that this integrity is preserved, that Live Oak Elementary School liabilities are paid promptly upon receipt of Live Oak Elementary income. As described in Chapter 8, one of the audit pitfalls peculiar to the construction industry is the use of money from one contract to pay the bills of another. To discourage this practice, some states have strictly enforced laws carrying stiff penalties if broken.

Billing Peculiarities to Look For.   The auditor will find that the larger the contract, the more elaborate the billing procedures. The contract will often call for detailed line-item control extending to the subcontractor level. A meshing of billing procedures with PERT (Program Evaluation and Review Technique) is not unusual.

Before beginning income auditing procedures, the auditor will have reviewed the contract, paying particular attention to billing instructions. The auditor makes a note to verify the contractor's compliance with these billing instructions. It is quite possible that compliance could become a problem.

The auditor should not pass up this opportunity to help the contractor with billing problems. At any rate, the auditor should realize that failure to solve these problems can have serious consequences. The ripple effect could trickle down to disgruntled subcontractors and suppliers, who ironically might have contributed to the problem by improper billing of their own. And, if delay in getting paid causes the contractor to pass up purchase discounts, it could affect the job estimates since these are an important part of the bidding strategy.

The consequences continue. Are the estimated costs to complete stated fairly in the analysis of work in progress? Further, are provisions for ultimate contract losses adequate?

THE CONTRACTOR'S DOCUMENTARY CHAIN
The Income Function

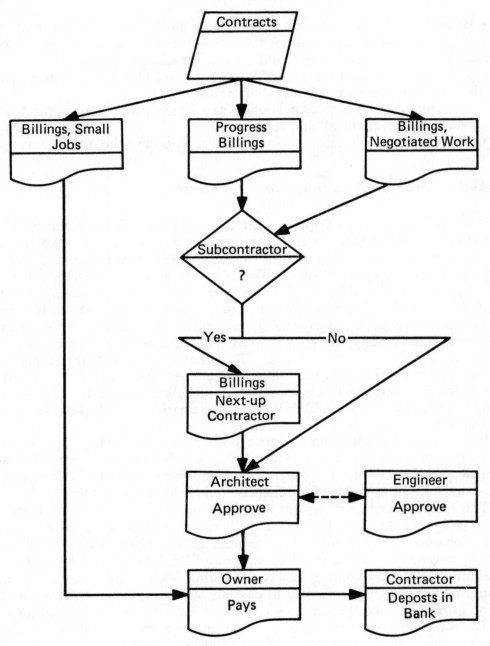

Figure 9–7

ORGANIZING THE WORKING PAPERS

The auditor begins to collect working papers with the notes taken during the initial contact with the contractor. The accumulation continues and accelerates as the audit gets under way. Audit plans, programs, objectives, instructions, procedures, flow charts, worksheets, schedules, extracts or copies of documents, notations, observations—every scrap of paper to show what the auditor plans to do and what he has actually done—will become a part of the working papers. A great variety of worksheets will show what has actually been tested, reviewed, counted, sampled, observed, matched, reconciled, vouched, verified, confirmed, examined, extended, footed, analyzed, and compared.

The preparation and accumulation of working papers should be purposeful and meaningful.[1] The old days when auditors tried to mystify clients and juniors by the preparation of worksheets covered with ticks, symbols, and codes is a thing of the past. Quite simply, working papers should aid the auditor and provide support for his opinion.[2] Clarity, consistency, and logic should prevail, so that the story of the auditor's accomplishments will be clear to everyone picking up the working-paper file.

A Simple and Effective Method for Organizing Working Papers

A simple yet effective method of organizing working papers entails using a folder for each account number series of the chart of accounts. Assuming that the contractor is using the chart of accounts illustrated in Figure 5–1, working papers pertaining to "Cash in bank—general" would be marked 102. All the working papers for this and other 100-Series accounts will be filed in one folder, representing a handy reference of work done in auditing current assets.

Working papers for the 200-Series of accounts, land and depreciable assets, can also be arranged in a neat package. The only precaution needed is the separation of depreciation schedule for each account. This might mean breaking out the corresponding depreciation, if the contractor's accountant hasn't already done so, rather than using Account 245 for total accumulated depreciation. If broken out to match each asset account, this would mean that 206 would be used for accumulated depreciation, building; 211 for accumulated depreciation, office furniture and equipment; and so on.

Since Account 735, depreciation, is also affected, it will be necessary for the auditor to make a notation here, giving reference to the detail contained in the depreciation schedule filed in 205 through 221.

Working Papers for Analysis of Work in Progress

A look at the worksheet illustrated in Figure 3–1 will show that several accounts are involved. For example, column 2, billings to date, is a part of 120, accounts receivable; while Column 3, costs to date, is a part of 604, cost of contracts.

Column 4, unearned billings over cost, make up account 314 in its entirety. The same is true of Column 12, unbilled costs and earnings, and account 125, costs and earnings over billings.

Column 6, estimated costs to complete, is practically a function of Column 3, costs to date; this, in turn is part of Account 604, cost of contracts. In view of the close relationship between Columns 6 and 3, most auditors prefer to file the analysis of work in progress under 604, cost of contracts. Other affected accounts will therefore contain a reference to 604.

The Use of Supplemental Folders to Organize Working Papers

It might be necessary to have supplemental folders. For example, if the contractor's inventory worksheets are voluminous, a single sheet marked 130 at the bottom might be put in the working-paper folder with the notation, "See separate folder for inventory worksheets."

Using the General Information Folder

The kind of information that belongs in the general information folder has been covered in detail in Chapter 8, under the section entitled: "How to Find and Use Background Information." Actual copies or extracts would be included in this folder, together with pertinent notations and observations by the auditor. Subdivisions within the folder are usually accomplished by tabs, although for voluminous material, separate folders within the general information folder might be practical.

HOW TO SIMPLIFY WORK WHEN CONDUCTING THE AUDIT

Work simplification is best accomplished by splitting the work to be done into component parts, and assigning each part to an individual. This, in effect, is what the audit plan illustrated in Figure 8–1 is designed to accomplish.

Please note that the audit plan follows an arrangement compatible with the organization of the working papers. First comes the general information; then, with some admixture, is the basic pattern of the chart of accounts; finally, the various reports and the financial statements bring the plan to an end.

The secret to work simplification is the use of the plan as a control device to assure the orderly and timely accomplishment of assignments. Each segment of the plan should be done completely, including not only the audit of primary accounts, but also all secondary accounts. For example, the testing of job costs, payroll, and general and administrative expenses covers a lot of territory, including the analysis of work in progress and all of its own spin-offs, as well as other accounts.

The auditor in charge, in making assignments, must be sure that the performing auditor understands that complete coverage of all related accounts is expected. Auditing, at its best, is a complicated task. Work simplification can only go so far. Actually, it consists primarily of trying to keep the audit from becoming more involved than it already is. Complete understanding of assignments, based on the audit plan, is the only way to avoid unnecessary complications.

SPECIAL TREATMENT FOR PERCENTAGE OF COMPLETION CONTRACTORS

This chapter has outlined all the techniques required to conduct a complete audit for any company in the construction industry. However, if the contractor uses the percentage of completion method as most of them do, at least for management purposes, the auditor will face certain complex problems that require special treatment beyond the procedures covered in this chapter. In the next chapter, the auditor will discover innovative methods for dealing with these problems.

Notes: Chapter 9

1. *Codification of Statements on Auditing Standards*, Sections 320A and 320B, © 1977 by the American Institute of Certified Public Accountants, Inc., New York.
2. Section 338.02, op. cit.

10

HOW TO HANDLE
THE AUDIT PROBLEMS OF
THE PERCENTAGE OF
COMPLETION CONTRACTOR

The McKesson & Robbins case was a traumatic experience for the accounting profession. Auditing procedures, which previously had leaned heavily on documentation, suddenly had to give way to the new requirements observing the actual taking of inventory and confirming accounts receivable through independent verification.

The accounting profession was shocked into reform by the Securities and Exchange Commission (SEC) hearings in 1939, which disclosed that $10 million out of $19 million of McKesson & Robbins fictitious assets consisted of nonexistent inventories. The reaction was to move from passive to active auditing, discarding total reliance on the client's documents for the physical and independent verification of assets.

THE FOUR SEASONS CASE

During the early 1970s, the auditors, managers, stockbrokers, and principal stockholders of Four Seasons Nursing Centers of America, an Oklahoma City construction firm, had to defend themselves in dozens of lawsuits, the principal one in New York City. Prestigious American and European investors and stockbrokers were suddenly caught in what the U.S. Attorney, Gary Naftalis of New York City, called "probably the biggest security fraud case ever filed." With losses to investors in the $200 million area, it seemed to dwarf the McKesson & Robbins case.

The New York City trial raised many issues, but the one that should concern auditors in the construction industry is the allegation that management had fraudulently overstated the numerator and understated the denominator of the percentage of completion fraction. The significance is that if the numerator is overstated and the denominator understated, it results in both an overstated percentage of completion and an overstated earned income.

The Ratchet Effect

Auditors should note the ratchet effect. Not only is the percentage of completion overstated as a result of an exaggerated numerator and an understated denominator, but the low denominator, a function of an understated estimated cost to complete the job, results in an overstated estimated gross profit on the job. The result is an overstated percentage of completion applied to an overstated estimated gross profit.

The Four Seasons Drama

In the Four Seasons case, the ratchet effect took over in a dramatic way. As earnings per share took off, the price of the stock went from $11 per share to over $100, split two-to-one, and kept going up. Investors here and in Europe rushed to get on the bandwagon. Four Seasons raised over $100 million in the last few months of 1969 through stock sales and other financing, then by June 30, 1970, it filed for reorganization under Chapter 10 of the Federal Bankruptcy Act of 1898, subsequently repealed by the Bankruptcy Reform Act of 1978, which includes all reorganizations under Chapter 11.

Why No Shock Waves from Four Seasons?

The question one might ask is, why didn't Four Seasons produce the shock waves among accounting professionals that McKesson & Robbins did? The answer is that McKesson & Robbins was a simple overstatement of assets, and therefore the cure was also simple: observe and confirm.

In Four Seasons, the problem was one of income determination, certainly more subtle and complex than the simple nailing down of assets. A quick, direct reaction by the accounting profession was neither required nor attainable.

The American Institute of Certified Public Accountants (AICPA) has been concerned with the problem of determining income of percentage of completion contractors long before the Four Seasons episode. The official AICPA pronouncement of May 1965, *Audits of Construction Contractors*, superseded their 1954 publication. A major revision in 1981, *Construction Contractors*, is a vast improvement over the 1965 publication. But the auditor is still left up in the air on certain vital issues, as we shall see.

HOW THE AICPA LOOKS AT CONSTRUCTION IN PROGRESS

Here, for example, is an overview of construction contractors as the AICPA deals with construction in progress:

- Do what is reasonable.
- In case of doubt, retreat to zero estimated gross profit.
- Be suspicious of costs to date.
- If costs to date clash with measurements by outsiders such as architects, engineers, inspectors, and others, then disallow some of these costs or disregard them entirely in accepting the outsiders' percentage of completion.
- Use your own judgment as to what costs you will disallow.
- However, as a rough guide, you might disallow costs that represent uninstalled material that is not unique to the job.

WHY ZERO ESTIMATED GROSS PROFIT IS NOT THE ANSWER

It seems as if the AICPA, in not offering the auditor more definitive guidance, is willing to settle for the generalized admonition to be carefully conservative.

The trouble with this kind of advice is that by following it, the auditor could be lulled into a false sense of security. For example, reducing estimated gross profit to zero, in the event that estimates are questionable, will not make everything all right. After all, questionable estimates might signal *a negative gross profit of huge proportions*. Failure to ascertain and disclose such a condition could mean deep trouble for the auditor.

THE CLEAN NUMERATOR THEORY

Old timers used to worry about "clean" and "dirty" surplus. The issue was whether surplus, or retained earnings as we now call it, should be kept "clean" of extraneous income items.

In the construction industry, there is something to be said in favor of the clean numerator theory. Let us see why.

In the popular cost-to-cost method, the percentage of completion is determined by the following fraction:

- The numerator equals costs to date.
- The denominator equals costs to date, plus estimated costs to complete the job.

Costs to date should be a clean-cut, straightforward figure. Distortion should come only from two sources: fraudulent documentation or erroneous cut-off. Either should be detected and corrected by the auditor.

Theory vs. Practice in Determining Costs to Date

The AICPA position that certain subcontractor costs incurred during early stages of the job, and that certain material costs representing uninstalled material not unique to the job might be disregarded, is hard to defend in actual practice. If the auditor insists in following it, he might expect this kind of reaction on the part of the contractor:

"If this material is not unique to the job, what is it doing here anyway?" Or,

"I've spent several thousand dollars getting this sand delivered to the job site by one of my subs. He has complied with his contract and I have paid him his money. The sand is setting here on the job site, ready for me to use for fill work. Are you telling me that I can't count this sand as part of my job costs just because it is a cost incurred during early stages of the job and that it hasn't been installed, and finally, that it is not unique to the job?"

Beware the Dangerous Practice of Messing with the Numerator

The AICPA position of allowing adjustments to costs to date, in order to arrive at a more realistic percentage of completion, can get the auditor in trouble. For example, if costs to date are incompatible with more determinable measurements of percentage of completion, then the adjustment should be made in the estimated-cost-to-complete portion of the denominator, not by eliminating costs contained in the numerator. Indeed, failure to adjust the denominator can distort earned income quite seriously. And the auditor's tampering with the numerator can get him into trouble.

Why the Auditor Should Not Tamper with the Numerator

The auditor can competently test only those factors that measure financial progress toward completion. He is not an architect or an engineer. He should resist the temptation to tamper with the numerator in order to make it compatible with measurements that he might not fully understand. Here are more reasons why he should resist temptations to mess with the numerator, and instead should concentrate on adjustments to the denominator.

• A verifiable numerator representing costs to date should be allowed to stand as a financial measure of costs versus total costs.

• If the cost-to-cost fraction produces something other than a factual percentage of completion, then the required adjustment should be made via the estimated-cost-to-complete portion of the denominator.

• If the auditor has problems with the contractor's estimated costs to complete, he cannot hide behind a zero estimated gross profit. To do so is to risk a charge of failing to use due care in disclosing a potentially serious loss.

• If there are significant differences between the contractor's and the outsider's percentages of completion, the auditor should be alerted to possible serious trouble, and should reconcile differences by following procedures for testing estimated costs described in the next two sections.

COST-TO-COST VS. OTHER PERFORMANCE MEASUREMENTS

Let us take the following example from the previously mentioned AICPA publication[1] and analyze the consequences of using performance measurements to overrule financial measurements.

Contract (Revenues)	$1,000,000
Billings to Date:	
First Year	200,000
Second Year	750,000
Third Year	1,000,000
Costs to Date:	
First Year	$ 300,000
Second Year	650,000
Third Year	900,000
Estimated Gross Profit	100,000
Percent Gross Profit	10%
Percent Completed:	
First Year	25%
Second Year	75%
Third Year	100%

The First Year. Assuming facts as shown above, the auditor might conclude that the difference between the first year percentage of completion of 25 percent, and the cost-to-cost percentage of completion of 33.33 percent ($300,000/-$900,000), might indicate questionable estimated costs to complete, and that this might call for a retreat to zero earned income. Instead of facing the issue of whether to use estimated gross profit of either $25,000 or $33,333, depending on which percentage of completion he will accept, the auditor might be tempted to say, "Oh, to heck with it, let's make it zero."

Does this satisfy the "due care" criterion of the AICPA standards of performance for the auditor?[2] Of course not. For example, if only 25 percent of the work has been done, and 33.33 percent of the money has been spent, maybe the total estimated costs should be $1.2 million ($300,000/.25), indicating an estimated gross loss of $200,000, rather than an estimated gross profit of $100,000.

The Second Year. If, at the end of the second year, 75 percent of the work has been done, with only 72.22 percent ($650,000/$900,000) of the money gone, maybe total estimated costs should be $866,666 ($650,000/.75), indicating an estimated gross profit of $133,333, rather than $100,000.

The Auditor's Dilemma. What's going on? If we try to equate the given percentage of completion to actual costs, we end up with a minus 200 percent gross profit for Year 1, and a plus 13.33 percent gross profit for Year 2. It is obvious that, in this particular example, the auditor cannot make the estimated percentages of completion of 25 and 75 percent fit the realities of actual costs without producing wild variations to total estimated costs. Certainly, this is not a fair presentation of what's really going on, any more than it would be to reduce gross profit to zero.

Alternative Methods of Recognizing Revenue and Costs

The AICPA publication previously cited gives two alternative methods of recognizing revenue and cost of revenue. These are shown in Figure 10–1, together with our own alternative, C, which uses the cost-to-cost method to determine the percentage of completion.

Alternative A. The majority of the members of the AICPA committee working on the Exposure Draft favored Alternative A. In this method, the percentages of completion of 25 and 75 percent, for Years 1 and 2 respectively, were applied to total estimated revenue of $1 million and total estimated costs of $900,000, to arrive at earned revenue and cost of earned revenue. Although both Alternative A and B produced the same gross profit, Alternative A was preferred because the gross profit percentage was a steady 10 percent, and in addition, costs of earned revenue were adjusted to match the earned revenue recognized.

Alternative B. The minority group liked Alternative B because costs of $300,000 were recognized in full. Earned revenue therefore equaled actual costs, plus the recognized gross profit of $25,000. By throwing actual costs plus gross

COST-TO-COST AS A COMPROMISE ALTERNATIVE

	Method		
	Alternative A	*Alternative B*	*Alternative C*
Income Statement			
Year 1			
Earned revenue	$250,000	$325,000	$333,333
Costs of earned			
revenue	225,000	300,000	300,000
Gross profit	$ 25,000	$ 25,000	$ 33,333
% of gross profit	10%	7.7%	10%
Year 2			
Earned revenue	$500,000	$400,000	$388,898
Cost of earned			
revenue	450,000	350,000	350,000
Gross profit	$ 50,000	$ 50,000	$ 38,898
% of gross profit	10%	12.5%	10%
Year 3			
Earned revenue	$250,000	$275,000	$277,769
Cost of earned			
revenue	225,000	250,000	250,000
Gross profit	$ 25,000	$ 25,000	$ 27,769
% of gross profit	10%	9.1%	10%
Balance Sheet Debit (Credit)			
Year 1			

Cost of uncom-
      pleted contracts
      and estimated
      profit in excess of
      billings
	$125,000		

Unbilled revenues		$125,000	$133,333
Year 2			

Excess of billings
      over costs in-
      curred and esti-
      mated earnings
      on uncompleted
      contracts			

Excess billings	$ (25,000)	$ (25,000)	$ (27,769)

Figure 10–1

profit into earned revenue, Alternative B causes the gross profit percentage to vary from year to year. This bothered advocates of Alternative A, but did not bother proponents of Alternative B, who thought that variations in the gross profit percentage from year to year were more representative of actual conditions.

Alternative C. Alternative C is presented in Figure 10–1 as a compromise. It applies the percentage of completion of 33.33 percent, based strictly on cost-to-cost, to the total estimated revenue of $1 million, in order to arrive at the $333,333 earned revenue figure. Actual costs of $300,000 are recognized in full. This should please those favoring Alternative B. Advocates of Alternative A should also be happy because actual costs agree with the percentage of completion of 33.33 percent, and the gross profit percentage is a steady 10 percent for all years.

Adjusting Entries. The balance sheet debit of $125,000, shown in Figure 10–1 for Year 1 and Alternative A, is the contra of the following credit entries:

Earned revenue	$ 50,000
Cost of earned revenue	75,000
Total credits	$125,000

The balance sheet debit of $125,000 for Year 1 under Alternative B is the contra of additional earned revenue of $125,000, recognized and added to the $200,000 billed.

The balance sheet debit of $133,333 for Year 1 under Alternative C is the contra of the additional earned revenue of $133,333, recognized and added to the $200,000 billed.

In Year 2, the balance sheet credits result from overbilling as follows:

	Alternatives A, B	Alternative C
Costs to date	$650,000	$650,000
Gross profit to date	75,000	72,231
Total	$725,000	$722,231
Billed to date	750,000	750,000
Excess billings	$ (25,000)	$ (27,769)

Is Alternative C a Solution? Alternative C might offer a happy compromise between Alternatives A and B, but it does little to reduce the auditor's anxiety. He knows that all three alternatives assume an immutable estimated total cost of $900,000. But under certain conditions described in the first and second year subsections above, it will vary from a high of $1.2 million to a low of $866,666. Where does this leave the auditor?

For one thing, the auditor must subject the total estimated cost figure to rigorous tests. This can best be accomplished by using the task-cost analysis techniques described in the following section.

HOW THE AUDITOR HANDLES PERCENTAGE OF COMPLETION DIFFERENCES

Let us continue the illustration presented in the above section, using amounts for Year 1 as follows:

Contract	$1,000,000
Total estimated costs	900,000
Billed to date	200,000
Costs to date	300,000

Suppose that the contractor, sticking with a strict cost-to-cost formula, states that he is 33.33 percent complete. Now suppose that the architect disagrees, stating that the percentage of completion is 25 percent.

Who is right? Perhaps neither.

STEP-BY-STEP PROCEDURE FOR TESTING ESTIMATED COSTS

More to satisfy himself rather than to try to resolve differences in the percentage of completion, the auditor proceeds as follows to determine the best possible way to test the key figure: total estimated costs. Here is how it's done:

• Set up the contractor's figures on a work sheet, using the format for analysis of work in process presented in Figure 3–1, except that the elements will be arranged vertically instead of horizontally. See Figure 10–2, Step 1.
• Subject the contract revenue to the auditing procedures described in Chapter 9.
• Do the same thing to billings to date and costs to date.
• Enter the amounts in the worksheet as shown in Figure 10–2, Step 2.
• Subject the estimated cost to complete ($600,000) to the task-cost analysis techniques.

The specific audit procedures to carry out the last step listed above will be described in the section that follows, and will be illustrated in Figures 10–3 and 10–4. The results will then be entered on the worksheet illustrated in Figure 10–2 as Step 3.

Contractor's Construction Company
Analysis of Work in Progress - Job 698
FYE October 31, 19___

PREPARED BY: W.R.J.   DATE: 11/18/

			Per Contractor	Per Audit	Adjustments to Contract Increases	Decreases
			Step 1	Step 2		
⟨1⟩	Contract or total estimated revenue		1000000	998500		1500
⟨2⟩	Billings to date		400000	400000		
⟨3⟩	Costs to Date		300000	299800	①	200
⟨4⟩	Billings over costs					
⟨5⟩	Costs over billings		100000	99800		200
				Step 3		
⟨6⟩	Estimated costs to complete		600000	639900	39900	
⟨7⟩	Estimated gross profit		100000	58800		41200
⟨8⟩	Percent gross profit		10.00	5.89		4.11
⟨9⟩	Percentage of completion		33.00	31.90		1.10
⟨10⟩	Billings over costs - earned					
⟨11⟩	Billings over costs - unearned					
⟨12⟩	Unbilled costs and earnings		133333	118577	②	14756

Kraftbilt BOX 800 TULSA OK 74161 5007A IVORY; 5207A GREEN; 5407A WHITE   PRINTED IN U.S.A.

Figure 10–2

Contractor's Construction Company

Estimated Costs to Complete Job 698

FYE October 31, 19 ___

PREPARED BY W. R. J.   DATE 11/18

	Per Take-off	Costs to Date	Balance Remaining	Costs to Complete
Labor hours	25146	7946	17200	18600
Labor costs	326900	103300	223600	260600
Material	136250	46100	90150	92100
Equipment	285200	100200	185000	185000
Miscellaneous	6950	2100	4850	5800
Subcontractors	144700	48300	96400	96400
Total	900000	300000	600000	639900

Figure 10–3

How to Use Task-Cost Analysis to Test Estimated Costs to Complete

The contractor in this example has shown estimated cost to complete of $600,000—total costs of $900,000 less costs to date of $300,000. The auditor must be prepared to validate this figure or to disagree with it, and if so, why. The auditor does this by a process of inductive reasoning, which we will call task-cost analysis.

The Basic Task-Cost Program.   The program is as follows:

• Compare labor hours, as well as each of the various cost elements, to comparable figures shown in the job takeoff.
• Prepare a worksheet as illustrated in Figure 10–3.
• Analyze each task to be performed in terms of balance of estimated hours and cost remaining to accomplish the task.

To carry out the last step listed above, the auditor will subject each element to further examination.

Labor Hours.   The auditor must refer to the takeoff to prepare the analysis of labor hours illustrated in Figure 10–4. He divides his analysis into two parts: Part I for completed tasks and Part II for tasks yet to be completed.

Please note that the problem begins to show up in Part I, where there is an overrun of 400 hours.

The auditor proceeds to Part II, and after discussing each task with the estimator, the contractor, and the job foreman, comes to the conclusion that before the job is over, there will more than likely be a manhour overrun of 1,400, as indicated by the total of Parts I and II, Figure 10–4.

Labor Costs.   The auditor concludes that labor costs are essentially a function of labor hours. However, although labor costs of $13.00 per hour used in the takeoff were in agreement with the cost experience for completed jobs, the auditor recognized inflationary factors, and with the concurrence of the contractor and his estimator, changed the rate to $14.00 per hour for the work remaining to be done. This adjustment is reflected in the labor costs to complete ($260,000) shown in Figure 10–3.

Material.   Most material purchases were controlled by purchase orders, which in turn matched quotes furnished by suppliers who had taken inflationary factors into account. The contractor's accounting system provided an element-by-element comparison of takeoff versus actual material costs, as illustrated in Figure 4–4. In addition, it had available the variations of the delivery report shown in Figure 4–5, to show dollar amounts of undelivered material by purchase order.

The 2 percent upward adjustment to estimated costs to complete was suggested by the auditor to cover purchases of items omitted from the takeoff. The contractor agreed that the 2 percent increase over takeoff costs was reasonable.

Contractor's Construction Company
Analysis of Labor Hours — Job 698

PREPARED BY W.R.J.   DATE 11/18/

Task			Per Take-off	Hours to Date	Balance Remaining	Estimated Hours to Complete	<Over> Under Balance
Completed Tasks - Pt. I			3250	3650	<400>	- 0 -	<400>
Tasks in progress - Pt. II							
1008			1516	801	715	890	<175>
1026			1008	598	410	631	<221>
2102			2109	1099	1010	1201	<191>
2316			2076	1363	713	596	117
4110			1969	1108	861	808	53
5001			2172	1170	1002	1128	<126>
Total Pt. I and Pt. II			25146	7946	17200	18600	<1400>

Kraftbill BOX 600 TULSA OK 74101 5007A IVORY; 5207A GREEN; 5407A WHITE   PRINTED IN U.S.A.

Figure 10–4

Equipment.   Determining equipment needed to complete the job is pretty cut-and-dried, as explained in Chapter 3. Amounts needed to complete the job should represent undelivered amounts, as illustrated in Figure 5–5. Inflation will be a problem, depending on the terms of the suppliers' quotations. For example, the supplier might try to hold prices for only a specified time period.

Miscellaneous.   Miscellaneous costs are a mixture of task-oriented costs and costs to cover anticipated contingencies. The auditor must discuss these costs with the contractor and his staff. Precise, task-oriented costs can be pinned down by the task-cost analysis techniques described in Chapter 3. Contingency items can also be isolated by determining whether the contingency has occurred, and if not, whether provisions for its occurrence require adjustment. In our example shown in Figure 10–3, let us assume that elimination procedures showed a need to increase the estimated costs to complete from $4,850 to $5,800.

Subcontractors.   If the contractor's documentation will support the balance remaining figure of $96,400, there is no need for further adjustment. The reason is that subcontractors will be held to the amounts they quoted to the contractor.

Adjustments and Reconciliations Resulting from the Task-Cost Program

Estimated costs to complete of $639,900, shown in the worksheet illustrated in Figure 10–3 under Step 3, allows the auditor to proceed with final adjustments and reconciliations. Estimated gross profit of $58,800 is the total estimated contract revenue of $998,500, minus costs to date of $299,800, minus estimated costs to complete of $639,900.

Unbilled costs and earnings represent costs of $99,800, plus that portion of the estimated gross profit earned, this amount being $18,757 or $58,800 times the percentage of completion of 31.90 percent.

Two changes to the contractor's representation, as shown in Figure 10–2, require adjustments to the financial records:

- The $200 decrease in costs to date.
- The $14,756 decrease in unbilled costs and earnings.

Adjusting entries would be as follows:

	Dr	Cr
Accounts receivable	$200	
Job costs		$200
Contract revenue	$14,756	
Unbilled costs and earnings		$14,756

The $41,200 reduction in estimated gross profit shown in Figure 10–2 can be reconciled as follows:

Increase in estimated costs to complete	$39,900
Decrease in total estimated revenue	1,500
Less decrease in costs to date	(200)
Decrease in estimated gross profit	$41,200

Please note that the relatively minor reduction of 1.43 percent in percentage of completion shows little relationship to the large reduction in estimated gross profit. This further proves that the key figure in the analysis of construction in progress is the estimated costs to complete the job. Adjustments to the numerator of the cost-to-cost fraction, made in an attempt to agree with a given percentage of completion, are not only futile, but could prove to be quite dangerous if, in so doing, the auditor fails to see the real problem hidden away in the denominator.

PREPARING THE AUDIT REPORT

After completing the audit itself, the auditor faces the task of preparing the audit report. The chapter that follows provides a step-by-step procedure for performing this most important function.

Notes: Chapter 10

1. *Construction Contractors*, pp. 161–2, Appendix 3, © 1981 by the American Institute of Certified Public Accountants, Inc., New York.
2. *Codification of Statements on Auditing Standards*, Au Sec. 230, p. 27, (© 1977) by the American Institute of Certified Public Accountants, New York.

11

PREPARING THE AUDITOR'S STANDARD REPORT AND RELATED INFORMATION

The auditor who does a good job in conducting the audit and documenting his findings will end up with a solid set of working papers. With this kind of back-up, the preparation of the audit report should present no real problems. To a great extent, the task is one of extracting pertinent facts from information already carefully organized in the working papers.

The problem, at this point, is more mental than procedural, more a matter of being keenly attuned to professional polish and user satisfaction than to the display of auditing skills. Let us, therefore, emphasize these two points as we consider what it takes to accomplish a successful wrap-up of the audit engagement.

THE AUDITOR'S STAKE IN THE AUDIT REPORT

Let us assume that the auditor, through a combination of fatigue and complacency, allows himself to slip in accuracy, completeness, and understandability. Let us further assume that these conditions find their way into the audit report.

No matter how brilliantly the auditor has performed in conducting the audit, he now becomes a failure in the eyes of his supervisor. And if the supervisor is not able to patch things up, the whole firm is exposed to possible charges of incompetence and even malpractice.

Let's face it. The audit report is the only thing outsiders will see. Therefore, rightly or wrongly, the auditor will be judged on it alone, and the great work he might have done in building up the underlying basis for his audit report will make little difference to the ordinary user.

233

ASSURING COMPLIANCE WITH AICPA REQUIREMENTS

Reporting standards of the AICPA pertain mostly to the auditor's standard report, consisting of its basic financial statement and integral components as follows:

- Balance sheet
- Statement of income
- Statement of retained earnings or changes in stockholders' equity
- Statement of changes in financial position
- Description of accounting policies
- Notes to financial statements
- Schedules and any explanatory material that is part of the basic financial statements

THE AUDITOR'S SHORT-FORM REPORT

The auditor forms an opinion, then expresses it via the common short-form report, consisting of the two-paragraph statement wherein the auditor proclaims (1) the scope of his examination, and (2) renders an opinion. Bankers will sometimes say, "as long as I see only two paragraphs, I'll think that everything is OK and I'll accept the auditor's report. If there is an extra paragraph, I'll begin to worry about it, thinking that the auditor is trying to put something over on me." This is an over-simplification of the two-paragraph clean opinion. But see subsequent sections for exceptions, qualified opinions, and disclaimers of opinion.

What Happened to the Long-Form Report?

The less common long-form report has been superseded by the report on information accompanying the basic financial statements. This report is subject to a separate set of disclosure ground rules,[1] and will be covered in the section that follows, together with the report on internal accounting control,[2] which replaces the former report on internal control.

The Need to Comply with Reporting Standards

It is assumed that the auditor is already familiar with reporting standards that apply to all audits, not merely those involving construction contractors.

These are contained in SAS (Statements on Auditing Standards). Numbers 1 through 15 have been codified by the AICPA,[3] while subsequent releases are published as separate publications when they are issued.

Whether the audit involves a construction contractor or someone else, compliance with AICPA reporting standards is mandatory[4] for the CPA. In summary, the auditor is required to make sure that his statement reveals:

1. Whether financial statements are prepared in accordance with generally accepted accounting principles
2. Whether such principles are consistent with those of the preceding period
3. Whether there is adequacy of informative disclosure on the financial statements
4. Whether the opinion paragraph:
   - Complies with auditor's standard report
   - Discloses departures from a standard
   - Is an unqualified opinion
   - Is a qualified opinion within AICPA criteria
   - Is an adverse opinion
   - Is a disclaimer of opinion
   - Is an inappropriate, piecemeal opinion
   - Includes comparative statements
   - Considers subsequent events

THE AUDITOR'S CHOICE IN RENDERING AN OPINION

The auditor should be careful not to give an unqualified opinion if he is not in a position to do so. He should note carefully the following AICPA admonition regarding the fourth standard of reporting:

> The report shall either contain an expression of opinion regarding the financial statements, taken as a whole, or an assertion to the effect that an opinion cannot be expressed. When an overall opinion cannot be expressed, the reason should be stated. In all cases wherein an auditor's name is associated with financial statements, the report should contain a clear-cut indication of the character of the auditor's examination, if any, and the degree of responsibility he is taking.[5]

If the opinion is not a clean or unqualified opinion, it must then be:

- A qualified opinion,
- A disclaimer of opinion, or
- An adverse opinion

The Auditor's Qualified Opinion

The main characteristic of a qualified opinion is the presence of an "except for" or a "subject to" condition, either at the end of the scope paragraph or as a separate paragraph between it and the opinion paragraph. The auditor might want to refresh his memory by consulting the several examples given in the AICPA Statements on Auditing Standards.

With reference to the construction industry, the auditor should be aware of the fact that the AICPA is debating the problem of making the use of percentage of completion accounting mandatory in the case of long-term contracts. If this rule is adopted, and if the auditor fails to convince the contractor to use it, then it might not be possible for the auditor to give even a qualified opinion. This is too significant an item to be explained away by the standard "except for" or "subject to" phrase.

The Auditor's Disclaimer of Opinion

The auditor in this case is saying that because of serious departures from auditing standards, he is not in a position to give an opinion. Omission of auditing standards, incomplete disclosures, restrictions imposed by the contractor, or lack of independence on the part of the auditor are examples of conditions that prevent the auditor from expressing an opinion.

The construction industry auditor should note that we have insisted on visits to job sites as an important requirement of the "due care" criterion of AICPA auditing standards. Please refer to the section in Chapter 8 entitled "Audit Pitfalls Peculiar to the Construction Industry." Failure to visit job sites must be considered a serious omission, as serious as failure to visit branch offices. Most authorities consider the latter serious enough to require a disclaimer of opinion.

The Auditor's Adverse Opinion

This event in ordinary audits is also rare. The auditor would have to be faced with a set of circumstances such that:

• He realizes that financial statements are not fairly presented in conformity with generally accepted accounting principles.
• He has run into a situation where the contractor refuses to present financial information fairly or to make adequate disclosures.
• He is sure of himself and can back up the serious charges underlying the adverse opinion.

In rendering an adverse opinion, the auditor gives his reasons in a separate paragraph. Then he expresses an adverse opinion, using language similar to the following:

> In our opinion, because of the effects of the matters discussed in the preceding paragraph, the financial statements referred to above do not present fairly, in conformity with generally accepted accounting principles, the financial position of X Company as of December 31, 19XX, or the results of its operations and changes in its financial position for the year then ended.[6]

Considering the usual pressure by banks and surety companies for a "clean" audit report, it is inconceivable that the auditor would not be able to convince the construction contractor to use generally accepted accounting principles in the presentation of financial statements. There are a couple of exceptions, depending on the final posture taken by the AICPA. For example:

• If the AICPA makes it mandatory to use the percentage of completion method on long-term contracts, the contractor might refuse to do so.
• If the AICPA makes it mandatory to eliminate certain costs in the numerator of the cost-to-cost fraction used in computing the percentage of completion, the contractor might refuse to go along for reasons discussed in Chapter 10.

If either of the two conditions develop, it is quite possible that the auditor would find himself in such a position that he would have no choice but to render an adverse opinion.

The Auditor's Use of Notes to the Financial Statements

Disclosure of significant accounting policies is a requirement of APB Opinion No. 22, and is usually presented as the first note or preceding the first note to the financial statements, although the choice of format is flexible.

The usual practice is to entitle the first note "Summary of Significant Accounting Policies," and to have it contain a statement that the contractor follows practices common to the construction industry and that he conforms with generally accepted accounting principles.

Subsequent notes will then disclose:

• Basis of consolidation
• Depreciation methods
• Amortization of intangibles
• Inventory pricing
• Translation of foreign currencies
• Recognition of profit on long-term construction contracts
• Recognition of revenue from franchising or leasing operations

SPECIAL DISCLOSURE REQUIREMENTS OF THE CONSTRUCTION AUDIT

In the construction industry, audit disclosure of the recognition of profit on long-term construction contracts means stating whether the percentage of completion or the completed-contract method has been used. The auditor should be alert, as pointed out elsewhere in this section, that the use of the percentage of completion method on long-term contracts might become mandatory.

Disclosure regarding percentage of completion must also be expanded to reveal whether the percentage was determined by use of the following methods:

- Cost-to-cost
- Architect or engineering estimates
- Other measures of performance

Finally, the auditor should state that, where significant differences were encountered between cost-to-cost and other measures of performance, the auditor reconciled these differences by means of task-cost analysis.

Special Disclosure Requirements for Percentage of Completion

Disclosure of methodology regarding percentage of completion contracts is not an AICPA requirement. However, as discussed in Chapter 10, its use is in keeping with the "due care" criterion of the AICPA standards of performance for the auditor. Disclosure is simply an assurance to the user of the financial statements that the auditor recognizes the consequences of imprecise determination of the percentage of completion method, and that his use of task-cost analysis is his way of assuring "due care."

HOW TO HANDLE INFORMATION TO ACCOMPANY FINANCIAL STATEMENTS

Information outside the basic financial statements consists of additional details that might be part of the accounting system, but conceivably could originate outside the system or even the firm.

If information accompanies the basic financial statements on which the auditor has expressed an opinion, there is an obligation to do something about it. Generally, this is what the auditor must do:

- Identify the accompanying information
- State whether it is additional analysis and not a required part of the basic financial statements

- Express an opinion on it or disclaim it, depending on whether or not auditing procedures to examine it have been used
- Either include it as part of the standard report or as a separate report

How the Auditor Handles Erroneous Accompanying Material

What happens if accompanying material misstates the facts? The auditor should attempt to revise it. If the contractor does not agree to the revision, the auditor either describes the misstatement, and of course gives no opinion, or refuses to include it in the audit report.

How Financial Statement Opinions Affect Accompanying Material

What if the auditor expresses an adverse opinion or disclaims an opinion on the basic financial statements? This will eliminate expressing an opinion on the accompanying information. To do so would mean rendering a piecemeal opinion, which of course is not allowed.

HOW THE AUDITOR HANDLES NONACCOUNTING INFORMATION

Finally, what about nonaccounting information? Normally, this means no opinion, although if the nonaccounting information is verifiable as a spin-off to the normal audit, the auditor might be in a position to express an opinion. For example, in the construction industry, a tabulation of employees by trade unions could easily be backed up by working papers supporting the examination of payroll records.

What to Do About Consolidated Statements

There is nothing in AICPA pronouncements pertaining to consolidated statements that does not apply *in toto* to the contractor. Therefore, nothing further will be said, except that the auditor should be aware of the fact that the same ground rules apply here as in other industries. Since the audit engagement usually entails the preparation of income tax returns, the auditor must also be aware that using consolidated income tax returns can help him take advantage of various carryovers such as the investment income tax credit and the net operating loss carryover of subsidiaries acquired by the contractor's corporation.

HOW THE AUDITOR'S REPORT CAN HELP THE OUTSIDER

For the construction industry auditor, there is good news and bad news insofar as the outsider is concerned. The bad news is that he will tear the audit report to pieces. The goods news is that he appreciates the report and knows what to do with it. What is so good about that? Simply that nothing pleases the auditor more than to have an appreciative audience.

What the Banker Is Looking for in the Audit Report

Accounting is the language of business, and most certainly a language the banker understands. Here is what the banker will be looking for:

- The usual ratios used by financial statement analysts.
- Accounts receivable, which are usually pledged to secure short-term loans. The banker will naturally want to know how good they are. An aging of accounts receivable in the notes portion of the financial statements will be a welcomed feature.
- Unbilled costs and earnings, at which figure the banker will cast a critical eye. The auditor, following task-cost analysis procedures, could provide the banker with assurances that over-optimism has not found its way into the financial statements.
- Changes in financial position; although the AICPA prefers the normal funds statement based on working capital changes, many contractors and their bankers favor presentation of this statement on a cash basis. The use of a net cash-flow figure for the period, as a reconciliation between beginning and ending cash balances, has great appeal and understandability for bankers and contractors nowadays when the cost of capital is so high.

What the Bonding People Are Looking for in the Audit Report

The principal concern of the security underwriters is simply this: Will the contractor perform or will we have to take over? Therefore, in addition to all the details that the banker is looking for, the bonding people will be looking toward performance indicators such as these:

- Analysis of Work in Progress. A job-by-job analysis must be made available to the surety underwriter, who, of all people, knows the danger, to both the contractor and the bonding company, of distortions caused by inflated percentage of completion figures. In addition to a detailed and complete analysis of work in progress, the auditor will want to comment, through appropriate notation, that he has employed task-cost analysis methods in the analysis of work in progress.

• Analysis of Completed Contracts. The gross profit percentage, reflected in the analysis of work in progress, will be more creditable to the bonding people if a similar track record is reflected by past performance. Therefore, an analysis of completed contracts is a valuable supplement to the bonding people.

• Working Capital. Because of the close tie-in between working capital and bonding capacity, any unusual item in current assets and current liabilities should be carefully explained in the notes accompanying the financial statements. Unbilled costs and earnings, and unearned billings over costs will be taken care of by the analysis of work in progress. However, an aging of accounts payable would be helpful.

A particularly touchy point with the bonding people is whether the contractor is current on the payroll withholding deposits. If there is a build-up in payroll withholding liabilities, the auditor should explain what is happening.

What the Investor's Looking for in the Audit Report

Quite frankly, construction firms attract few investors. Most construction firms are closely held corporations that evolved from the Mom and Pop mode. But for those firms that do go beyond this stage, here is what the investor will be looking for:

• What happened to my investment? The best place to find this out is the cash flow statement. The auditor should keep this in mind, and should be sure that all doubtful entries are explained.

• What about bonding company indemnification? Who else is involved besides the auditor? Again the auditor should clarify.

• Is the contractor going to make it? The investor is no different from the banker and the surety underwriter on this point. All have a stake in the contractor's well-being. Therefore, what interests the banker and the surety underwriter, as discussed above, will also interest the investor.

What Other Outside Users of the Audit Report Will Be Looking for

Outside users of the auditor's report include many others in addition to those discussed above. For example:

• Government entities who are required by policy or regulation to review an audited set of the contractor's financial statements. Situations will vary. Some Federal, state and municipal agencies require audited financial statements, either to accompany the bid forms or to be submitted as part of pre-qualification requirements. The auditor can be of great help to the contractor's personnel by showing them how to use the audit report, and if necessary, the audit working papers, to satisfy the needs of government entities.

• Suppliers desiring to set up a line of credit for the contractor will often ask for audited financial statements. Usually, the normal audit report will do, but the auditor should help the contractor meet the special demands of suppliers when they go beyond the contents of the audit report.

THE AUDIT REPORT ILLUSTRATED

Following is an illustration of the audit report. It is presented as an aid to understanding the points discussed in this chapter. However, it is not all-inclusive. And there are changes ahead, as indicated by several AICPA Exposure Drafts that are constantly in circulation.

The sample report, illustrated by Figures 11–1, 11–2, 11–3, 11–4, 11–5, and 11–6, together with accompanying notes (Figures 11–7 through 11–11), uses as an example a mechanical contracting firm, because heavy direct costs, together with substantial subcontractor and miscellaneous costs, are normal for such a

---

ASTRO MECHANICAL CONTRACTORS, INC.
and Its Wholly Owned Subsidiary,
KRIMP SHEET METAL CONTRACTORS, INC.

Table of Contents

Figure 11–1

firm. Opportunities to test the system for proper handling of these costs are present in abundance. Among these are:

- Work in progress
- Percentage of completion
- Task-cost analysis
- Uninstalled, nonunique material costs
- Estimated costs to complete jobs in progress

Finally, a mechanical contractor would be more apt to have a wholly owned subsidiary, something seldom found in other echelons of the construction hierarchy.

BENEDETTO AND COMPANY, INC.
Certified Public Accountants

The Shareholders and Board of Directors

Astro Mechanical Contractors

    We have examined the consolidated balance sheets of Astro Mechanical Contractors, Inc. and its wholly owned subsidiary, Krimp Sheet Metal Contractors, Inc., as of October 1, 19x1 and 19x2 and the related consolidated statements of income and retained earnings and changes in financial position for the years then ended. Our examinations were made in accordance with generally accepted auditing standards, and accordingly, included such tests of the accounting records and such other auditing procedures as we considered necessary in the circumstances.

    In our opinion, the financial statements referred to above present fairly the financial position of Astro Mechanical Contractors, Inc. and its wholly owned subsidiary, Krimp Sheet Metal Contractors, Inc. at October 31, 19x1 and 19x2, and the results of their operations and the changes in their financial position for the years then ended, in conformity with generally accepted accounting principles applied on a consistent basis.

Benedetto and Co Inc.

Certified Public Accountants

Kansas City, Missouri
December 18, 19x2

Figure 11–2

ASTRO MECHANICAL CONTRACTORS, INC.
Consolidated Balance Sheet
October 31, 19x2 and 19x1

Assets

	19x2	19x1
Current Assets		
Cash	$ 42,600	$ 38,300
Certificates of deposit	150,000	50,000
Contracts receivables (Note 2)	1,735,700	1,348,400
Unbilled costs and estimated earnings (Schedule 3)	75,300	63,800
Inventory at lower of cost or market on a first-in first-out basis (Note 3)	36,900	32,700
Prepaid expenses (Note 4)	15,600	12,300
Note receivable, subsidiary (Note 5)	30,000	50,000
Total Current Assets	2,086,100	1,595,500
Property and Equipment (Note 6)	523,100	426,500
Other Assets	1,500	1,500
Total Assets	2,610,700	2,023,500

LIABILITIES AND SHAREHOLDER'S EQUITY

	19x2	19x1
Current Liabilities		
Notes payable (Note 7)	131,700	204,200
Accounts payable (Note 8)	728,600	768,200
Unearned billings over costs (Schedule 3)	46,200	52,800
Accrued income taxes payable	355,000	134,500
Other accrued liabilities (Note 9)	12,500	12,600
Deferred income taxes (Note 12)	100,300	67,200
Add: Installment payments due in one year	125,200	125,200
Total Current Liabilities	1,499,500	1,364,700
Long-Term Debt		
Real estate mortgage (Note 10)	150,000	175,200
Equipment mortgages (Note 11)	100,000	200,000
Less: Installment payments due in one year	(125,200)	(125,200)
Total Long-Term Debt	124,800	250,000
Total Liabilities	1,624,300	1,614,700

Figure 11–3

Shareholders' Equity

Common stock, $1 par value, 300,000 authorized, 250,000 issued and outstanding	250,000	250,000
Retained earnings	736,400	158,800
Total Shareholders' Equity	986,400	408,800
Total Liabilities and Equity	2,610,700	2,023,500

The accompanying notes are an integral part of these financial statements.

Figure 11–3, Cont'd

ASTRO MECHANICAL CONTRACTORS, INC.
Consolidated Statement of Income and Retained Earnings
Years Ended October 31, 19x2 and 19x1

	19x2	19x1
CONTRACT REVENUE	$10,404,200	$8,090,700
COST OF CONTRACT REVENUE	9,051,600	7,367,200
GROSS PROFIT	1,352,600	723,500
SELLING, GENERAL AND ADMINISTRATIVE EXPENSE—SCHED. 4	424,200	329,800
INCOME FROM OPERATIONS	928,400	393,700
OTHER INCOME		
Gain on sale of equipment	6,500	2,300
Interest income	4,600	3,090
Total other income	11,100	5,390
TOTAL INCOME	939,500	399,090
OTHER DEDUCTIONS		
Interest expense	42,000	27,000
NET INCOME BEFORE INCOME TAXES	897,500	372,090
INCOME TAXES (Note 13)		
Federal	320,500	120,100
State	34,500	14,400
Total	355,000	134,500
Net income (per share: $2.17 19x2 and $.95, 19x1)	542,500	237,590
RETAINED EARNINGS BEGINNING OF YEAR	218,900	(78,790)
LESS DIVIDENDS	25,000	
RETAINED EARNINGS END OF YEAR	786,400	158,800

The accompanying notes are an integral part of these financial statements.

Figure 11–4

ASTRO MECHANICAL CONTRACTORS, INC.
Consolidated Statement of Changes in Financial Position
Years Ended October 31, 19x2 and 19x1

	19x2	*19x1*
Source of funds:		
From operations:		
Net income	$542,500	$237,500
Charges (credits) to income not involving		
cash and cash equivalents		
Depreciation and amortization	51,600	41,500
Deferred income taxes	33,100	10,500
Gain on sale of equipment	(6,500)	(2,300)
	620,700	287,200
Proceeds from equipment sold	15,000	15,000
Net charges (credits) to income resulting from		
costs and estimated earnings on		
uncompleted contracts	(18,100)	3,600
Increase in accrued income taxes payable	220,500	72,100
Decrease in note receivable, subsidiary	20,000	5,000
Total	858,100	382,900
Use of funds		
Increase in contracts receivable	387,300	220,000
Increase in inventory	4,200	1,300
Increase in prepaid expenses	3,300	200
Increase in property and equipment	96,600	15,900
Decrease in notes payable	72,500	20,600
Decrease in accounts payable	39,600	5,600
Decrease in other accrued liabilities	100	500
Decrease in real estate mortgage	25,200	25,200
Decrease in equipment mortgages	100,000	31,800
Increase in dividends	25,000	
Total	753,800	321,100
Increase (decrease) in cash and certificates of		
deposit for the year	104,300	61,800
Cash and certificates of deposit		
Beginning of year	88,300	26,500
End of year	192,600	88,300

The accompanying notes are an integral part of these financial statements.

Figure 11–5

	October 31			October 31
	19x2			19x1
ASTRO MECHANICAL CONTRACTORS, INC. and Its Wholly Owned Subsidiary, KRIMP SHEET METAL CONTRACTORS, INC. Earnings from Contracts Year Ended October 31, 19x2 **Schedule 1**	Revenues Earned	Cost of Revenues	Gross Profit	Gross Profit
Contracts completed during year	$ 2,435,700	$1,786,900	$ 648,800	$420,000
Contracts in progress at year-end	7,836,500	7,254,700	581,800	288,500
Management contracts, fees earned	132,000	10,000	122,000	15,000
Unallocated indirect and warranty costs				
Minority interest in joint venture				
Charges on prior year contracts				
	10,404,200	9,051,600	1,352,600	723,500

Figure 11–6

ASTRO MECHANICAL CONTRACTORS, INC.
and Its Fully Owned Subsidiary,
KRIMP SHEET METAL CONTRACTORS, INC.

Schedule 2

Contracts Completed
Year Ended October 31, 19x2

Contract Number	Type	Contract Totals			Before November 1, 19x2			During Year Ended October 31, 19x2		
		Revenue Earned	Cost of Revenues	Gross Profit	Revenue Earned	Cost of Revenues	Gross Profit	Revenue Earned	Cost of Revenues	Gross Profit
1008	A	$2,006,600	$1,697,600	$ 309,000	$1,059,200	$ 870,000	$189,200	$ 947,400	$ 827,600	$119,800
1011	B	500,000	420,000	80,000	185,000	150,000	35,000	315,000	270,000	45,000
1402	A	1,200,000	641,700	558,300	819,300	527,500	291,800	380,700	114,200	266,500
1621	B	809,000	627,500	181,500	160,500	120,500	40,000	648,500	507,000	141,500
Small Contracts		160,100	80,100	80,000	16,000	12,000	4,000	144,100	68,100	76,000
		$4,675,700	$3,466,900	$1,208,800	$2,240,000	$1,680,000	$560,000	$2,435,700	$1,786,900	$648,800

Contract Types
A—Fixed Price
B—Cost-Plus-Fee

Figure 11-7

ASTRO MECHANICAL CONTRACTORS, INC.
Analysis of Work in Progress
October 31, 19x2

Schedule 3

	Total Contract	Billings to Date	Costs to Date	Billings Over Costs	Costs Over Billings	Estimated Cost to Complete	Estimated Gross Profit	Percent Complete	Gross Profit Earned	Billings Over Costs Earned	Billings Over Costs Unearned	Unbilled Costs & Earnings
Beverly Heights Bldg.	$ 1,071,000	$ 822,000	$ 831,000	$	$9,000	$ 240,000	–0–	78	–0–	$	$	$ 9,000
Home Base, Inc.	500,000	320,000	312,000	8,000		178,000	10,000	64	6,400	6,400	1,600	
Real Place I	1,900,000	864,600	755,500	109,100		786,500	358,000	49	175,400	109,100		66,300
Tertiary Refining Co.	16,000,000	5,754,600	5,310,000	444,600		9,578,900	1,111,100	36	400,000	400,000	44,600	
Total	$19,471,000	$7,761,200	$7,208,500	$561,700	$9,000	$10,783,400	$1,479,100	40[a]	$581,800[b]	$515,500	$46,200	$75,300

(a) Based on total cost-to-cost, resulting in aggregate percent complete.
(b) Sum of gross profit earned for each job and not a product of aggregate percent complete.

Figure 11-8

ASTRO MECHANICAL CONTRACTORS, INC.
and Its Wholly Owned Subsidiary,
KRIMP SHEET METAL CONTRACTORS, INC. **Schedule 4**

Selling, General and Administrative Expense

	19x2	19x1
Officer salaries	$106,000	$ 82,500
Other salaries	120,000	95,200
Advertising	3,600	3,000
Auto and truck	25,500	18,000
Bad debts	3,500	2,700
Company meetings	2,100	1,900
Contributions	1,300	1,800
Depreciation	51,600	41,500
Dues and subscriptions	5,100	4,100
Entertainment and travel	10,200	5,000
Equipment rental	22,500	17,500
Freight	1,500	1,200
Insurance	9,800	7,500
Licenses and permits	6,200	4,800
Maintenance	1,800	1,400
Office expense	6,100	5,900
Taxes, other than income	6,900	5,200
Telephone	3,800	2,900
Outside services	8,900	6,800
Professional services	9,800	7,600
Tool expense	10,000	7,800
Utilities	8,000	5,500
	$424,200	$329,800

Figure 11–9

BENEDETTO AND COMPANY, INC.
Certified Public Accountants

The Shareholders and Board of Directors

Astro Mechanical Contractors

Our examination of the basic financial statements presented in the preceding section of this report were made primarily to form an opinion on such financial statements taken as a whole. The additional information, contained in the following pages, is not considered essential for the fair presentation of the financial position of Astro Mechanical Contractors, Inc., the results of its operations, or the changes in its financial position in conformity with generally accepted accounting principles. However, the following data were subjected to the audit procedures applied in the examinations of the basic financial statements, and in our opinion are fairly stated in all material respects in relation to the basic financial statements taken as a whole.

Benedetto and Co. Inc.

Certified Public Accountants

Kansas City, Missouri
December 18, 19x2

Figure 11-10

ASTRO MECHANICAL CONTRACTORS, INC.
Notes to Consolidated Financial Statements
October 31, 19x2 and 19x1

1. SIGNIFICANT ACCOUNTING POLICIES

Primary Functions and Operating Cycle

The company is a mechanical contractor engaged in plumbing, heating, air conditioning, process piping, and ventilating for commercial, industrial, and institutional construction. Work is obtained either through the bidding process or negotiation. It consists of fixed-price contracts, cost-plus-fee contracts, fixed-price contracts with incentive and penalty provisions, and project manager contracts.

The company's fully owned subsidiary takes care of the sheet metal and ventilation work. Occasionally the company will joint venture a large

Figure 11-11

job with another mechanical contractor, although at present no such arrangements are in force.

Because of the wide variety of work done, there is no real operating cycle. However, the company is geared to perform large contracts extending over a period of two years or more. It is company policy to go after such contracts.

In view of company policy stressing long-term contracts, it would seem that elimination of current and noncurrent classification of balance sheet items would be indicated. However, such classification has been retained for two reasons. First, the bulk of the contracts are still completed in less than two years. Second, working capital evaluation essential to outsiders pretty well dictates a current-noncurrent division of assets and liabilities.

Principles of Consolidation

Included in the consolidated financial statements is the company's fully-owned subsidiary, Krimp Sheet Metal Contractors, Inc. The company has eliminated significant inter-company transactions.

Revenue and Cost Recognition

The percentage of completion method is the basis for recognition of revenue on fixed-price and modified fixed-price, long-term contracts. Management insists on the use of the cost-to-cost method to determine percentage of completion, and we agree since we feel that it is simpler, more understandable, and easier to verify than other measurements of performance. Estimated costs to complete a job are determined by task-cost analysis techniques, by which each task remaining to be accomplished is analyzed and priced. Since the cost-to-cost function consists of cost to date as the numerator, and cost to date plus estimated costs to complete as the denominator, the percentage of completion is automatically adjusted for cost efficiencies or deficiencies via the estimated cost to complete factor.

Cost-plus-fee contracts are measured by adding pro-rata fees to costs incurred. Contract management projects are recognized only as the fee is earned and billed, as specified in the contract.

Job costs include labor, material, equipment, miscellaneous, and subcontractor costs, as well as certain indirect costs such as supervision, travel, supplies, tools, repairs, and depreciation when direct allocation to jobs can be readily determined.

Selling, general, and administrative expenses are charged to the period in which they are incurred.

A month-by-month analysis of work in progress, utilizing task-cost analysis of work remaining to be done, is used to determine provisions for estimated losses. Such analysis is shown in Schedule 3. It is the basis for the current asset, "unbilled costs and estimated earnings" and the current liability "unearned billings over costs." Increases to the current asset increases contract revenue, and increases to the current liability decreases contract revenue.

Figure 11–11, Cont'd

Project incentives and claims are recognized only upon reasonable assurance of realization.

Property and Equipment

The company uses straight-line depreciation and amortization over the useful life of the assets. Management is conscious of the trade-off between useful life and the investment credit, with preference given to maximization of the investment credit.

Pension Plan

Nonunion employees are covered by the company plan. Union employees are covered by their respective union plans, to which the company contributes in accordance with the various union contracts. Costs, including amortization of prior service costs and accrued costs, are charged to earnings.

Translation of Foreign Currencies

No foreign contract revenue has been recorded during the current or previous year. However, prior to that time, the company has done work in Mexico through joint venture with a Mexican firm. See Note 14, SUBSEQUENT EVENTS.

Income Taxes

The company and its subsidiary use the completed-contract method for tax purposes and the percentage of completion method for financial statements. Deferred taxes resulting from timing differences are provided for in the financial statements.

2. CONTRACT RECEIVABLES

	October 31 19x2	October 31 19x1
Contract receivables		
Billed		
Completed contracts	$ 261,000	$ 207,600
Contracts in progress	989,800	700,200
Retained	451,600	417,500
Unbilled	59,600	43,300
	$1,762,000	$1,368,600
Less: Allowance for doubtful collections	26,300	20,200
	$1,735,700	$1,348,400

A total of $11,500 of the October 31, 19x2 receivables in the retained category will not be collected until after the end of the next fiscal year.

Figure 11–11, Cont'd

3. INVENTORY PRICING

Inventories are stated at the lower of cost or market. The first-in first-out method is used. Excess material is credited to the job generating it and picked up in inventory at cost. There is a review of inventories every six months; obsolete items are sold for junk.

4. PREPAID EXPENSES

	19x2	19x1
Prepaid insurance	$10,500	$ 9,300
Prepaid equipment rental	5,100	3,000
	$15,600	$12,300

5. NOTES RECEIVABLE, SUBSIDIARY COMPANY

Note Dated October 31, 19x1, principal amount of $50,000.00, interest at 12 percent, monthly payments of $1,666.67, plus accrued interest, began November 30, 19x1. Maturity date is April 30, 19x4.

6. PROPERTY AND EQUIPMENT

	19x1		
Autos and trucks	$ 50,000	$ 10,000	$ 40,000
Machinery and equipment	196,500	85,600	110,900
Office equipment	8,000	2,000	6,000
Land	7,000		7,000
Building	312,500	49,900	262,600
	$574,000	$147,500	$426,500

	19x2		
Autos and trucks	$ 62,000	$ 12,000	$ 50,000
Machinery and equipment	261,100	55,000	206,100
Office equipment	13,000	3,000	10,000
Land	7,000		7,000
Building	312,500	62,500	250,000
	$655,600	$132,500	$523,100

7. NOTES PAYABLE

Ninety-day notes payable at 1½ points over prime rates are due the Third National Bank of Kansas City, Missouri. Selected contract receivables are used as collateral.

8. ACCOUNTS PAYABLE

Accounts payable include retainage due to subcontractors. Total is $135,400 as of October 31, 19x2 and $242,700 as of October 31, 19x1.

Figure 11–11, Cont'd

These are amounts held back from progress billings, pending satisfactory completion of jobs. These amounts will be paid within one year, with the exception of $3,900 representing retainage on a job started in August 19x2.

9. OTHER ACCRUED LIABILITIES

	19x2	*19x1*
Payroll withholding	$ 1,700	$ 4,900
Payroll taxes	1,000	2,200
Accrued interest	9,800	5,500
	$12,500	$12,600

10. REAL ESTATE MORTGAGE

Mortgage secured by real estate due in monthly installments of $2,100 plus interest at 10 percent through October 15, 19x8.

11. EQUIPMENT MORTGAGES

These are collateralized by equipment and are due in monthly installments of $8,333.33 plus interest at 10 percent through October 31, 19x3.

12. INCOME TAXES AND DEFERRED INCOME TAXES

	October 31 19x2	*October 31 19x1*
Currently payable, net of investment credits of $9,600 and $1,500	$230,000	$ 90,000
Deferred		
Contract related	123,000	43,000
Property and equipment related	2,000	1,500
	$355,000	$134,500

As of October 31 of respective years, deferred income taxes consisted of:

	October 31 19x2	*October 31 19x1*
Contract related	$ 96,800	$ 64,400
Property and equipment related	3,500	2,800
	$100,300	$ 67,200

Figure 11–11, Cont'd

13. BACKLOG

Balance October 31, 19x1	$12,300,000
Contract adjustments	895,000
New contracts year ended October 31, 19x2	7,061,200
	$20,256,200
Less: contract revenue, year ended October 31, 19x2	10,404,200
Balance October 31, 19x2	$ 9,852,000

14. SUBSEQUENT EVENTS

November 1, 19x2 and December 17, 19x2, the company entered into construction contracts in the amount of $2,200,000, including a joint venture with a Mexican firm totalling $1,010,000.

Figure 11–11, Cont'd

GETTING READY FOR THE TAX RETURN AND FOR TAX PLANNING

Practically all audit engagements require the preparation of income tax returns. While the next chapter is not all-inclusive, it will serve to stimulate the auditor into further research and updating. It will do the same thing for the tax practitioner, whether he be the auditor or someone else. In addition, it will identify pitfalls and how to avoid them, as well as opportunities for tax planning and how to take advantage of them.

Notes: Chapter 11

1. STATEMENT ON AUDITING STANDARDS NO. 29, *Reporting on Information Accompanying the Basic Financial Statements in Auditor-Submitted Documents,* p. 3, Copyright © 1980 by the American Institute of Certified Public Accountants, Inc.

2. STATEMENT ON AUDITING STANDARDS NO. 30, *Reporting on Internal Control,* p. 1, Copyright © 1980 by the American Institute of Certified Public Accountants, Inc.

3. CODIFICATION OF STATEMENT ON AUDITING STANDARDS, *Introduction,* p. 3, Copyright © 1977 by the American Institute of Certified Public Accountants, Inc.

4. APB OPINION NO. 22, *Disclosure of Accounting Policies,* p. 3, Copyright © 1972 by the American Institute of Certified Public Accountants, Inc.

5. STATEMENT ON AUDITING STANDARDS, *Reports on Audited Financial Statements,* p. 210, Copyright © 1977 by the American Institute of Certified Public Accountants, Inc.

6. *Ibid.,* p. 223.

12

TAX TECHNIQUES FOR THE CONSTRUCTION CONTRACTOR

No sooner had the Economic Recovery Tax Act of 1981, better known as ERTA, been passed, the biggest tax cut of them all, than we had to face the Tax Equity and Fiscal Responsibility Act of 1982, better known as TEFRA, the biggest tax increase ever passed. Other than questioning the wisdom of 180-degree turns in tax policy, one wonders whether it is possible to present tax tips for anybody, in this book or any book. But let's not give up.

This chapter is designed to give the tax practitioner tax tips—not complete guidance—on tax matters particularly troublesome to the construction contractor. If the reader is further inspired to research and update, so much the better. Updating is particularly significant, since the House Ways and Means Committee, as well as the Senate Finance Committee, are a restless bunch. Reading this chapter is only the beginning. The tax practitioner must keep up with the activities of these two committees.

The Internal Revenue Code casts a long shadow of uncertainty over every business decision, including those of the contractor. Lifting the shadow in its entirety is beyond the scope of this book. However, the gloom can be dispelled to a certain extent in those situations that are particularly troublesome to the contractor. How will this be done? By looking at those situations and providing useful, practical tax tips, along with the accounting records needed to back them up. The approach will be to guide the practitioner, and through him the contractor, around pitfalls encountered not only in tax strategy, but also in the daily decision-making process. Many a tax problem has had an innocuous beginning. The practitioner who is aware of these pitfalls will be able to do a better job in helping the contractor stay out of trouble.

GETTING READY FOR THE IRS AUDIT

Audits by the IRS, like Judgment Day, come when least expected. Getting ready for them and performing effectively during the audit itself are both desirable objectives. Both will be covered in this chapter, with heavy reliance on record-keeping techniques detailed in previous chapters.

The Importance of Record Keeping in Tax Management

One more word about record keeping: Certain tax situations require accounting specifics that the practitioner should be aware of and should crank right into the accounting system. The main idea is to avoid crash reconstruction projects when the IRS comes calling and starts asking questions for which there are no ready answers. What these accounting specifics are and how to deal with them will be covered in the sections that follow.

Working with the Internal Revenue Code

It is a good idea for the practitioner, and even the contractor, to get used to talking and thinking about tax problems in terms of pertinent sections of the Internal Revenue Code. Why? Because this is the common language of professionals in and out of the Internal Revenue Service. Regulations, rulings, announcements, court cases, legislative action, committee reports, and legislative history— all of these revolve around specific sections of the code. And all of these segments must be looked at. For example, the researcher will often find that committee reports and legislative history, revealing Congressional intent, will provide the clinching argument in squaring off against the IRS auditor.

For the contractor, tax section approach aids understanding and discussion. For the practitioner, such an approach is indispensable for intelligent discussion with the IRS, and also for updating and research.

Opportunity vs. Pitfall Approach to Tax Planning

The presentation that follows will show sections of the Internal Revenue Code having special impact on the construction industry. These are presented with respective tax strategy opportunities as well as corresponding pitfalls. Please note that this is not an all-inclusive presentation, and considering the state of flux in the tax scene, it is definitely not the last word.

Working with Investment Credit

Section 38, Investment in Certain Depreciable Property, lays down the general rule that a credit against income tax is allowed for qualified investments in certain depreciable property. Specifics concerning definitions, allowances, limitations, and recapture are in Code Sections 46 through 48.

Opportunities
• For the contractor who invests heavily in machinery and equipment, the investment credit presents an opportunity to shelter corporate income, and in the case of tax-option Subchapter S corporations, personal income. See Section 1371.

• The contractor can look into opportunities offered by generous investment credit and cost recovery deductions allowed for the rehabilitation of qualified buildings and certain historic structures.

• For the high bracket contractor-stockholder of a Subchapter S corporation, the practitioner must consider the possible trade-off between the investment credit and the Accelerated Cost Recovery System (ACRS). It might be that the various opportunities for accelerated cost recovery might prove more attractive than taking the investment credit. For example, ACRS permitted by Section 168, along with the decision to expense certain depreciable assets made possible by Section 179, might be better than the investment credit. The investment credit takes on a new look, as shown in the section labeled "Pitfalls," below. But Section 179 write-offs were not affected by EFRA.

• For the contractor working with used components that are absorbed into the fabrication process, it is good to know that this use will not necessarily disqualify the finished product as a new item. The practitioner will find court cases in which the used property limitation was successfully bypassed with tremendous potential tax savings; for example, in the fabrication of oil and gas-drilling rigs.

Pitfalls
• Beware of new limitations and requirements to reduce the basis of property by 50 percent of the investment credit, prescribed by TEFRA.

• There is an option to forgo the 50 percent basis adjustment if you reduce your investment percentage by 2 points; for example, the 10 percent investment credit can be reduced to 8 percent; and the 6 percent investment credit can be reduced to 4 percent. There is also a new investment credit treatment, as well as a special ACRS for safe-harbor leasing arrangements.

• The investment credit is subject to the "at risk" provisions of Section 465.

• The practitioner should be aware of the latest limits on used property if the used property status cannot be bypassed.

• The contractor should understand the consequences of investment credit recapture, if the property is disposed of before the time period specified in claiming the credit, as well as in certain reorganizations.

• The investment credit and accelerated cost recovery can take a nasty turn when exposed to Sections 55, 56, 57, and 58, dealing with the alternative minimum tax. If the contractor succeeds in lightening or even eliminating tax liability by means of a passed-through investment credit, he or she should hold up the celebration until the practitioner figures the alternative minimum tax. In effect, the IRS says, "Okay, you've succeeded in reducing your taxable income via various credits including the investment credit, capital gains, and other such tax preference items. Now let's see what's left after we make several adjustments."

What's left might be a huge amount of income subject to the alternative minimum tax. TEFRA, if anything, has expanded the scope of includable items. So, while the contractor might have reduced or even escaped taxes by resorting to such things as capital gain deduction, accelerated depreciation on real property, accelerated depreciation on leased personal property, amortization of certified pollution control facilities in excess of normal depreciation, percentage depletion in excess of adjusted basis, and intangible drilling costs, he has to add them back and make other adjustments to arrive at the total that is subject to the alternative minimum tax. What's left, after all these adjustments, is subject to a 10 percent alternative minimum tax for amounts up to $20,000, and 20 percent for amounts over $20,000. In certain cases, this could double the amount of tax due, as compared to the regular tax.

Dealing with Work Incentive Programs

Section 40, Expenses of Work Incentive Programs, covers the general rule, and specifics are found in Sections 50A, 50B, 51, 52, and 53. A related type of credit is the targeted jobs credit of Section 480C.

Opportunities
• Nonunion contractors might find the generous tax credit quite attractive.
• Union contractors might as well forget the WIN and targeted job credits, since they are not free to hire such people.

Pitfalls
• Targeted jobs must meet certain rigid specifications.
• The hazards of employing such people in construction work are so formidable that they completely offset tax advantages.

Executive Bonuses Could Mean Gross Income Problems

Section 61, Gross Income Defined, is a sleeper. The practitioner might think that everybody knows what constitutes gross income. However, while advising the contractor on year-end executive bonuses, the practitioner might run into problems generated by Sections 83, 162, and 267.

Opportunities

• The usual objective is to permit the accrual basis corporation to accrue and deduct, while the cash basis recipient defers income until it is actually received.

• The IRS might say, "You can't have your cake and eat it," but the fact is that careful planning and meticulous execution of the plan will accomplish just that—accrual and deduction for the corporation, and deferral for the cash-basis taxpayer.

Pitfalls

• Section 83, Property Transferred in Connection with Performance of Services, requires that the fair market value of such property be included as gross income by the person receiving it. The definition of property is pretty broad and includes promissory notes. Whether or not the property is subject to substantial risks of forfeiture will determine whether it is nontransferable, and therefore not a taxable event. The practitioner should tread carefully in this very technical area.

• Section 162, Trade or Business Expenses, deals with deductibility of such expenses, including a reasonable allowance for salaries, or other compensation for personal services rendered. The key word is "reasonable." If the compensation is not out of line with personal contributions to a profitable company situation, then it is reasonable.

• Section 267, Losses, Expenses, and Interest with Respect to Transactions between Related Taxpayers, knocks out deductions otherwise allowed by Section 162, unless certain conditions are met when dealing with related taxpayers. There is no deduction allowed:

(1) If the bonus is not paid within 2½ months after the close of the corporation's tax year,

(2) If the recipient is on a cash basis and receives payment in a year different from that of the corporation, and

(3) If, at the close of the corporation's tax year or 2½ months thereafter, the recipient is a related taxpayer as defined in this section.

All three of the above conditions must exist before the accrual is disallowed.

• Objectives can be jeopardized by making the obligation to pay in the form of a note having fair market value, say one that is collateralized, unless operating under the 2½ month rule of Section 267.

• Another pitfall is failure to make the bonus "reasonable," thereby disqualifying it as a Section 162 deduction.

• The practitioner, thinking he's on safe grounds, might fail to research Sections 61, 83, 167, and 172 thoroughly, thereby inviting a calamitous disallowance.

Tax Pros and Cons of Group-Term Life Insurance

Section 79, Group-Term Life Insurance Purchased for Employees, prescribes ground rules for allowing deductions to the contractor while the employees recognize no income.

Opportunities
• TEFRA introduces new nondiscriminatory requirements. Generally, it takes away key employee discrimination by which expanded coverage could be worked out for key employees.
• If the plan survives new nondiscrimination requirements, the contractor can deduct the cost of group-term life insurance, and such cost is not income to the employee, provided the policy does not exceed the statutory limitation.
• Formulas for eligibility and computation of the tax-free insurance are precise but not overly complex.
• For the union contractor, this is an opportunity to provide nonunion employees with tax-free group-term life insurance.
• For the high profit contractor, this is another employee benefit that can act as an effective and valid tax shelter.

Pitfalls
• The practitioner should work out details of the plan with a qualified and reputable insurance agent, preferably a CLU (Certified Life Underwriter), to make sure that no problem is encountered by omitting union employees. Normally, these employees are covered by group-term insurance plans of their own, included in the union contract.
• Reporting requirements based on formulas prescribed in Section 79 must be met regarding insurance coverage in excess of the tax-free limit.
• The contractor must comply with age-bracket formulas for figuring gross income to employees, for any premiums representing that portion of the insurance coverage that is over the tax-free limit. Unfortunately, tables which determine nontaxable portions are out of date and unrealistically low. The IRS is working on updates, but in the interim, this could be a problem.

Pros and Cons of Health Insurance Plans

Section 106, Contributions by Employer to Accident and Health Plans, deals with conditions required to assure deductibility.

Opportunities
• Generally, contributions are deductible to the contractor and do not constitute income to the employees.
• These plans can be effective morale boosters for nonunion employees not

otherwise covered by such plans. Especially attractive to employees is the fact that TEFRA raised the old 3 percent floor for medical expense deduction to 5 percent of adjusted gross income. In effect, medical expense deductibility is a thing of the past in all but catastrophic cases. Therefore, employer accident and health plans might be the only way for the employee to overcome the effects of the new, expanded, nondeductible limits.

Pitfalls
• If the plan is covered by outside insurance, nondiscrimination requirements have been greatly relaxed; but if the plan is a self-insured plan, nondiscrimination requirements and special conditions are many, and the practitioner should know exactly where his client fits in.
• One of the peculiarities is that payment to a fund or a trust will satisfy general rules, but payments to accident and health plans offering options for accumulated sick leave payments will trigger gross income to the employee.

What the Contractor Should Know About Furnished Meals or Lodging

Section 119, Meals or Lodging Furnished for the Convenience of the Employer, will often apply to the contractor. For example, he will often run into situations in which he will furnish meals to his employees. More rarely, he will furnish lodging. Furnishing meals can be a common occurrence. Preparing a bid is often a deadline-fighting experience in which meals are brought in while everyone works right up to bid time. Lodging is sometimes furnished at the job site, sometimes at the contractor's trailer house.

Opportunities
• Meals are deductible and are not gross income to the employee if furnished on the business premises for the convenience of the contractor.
• Lodging must meet the test of (1) being furnished on the business premises, (2) for the convenience of the employer, and (3) accepted as a condition of employment.
• If the above conditions are met, IRS regulations permit exclusion from the employer's gross income those charges made to employees for meals and lodging; for example, through payroll withholding.
• Also, if such conditions are met, the value of meals and lodging is excluded from the employees' gross income.
• The example in Regulations cites construction projects at a remote job site in Alaska, but conditions could fit other less remote job sites.

Pitfalls
• Employer-furnished meals are deductible under conditions cited above, but cash reimbursement for meals has unfortunately become such an issue that

the IRS has challenged the nonincome feature right up to the Supreme Court. See R. J. Kowalski, Section 434 U.S. 77 77-2 USTC. Also see "Tax Consequences of Day-to-Day Decisions," this chapter.

• Travel pay is often a part of the union contract and usually a nontax item, although it has drifted back and forth from the nontax category.

• Reimbursable travel expense is no real problem, provided there is reporting and accountability by the employee. Meals and lodging paid for overnight travel can be reimbursed tax free to the employee, and will pass the "as if" reporting test if the daily reimbursement does not exceed prescribed per diem rates. But see Section 274 for other conditions to be met.

Tax Tips on Construction Period Interest and Taxes

Section 189, Amortization of Real Property, Construction Period Interest and Taxes, requires capitalization of these two expenses, normally deductible under Section 162. The construction period extends from the beginning of construction and ends with the property being turned over to the owner or offered for sale. Taxpayers affected are (1) the individual owners, (2) tax option or Subchapter S Corporations, (3) personal holding companies, and (4) estates and trusts. Property affected originally included several categories, but now seems to be settling down to only residential real property, with low income housing exempted. However, EFRA expanded the rule to include the construction of nonresidential real property by regular corporations.

Opportunities
• We are dealing with the contractor in the additional role as developer.

• The nondeductibility of construction interest and taxes affects the contractor-developer in many ways: (1) individually, (2) as a recipient of pass-through transactions of tax option corporations, (3) under conditions resulting from personal holding company status, and (4) with respect to the peculiar consequences of estates and trusts, as well as nonresidential construction by regular corporations.

• Section 190, Expenditures to Remove Architectural and Transportation Barriers to the Handicapped and Elderly, permits expenditures to be treated as a deduction and therefore should be considered.

• Section 191, Amortization of Certain Rehabilitation Expenditures for Certified Historical Structures, must also be considered, since amortization over a compressed period of time is permitted.

Pitfalls
• Failure to recognize the changing role of the construction contractor when he becomes an owner-developer.

• Failure to examine in detail code, regulations, and cases under Sections 189, 190, and 191.

Why Travel and Entertainment Expenses Are Disallowed

Section 274, Disallowance of Certain Entertainment, Etc. Expenses, in effect states that entertainment activities should be tied into a bona fide business discussion, and entertainment facilities should be used in connection with such activities.

Opportunities

• Several exceptions and documentation requirements should be brought to the attention of the contractor, who often obtains his best contracts as a result of activity taking place outside the estimating room.

• Contractors successful in getting negotiated work are heavy investors in "Entertainment, Etc. Expenses," and can get around the negative provisions of Section 274, provided they observe certain precautions.

• The practitioner who can offer expert guidance through the maze of Section 274 technicalities can help establish company policy that will assure deductibility of travel, entertainment, and gifts, usually lumped together under the common title of travel and entertainment (T & E).

• Dues to social, athletic, or sporting clubs are treated as items with respect to facilities; the use of facilities must satisfy the rule of use under specified conditions, and should be used primarily for business. The word "primarily" means more than 50 percent.

• Tax strategy for travel and entertainment (T & E) must assure record-keeping that reflects: (1) the amount of such expense, (2) the time, place, or description of the gift, (3) the business purpose, (4) the names of persons entertained or to whom gifts were given, and (5) the business relationship to the taxpayer of the recipients. Notations can be made on the credit card ticket to satisfy the record-keeping requirements of Section 274.

• If travel is lumped together with entertainment expenses during the IRS audit, the practitioner must handle it separately since substantiation requirements differ.

• Business purpose of the travel expense can usually be established without too much trouble, provided care is taken to weed out personal benefits.

• Cost of spouse's travel may or may not be deductible. Some cases show a surprising allowance for the spouse's travel, depending on the business relevance of the spouse's presence.

• Special deductibility conditions govern travel outside the United States.

• Entertainment before or after a substantial business discussion is an exception to the "directly related to business" requirement. In other words, such entertainment qualifies as a deduction.

• Another exception to the general rule permits deduction for business meals in surroundings generally considered to be conducive to business discussions. The key word is *conducive*. In fact, an actual business discussion is not required, and under special conditions, the contractor could sponsor an event and would not even have to be present.

• Of special interest to the contractor is reimbursement for travel under the $44 rule.

  • Normally, an employee accounts for expenses and is reimbursed. The result is a deduction for the employer and no taxable income to the employee.

  • If the per diem allowance does not exceed the greater of $44 or the maximum per diem rate authorized to be paid by the Federal government in the locality in which travel is performed, an accounting will be deemed to have been made.

  • This same rule applies to a mileage allowance not in excess of 20 cents per mile.

  • Careful updating is required before relying on this rule, since the original Revenue Ruling (80–62) has been amended many times.

Pitfalls

• With so many technicalities and exceptions, not to mention the common travel and entertainment (T & E) practice of spending first and worrying about it later, pitfalls are a real and constant presence.

• Use of country club facilities by the contractor's spouse and children can tilt the personal use factor up to or over the 50 percent mark, so that the "primarily for business" requirement cannot be satisfied. Therefore, all expenses related to country club facilities will be disallowed.

• The more than 50 percent rule required for qualification as primarily for business use for company automobiles and airplanes is also put in jeopardy by heavy personal use. The measurement for automobiles is the number of miles driven and for airplanes, hours flown.

• Company sponsored recreational facilities lose deductibility for that portion representing use by anyone having a 10-percent or greater interest in the company.

• Gifts are limited to $25 per year, per person.

• Foreign travel has limitations as to time, frequency, and personal benefits.

• There is no way that lavish or extravagant entertainment can be assigned a business purpose.

• Business meals taken in noisy entertainment facilities will fail the test of surroundings generally considered to be conducive to business discussions.

Problems of Transfers to Controlled Corporations

Section 351, Transfer to Corporation Controlled by Transferor, states the general rule that if a person or persons transferring property to a corporation maintains control immediately after the transfer, no gain or loss is recognized.

Control is defined in Section 368(c) as ownership of at least 80 percent of the voting stock issued, and 80 percent of all other stocks issued.

Opportunities
• The contractor can transfer property bought at a bargain, stepping up the value so that he receives stock with a much higher book value than he paid for the property.
• This is a tax-free exchange, since no tax is due on the difference between the basis of the property transferred and the book value of the stock issued.

Pitfalls
• The assets must belong to the contractor and not to a corporation.
• The trouble with a corporation owning the assets is that, once it has served its purpose as a conduit, the contractor might be tempted to liquidate it or "collapse" it.
• Under such conditions, he runs into Section 341, which triggers ordinary income on the gain between what the contractor paid for the assets and what he got for them in the way of stock; this is quite different from a tax-free exchange, which postpones settlement under more favorable capital gains treatment.
• The transaction, if properly handled, is tax-free for the time being, which means tax deferral, not tax avoidance. Scrupulous observance of the steps spelled out in Regulation 1.251.3(a) must be met, in order to assure trouble-free deferral.

Regulations on Completed-Contract Method of Accounting

Section 451, General Rule for Taxable Year of Inclusion, has been changed by TEFRA insofar as long-term construction contracts are concerned. What are long-term construction contracts? Those lasting over three years. Counting begins when first costs are incurred, exclusive of bid preparation costs. For example, the contractor is the successful bidder on June 1, 198x. On June 5, 198x he goes to the City Hall and gets a building permit, paying $100. He starts counting on June 5, 198x.

Another condition for coming under TEFRA's requirements on the special treatment of long-term contracts is that the contractor must have had average annual gross receipts of over $25 million for the three preceding tax years.

To the contractor who qualifies under the three-year and the $25 million ground rules, TEFRA means that the completed-contract method can no longer continue to be used to defer income and costs on completed contracts while taking current deductions for so-called indirect costs (treated as period costs prior to TEFRA). Definitions become important. What are costs and expenses allocable to long-term contracts? What are indirect costs? During the transition period, these definitions can make sizeable differences in the tax bill. For example,

For Taxable Years Beginning in:	Percentage of Indirect Costs Currently Deductible:
1983	66⅔
1984	33⅓
1985	0

Opportunities

• The tax practitioner, by studying aggregation and segregation rules prescribed in IRS regulations, can avoid the unnecessary inclusion of the contractor's gross income in the over $25 million category.

• Careful timing of expenses can also avoid an inadvertent borderline inclusion of expenses in the over-three-year category.

• There are certain costs that will continue to be currently deductible, and the tax practitioner, working with the contractor's accountant, can save the contractor an unnecessary loss of current period deductions by carefully accounting for these costs.

Pitfalls

• For those years in which indirect costs continue to be currently deductible, careful segregation of direct and indirect costs is a must, in order to avoid costly and unnecessary tax assessments down the line.

• The contractor who fails to consider the cash-flow effects of being denied current or period deductions for indirect costs will soon find himself in a serious cash-flow squeeze.

How to Avoid Personal Holding-Company Status

Section 541, Imposition of Personal Holding-Company Tax, calls for a tax of 50 percent, in addition to the regular corporate taxes on undistributed personal holding-company income. Related sections are 542 through 547. A holding company is a corporation with (1) passive income (as defined in these sections) of at least 60 percent of its adjusted ordinary income (also defined in these sections), and (2) with 50 percent of its stock owned by not more than five individuals. These are the general rules. There are several exemptions, specific conditions, and definitions. Both conditions stated above must exist before a corporation becomes a personal holding company.

Opportunities

• The ordinary construction company would seldom if ever qualify as a personal holding-company.

• Related corporations engaged in rental activities, for example, must be structured to avoid personal holding-company status.

• If the contractor wants to engage in activities producing passive income, he might do so in his own name or in a partnership arrangement.

• However, new Subchapter S regulations permit liberalization of passive income limitations. If the contractor is involved in passive income, he should look into these new regulations, taking into account the use of a Subchapter S corporation. This option provides a conduit for passive income without getting into the holding-company trap, while providing the usual corporate umbrella regarding limited personal liability.

Pitfalls

• For the holding company, there is the additional 50 percent tax.

• For individuals and partnerships, there are the pitfalls of related taxpayers and the "at risk" provisions of Section 465.

Pros and Cons of the Subchapter S Corporation

Subchapter S, Election of Certain Small Business Corporations as to Taxable Status, deals with Code Sections 1371 through 1379. A qualifying Subchapter S corporation retains the legal attributes of a corporation, but is generally not subject to income tax. Taxable income or losses are passed through to stockholders in basically the same manner as in a partnership.

Opportunities

• For the construction contractor getting started in the business and suffering the usual early-years' losses, the appeal of having the losses passed through to offset other personal income is quite attractive.

• Suppose the corporation begins to prosper and the prosperity passes on to the contractor, putting him into a high-income tax bracket? At that point, it might pay to deliberately perform an act that will terminate the Subchapter S status, thereby placing taxable income in the relatively lower corporate tax rates.

• Dividends payable at the end of the corporate tax year can sometimes be deferred. For example, taxable income in the form of dividends distributed to the calendar year stockholder on January 31, 19xx becomes taxable on April 15, 19xy.

Pitfalls

• The shareholders' portion of the net operating loss is generally limited to the stockholders' basis in the stock, plus the indebtedness of the corporation to the stockholders.

• Distributions made to stockholders during the stockholders' taxable year are ordinary income to them.

• Distributions must be reported on Form 1099.

• Dividends must be reported on Form K-1.

• Under certain conditions described in Section 138, a Subchapter S corporation can be subject to tax. Basically, the tax depends on certain capital gains and other taxable income criteria.

• There are limitations on passive investment income, although the Subchapter S Revision Act of 1982 practically eliminates these limitations.

• This same act loosens up eligibility requirements. At the same time, it tightens up on the retroactive revocation of Subchapter S status. It moves the Subchapter S corporation away from the tax-year ending to calendar-year ending, thereby putting a clamp on deferral of income where fiscal years differ from the taxpayer's normal calendar-year ending.

• A problem is created for new Subchapter S corporations required to use calendar-year accounting, or for old Subchapter S corporations forced into the same thing when there is a change in stock ownership. Tax benefits based on different year-endings between the Subchapter S corporation and the taxpayer will thus be eliminated.

EVALUATING TAX SHELTERS

What is a tax shelter? It's anything that will reduce taxable income. The IRS has attacked tax shelters not so much because they are evil in themselves, but because some of them encourage tax avoidance as opposed to the tax deferral option, which is permissible under certain conditions. Another IRS peeve is that the most effective tax shelters are available only to the select few who can afford high-risk ventures in the first place.

Most tax shelters have been shut down. The last one to go was a straddle plan, whereby the taxpayer sold short and borrowed against the government bond he sold short, to cover his short sale. Interest due to the owner of the bond was currently deductible. The tax cycle evolved into three parts: leveraged deductions during the first year, breakeven during the second year, and capital gains for the third year. Unfortunately, one of several technical correction tax acts has virtually shut down this last remaining tax shelter.

Are Tax Shelters Worthwhile for the Contractor?

What he should ask himself is whether he wants to get involved at all. Is tax deferrence so attractive that the contractor can justify throwing good money after bad? For example, does he want to put his hard-earned money in high-risk oil and gas ventures, merely because they offer opportunities to write off a large part of the investment via intangible drilling costs? The contractor, even if he is at the top personal tax bracket of 50 percent, should ponder the wisdom of spending a dollar to gain a fifty-cent deduction.

For the corporation with even lower tax brackets, the expenditure of cash to shield a lesser amount of tax liability must be viewed even more critically. In this case, the tax shelter *per se* takes second place to such things as positive cash flow benefits; for example, those afforded by accelerated cost-recovery.

Tax Shelters Get Special IRS Attention. Many tax shelters, such as the investment credit, interest expense, and cost recovery deductions in real estate investment projects, are now limited to the at-risk limitations of Section 465. Look out for Section 465 because even the previously allowed at-risk losses will be recaptured if amounts at-risk drop below zero, for example, by an increase in nonrecourse indebtedness. This feature, and certain specific tax-shelter conditions, are part of the continuing effort to eliminate tax-shelter abuses.

Exotic Tax Shelters Are Being Shut Down. If the old stand-bys such as coal commodity options and futures, equipment leasing, farm operation, motion pictures, publications, oil and gas, and real estate are now getting closer scrutiny, it goes without saying that questionable, exotic tax shelters will bring on the immediate wrath of the IRS. The IRS has just about shut them all down.

Pros and Cons of Tax Shelters. The contractor should ask himself these questions before investing in a tax shelter:

- What am I getting, other than a reduction of income or an additional deductible expense?
- Suppose that there eventually is a return on my investment; will it be better than the return from investing in my own business?
- What about plowing money back into my own business; is it not better to:
    - Build up a cash reserve to provide self-financing, thereby saving the high cost of short-term loans?
    - Build up net working capital, thereby enjoying all the advantages of stepping up to the level of the big contractor, and leaving behind the dog-eat-dog competition of the under-financed contractor? Chapter 4 treats this matter in detail.

Employee Benefit Plans as Tax Shelters. A tax shelter normally not included in the usual menu is the general area of employee benefits such as medical reimbursement plans, profit-sharing plans, and retirement plans. The economic benefits of such plans, strictly speaking, are no different from other tax shelters, but the intangibles in the form of employee morale, loyalty, and stability must not be overlooked. Also, for the union contractor, these plans, if properly put together, can mean substantial tax-free benefits for himself and his nonunion staff members.

Tax-Free Investments Are Not for the Contractor. As a rule, this is a luxury the contractor cannot afford. Greater benefits are available from internal rate of return than from tax-free investments in municipal bonds and the one-shot "All-Savers Certificates."

Tax Consequences of Day-to-Day Decisions

The practitioner will more than likely be called in by the contractor to give advice about the tax consequences of major decisions such as capital investment opportunities and the adoption of employee benefit plans. Minor, day-to-day decisions are easily overlooked. Often these can trigger tax problems of major proportions. Let's take a look at both of them, the major ones as well as the minor ones.

Tax Consequences of Capital Investment Decisions

Normally, these are among the major decisions the contractor will make. Financial aspects such as the cost of capital tend to stand out. However, tax planning options are many, and these have a bearing on the outcome of the financial forecasts. The tax practitioner must run these out, taking into account the investment credit, the accelerated-cost recovery system (ACRS), tax preference consequences, and the alternative minimum tax. The financial consequences of tax elections and options are so important and long-lived that the tax practitioner cannot afford to overlook any of them.

Tax Consequences of Employee Benefit Plans

This is another major decision. A formal plan engineered by insurance and legal experts will be on safe grounds, but what about seemingly harmless fringe benefits such as meals and lodging provided for the convenience of the contractor? The only thing to be said to the practitioner is, "Be careful and thorough." The IRS seems to have a fixation on employer-furnished meals, as pointed out previously in this chapter. The gist of the whole matter is the IRS desire to count the value of meals as wages subject to withholding. The courts say no. The IRS counters by producing regulations that require including the value of such meals as gross income, which, if not subject to withholding, must nevertheless be reported as part of gross income in the employee's W-2.

Congress has continued to forbid the Treasury Department from issuing regulations regarding fringe benefits. The reason is fear that regulations might go too far, including as an extreme, fringe benefits representing nothing more than normal comfort provisions to employees. But the IRS has seized on court decisions to say, "Yes, the value of employer-provided meals can be included in W-2 income," but, "No, they are not subject to withholding tax."

The contractor and his practitioner must recognize that the IRS will keep hammering away in this area. They must keep up with each case as it develops. Fringe benefits will have to be watched so that they do not exceed the negative provisions of Section 274, for example. The contractor must be aware of the

Section 274 limitations on per diem and mileage allowance, so that payments for travel meet the "as if reporting" requirements.

Tax Consequences of Travel and Entertainment Decisions

Seemingly innocent, day-to-day decisions such as letting the family use country club facilities can have serious consequences. The practitioner must keep up with Section 274 cases, and alert the contractor to any new twists. The contractor must at least read what has been said about Section 274 in this chapter.

ACCOUNTING RECORDS NEEDED TO BACK UP THE TAX RETURN

A good set of accounting records will normally suffice as a back-up to the tax return. If the contractor has followed advice contained in this book on the documentary and accounting basis for a reporting system, he will be on safe grounds. All that is left to become ready for the IRS auditor is minor.

IRS Audits and a Good Set of Files

Documentation is the name of the game when coping with the IRS auditor. It sounds simplistic, but many an IRS disallowance has stood up because the taxpayer could not come up with the necessary documentation. "I know," the contractor will say, "that I had a complete travel report from Joe Smith when he accounted for the $1,000 travel advance. Now, what did I do with it?" Picture the situation: The bookkeeper wrote the check for $1,000. The contractor signed it. Joe Smith turns in tickets worth $900. The $100 is deposited (debit bank account) and the bookkeeper credits travel expense for $100. Then the $900 worth of documentation is lost or misfiled. Everybody thinks they've done their job, but the IRS comes in two years later and asks for documentation for the $900. Can the contractor produce it? If not, the IRS agent can cite Section 274 and disallow it.

Meeting Section 274 Requirements. This is a negative section that tells us what the IRS will not allow and why. The secret of success is record-keeping. As stated in previous sections, a notation on the credit-card ticket will suffice. Or, a diary of sorts, showing all the required Section 274 information, should be kept.

Adjustments for the Completed-Contract Basis. Most contractors using the percentage of completion basis for long-term contracts will use the completed-contract method for tax purposes. The adjustment to the books at the end of the contractor's fiscal year consists of deferring both the income from contracts in progress and its related costs. The entry deferring income and costs for contracts in progress is reversed at the beginning of the next fiscal year so that, in effect, the contractor's books are placed back on the percentage of completion basis.

HOW TO HANDLE THE IRS AUDIT

The dreaded notice from the IRS, that the contractor's tax return for year 19xx is to be audited, usually leads to a state of shock for both the contractor and his practitioner. This, of course, is not always the case. The experienced practitioner will recall past audits in which the IRS field auditor proved to be a reasonable guy or gal who was trying to do a good job.

In most cases, issues are resolved and the audit is closed at field level. In a few cases, the tax practitioner will have to appeal. From then on, the appeal can go back and forth, either in favor of the taxpayer or the IRS. Finally, it reaches the highest court of appeals. Occasionally, this can mean the Supreme Court.

At the field and conference levels, the tax practitioner can do a good job. If the case is complex and is not resolved at these levels, it is best to bring in a tax attorney who can carry it on through the higher levels.

For the tax accountant, dealing with the IRS audit usually means satisfying documentation requirements at the field audit level. In other words, it means cooperating with the IRS agent and being able to produce the necessary documentation. The secret of good documentation is still trite: a good accounting system, backed up by a good filing system.

If issues go beyond documentation, the practitioner should quickly evaluate the situation, and if resolution of the issues begins to get into matters of law rather than accounting, it might be time to call in the tax attorney. The accountant should remember that the true sign of a professional is the ability to recognize limitations. A practitioner who says, "So far can I go, and no further" is being a wise professional.

TAX TIPS FOR THE CONTRACTOR GOING OUT OF BUSINESS

When the contractor calls it quits, he runs into a completely new set of tax consequences. Here are a few tips that are being passed on directly to the contractor.

• If you are contemplating bankruptcy or reorganization under the Bankruptcy Reform Act of 1978, the first thing you should do is get yourself a good attorney, one who specializes in this very complex field.

• Be sure that all withholding taxes have been paid. If the IRS learns that you are thinking of going out of business, it will immediately levy an assessment on you personally for all unpaid withholding taxes. This is what is known as the "100 percent penalty." Not even personal bankruptcy will discharge this obligation.

• Most bonding companies will concur with the need to pay withholding taxes first. A few not-too-ethical bonding companies might try to talk you into taking care of suppliers and subcontractors first, thereby shifting to you potential responsibilities under payment bonds.

• Be sure that your accounting records are in good shape and up to date.

• Be sure that your accountant is the last employee to go. Your attorney will need a great amount of information that only your accountant can furnish.

• If you have personally loaned money to the corporation and see no way of getting it back, consult your CPA about converting your loan into Section 1244 stock. If you do this, you can take an ordinary loss with carry-back and carry-forward features. Otherwise, your loan becomes a long-term capital loss, currently limited to a yearly deduction of $3,000 ($1,500 if married and filing a separate return), and furthermore, it will cost you $2 for every $1 you are allowed to deduct.

• Good luck, and keep your cool.

INDEX